Chicago Public Library

Form 178 rev. 1-94

PARTING AT THE CROSSROADS

PRINCETON STUDIES IN AMERICAN POLITICS:
HISTORICAL, INTERNATIONAL, AND
COMPARATIVE PERSPECTIVES

SERIES EDITORS

IRA KATZNELSON, MARTIN SHEFTER, THEDA SKOCPOL

A list of titles
in this series appears
at the back of
the book

PARTING AT THE CROSSROADS

THE EMERGENCE OF HEALTH INSURANCE IN THE UNITED STATES AND CANADA

Antonia Maioni

PRINCETON UNIVERSITY PRESS   PRINCETON, NEW JERSEY

Library of Congress Cataloging-in-Publication Data
Maioni, Antonia.
Parting at the crossroads : the emergence of health insurance
in the United States and Canada / Antonia Maioni.
p. cm. — (Princeton studies in American politics)
Includes bibliographical references and index.
ISBN 0-691-05796-6 (cl : alk. paper)
1. Insurance, Health—United States. 2. Insurance, Health—
Canada. I. Title. II. Title: Emergence of health insurance
in the United States and Canada. III. Series.
HD7102.U4M32   1998
368.38′2′00973—DC21   97-43548   CIP   Rev.

This book has been composed in Galliard

Princeton University Press books are printed
on acid-free paper and meet the guidelines
for permanence and durability of the Committee
on Production Guidelines for Book Longevity
of the Council on Library Resources

http://pup.princeton.edu

Printed in the United States of America

1   3   5   7   9   10   8   6   4   2

à Pierre

Contents

Acknowledgments

WHEN I began working on this project, it was destined to be a dissertation on the development of the welfare state in the United States and Canada. What intrigued me was how these two countries were so close, and yet so different, in their social policy experience. Nowhere was this more evident than in health insurance, an area that, it seemed to me then, comparative welfare state scholars had not paid enough attention to. By the time I finished the dissertation, health policy had exploded onto the American political agenda, and interest in the Canadian comparison had resurfaced. Writing about the historical development of health insurance in the midst of a raging debate about health reform proved to be a challenging task. The inscription that inspired me as I was buried in archival research, "What is past is prologue," was surely fitting in this respect.

Completing this work was a long but constantly rewarding process. This would not have been possible, however, without the dedicated support of a great many people. I would like to thank first and foremost my dissertation supervisor at Northwestern University, John Stephens, who first sparked my interest in this topic, and who has provided constant guidance and encouragement since then. Thanks are also due to Charles Ragin and Bill Crotty for their patient help as members of the dissertation committee, and to Cathie Jo Martin who helped me formulate the initial research question. While at Northwestern, I also benefited from the guidance and friendship of a number of professors and fellow students, including Dennis Chong, the late R. Barry Farrell, Evelyne Huber, Kenneth Janda, Ben Page, Clarissa Brown, Julia Fiske, Nick Hockens, Ken Kollman, Lisa Ehrlich Trotter, and Alex Weiss. Special thanks also go to my dear friends Aili and Warren Tripp, who made living in Chicago a wonderful experience.

As I was transforming my dissertation into this book, I was fortunate to meet many dedicated health policy scholars, many of whom are actively committed to health care and engaged in the process of reform. They helped me recognize that the study of health policy is not simply an academic exercise in theory building, or just another interesting social-science puzzle. In fact, health reform is a critical issue that directly affects individual lives in the most profound way. Several people have commented on parts of this manuscript at various stages in its development, and have provided valuable criticism and insights. I would especially like to thank Keith Banting, André-Pierre Contandriopoulos, Ellen Immergut, Larry Jacobs, Ted Marmor, Jim Morone, Mark Peterson, Theda Skocpol, Rob Sullivan, Kent Weaver, and the anonymous reviewers who read the manuscript.

I am indebted to many colleagues and friends for their constant support. At the University of Ottawa, I was surrounded by a collegial group of people to whom I am grateful, in particular Caroline Andrew, who read and commented on the manuscript, and Manon Tremblay, without whom life as a neophyte assistant professor would have been very lonely indeed. I have also benefited from the intellectual environment at McGill University, where my colleagues provided inspiration and helpful advice as I completed the book, in particular Chris Manfredi, Hudson Meadwell, Mark Brawley, and Kathryn Stoner-Weiss. At the Université de Montréal, thanks are due to Alain Noël and Gérard Boismenu, who read parts of the manuscript, and to Laurence McFalls and Jane Jenson for their encouragement. I would also like to thank my good friends Marion Dove, Ann Corbett, and Claude Côté, and my family, especially Louis Maioni, Teresa Maioni, and Louise and Yves Martin, for helping to keep everything in perspective. A very special thank-you to my friends Axel and Magda van Trotsenburg for their generous hospitality in Washington, and to Romeo, Betty, and Cathy Maione, who always provided a home for me in Ottawa.

The final revisions were put to the manuscript while I was a visiting scholar in the North American Studies Program at Duke University. Thanks to John Thompson for his comments on the project and his warm welcome at the Canadian Studies Center, and, for their help and hospitality, to Louis Bélanger, Denise Young, and the Huber-Stephens family in Chapel Hill.

For their assistance in facilitating my research, I am indebted to the staff of the Government Publications collection of the Northwestern University Library, the Civil Reference Branch of the National Archives and Records Administration in Washington, D.C., the Reference Department at the State Historical Society of Wisconsin in Madison, and the Historical Resources Branch of the National Archives of Canada in Ottawa. For their help in obtaining access to certain restricted materials at the National Archives of Canada, thanks are due to Ian McClymont, Geoffrey Pearson, Paul Martin Jr., and the Canadian Labour Congress. I would like to express my appreciation for the services provided by the staffs of the Departments of Political Science at Northwestern University, the University of Ottawa, and McGill University. Thanks also to my research assistants, Sébastien Gagnon-Messier and Siobhán Harty.

I am grateful for the financial support provided by the following organizations: the Graduate School at Northwestern University; the Alumnae Board of Northwestern University; the Earhart Foundation; the School of Graduate Studies and Research, University of Ottawa; the McGill Faculty of Graduate Studies and Research; the Social Science and Humanities Research Council of Canada; and the Fonds pour la Formation de Chercheurs et l'Aide à la Recherche (FCAR-Québec). At Princeton University Press, I would like to thank Malcolm Litchfield for his support and encouragement. Thanks also to Joan Hunter for her assistance in copyediting the manuscript. Earlier versions of certain parts of this book have appeared, in different forms, in the *Journal of Health Politics, Policy and Law*, *Comparative Politics*, and *Politique et sociétés*.

My husband, Pierre Martin, has shared with me the entire run of this project, from its inception to the final editing, and his unwavering confidence has sustained me through it all. Little would have been possible without his endless patience and understanding, and so it is to him, with much love, that I dedicate this work.

IN MENTIONING the names of acts, bills, groups, journals, or organizations, acronyms or abbreviations have often been given. Names frequently used have been identified by the following abbreviations:

AALL	American Association for Labor Legislation
AAPS	Association of American Physicians and Surgeons
AARP	American Association of Retired Persons
AASS	American Association for Social Security
ACCL	All-Canadian Congress of Labour
AFBF	American Farm Bureau Federation
AFL	American Federation of Labor
AFL-CIO	American Federation of Labor–Congress of Industrial Organizations
AHA	American Hospital Association
AMA	American Medical Association
AMPAC	American Medical Association Political Action Committee
CCF	Co-operative Commonwealth Federation
CCL	Canadian Congress of Labour
CCMC	Committee on the Costs of Medical Care
CCUS	Chamber of Commerce of the United States
CEN	Central Files of the Social Security Board
CES	Committee on Economic Security
CFA	Canadian Federation of Agriculture
CHC	Canadian Hospital Council
CHIA	Canadian Health Insurance Association
CIO	Congress of Industrial Organizations
CLC	Canadian Labour Congress
CLIOA	Canadian Life Insurance Officers Association
CMA	Canadian Medical Association
CMAJ	*Canadian Medical Association Journal*
CNH	Committee for the Nation's Health
COHC	Columbia Oral History Collection
COPE	Committee on Political Education
CPMA	Canadian Pharmaceutical Manufacturers Association
DHEW	Department of Health, Education and Welfare
DNC	Democratic National Committee
DNHW	Department of National Health and Welfare
DOL	Records of the Department of Labor

DPNH	Department of Pensions and National Health
DRS	Records of the Office of Research and Statistics
EPF	Established Programs Financing Act
ESI	Employment and Social Insurance Act
ERISA	Employee Retirement Income Security Act
FERA	Federal Emergency Relief Administration
FSA	Federal Security Agency
GAO	U.S. General Accounting Office
GDP	Gross Domestic Product
HIDS	Hospital Insurance and Diagnostic Services Act
HMO	Health Maintenance Organization
H.R.	House of Representatives
JAMA	*Journal of the American Medical Association*
JCPC	Judicial Committee of the Privy Council
LSR	League for Social Reconstruction
MG	Manuscript Group
M.P.	Member of Parliament
NA	National Archives and Records Administration
NAC	National Archives of Canada
NAM	National Association of Manufacturers
NCSC	National Council of Senior Citizens
NDP	New Democratic Party
NFU	National Farmers' Union
NIRA	National Industrial Recovery Act
NPC	National Physicians' Committee
NRA	National Recovery Administration
OAA	Old Age Assistance
OASDI	Old-Age, Survivors' and Disability Insurance
OASI	Old-Age and Survivors' Insurance
OECD	Organisation for Economic Co-operation and Development
PAC	Political Action Committee
RG	Record Group
S.	Senate
SCPS	Saskatchewan College of Physicians and Surgeons
SFL	Saskatchewan Federation of Labour
SHSW	State Historical Society of Wisconsin
SSA	Social Security Administration
SSB	Social Security Board
TLC	Trades and Labor Congress
WMD	Wagner-Murray-Dingell Bill
UMW	United Mine Workers

PARTING AT THE CROSSROADS

CHAPTER ONE

The United States and Canada in Comparative Context

HEALTH INSURANCE represents a central pillar of the modern welfare state, both because it can be seen as a "social right" of citizenship and because it is the largest social policy expenditure for most countries. While the characteristics of payment and administration differ widely, every industrialized country has some form of government funding for health insurance. Although soaring health costs, pressure for fiscal reform, and concerns about access and quality of care are problems for many countries, nowhere else is the basic legitimacy of universal health insurance subject to the same fundamental scrutiny as in the United States. The absence of comprehensive, universal health insurance in the United States, and the highly charged nature of the political debate around the issue, thus offer an important puzzle to students of comparative politics and the welfare state.

This puzzle is even more compelling when the United States is compared with its closest neighbor, Canada. In contrast to European welfare states, rooted in either "statist" traditions or social-democratic welfare systems, these two countries are said to represent the "liberal" model of welfare state development that emphasizes individual initiative and opportunity, where social policy is more residual in nature and associated with the role of the market.[1] In a comparative context, there are many political and economic similarities that make the two "more alike to each other" than to other countries: In fact, the United States and Canada resemble one another in the very features that have been shown to influence welfare state expansion in industrialized societies.[2] The two countries had comparable timing of industrialization and have enjoyed similar levels of economic development and relative prosperity. Both have federal structures of government, in which subnational governments play a role in social programs. Neither has fully corporatist policy-making arrangements, nor strong social-democratic or labor parties, and the organized labor movement in both countries has been historically weak and fragmented. Having emerged as "new nations" in North America, the two

---

[1] Esping-Andersen, 1990, chap. 1.
[2] Kaim-Caudle 1973, 310; Kudrle and Marmor 1981, 88–91.

countries are generally considered to have comparable cultural characteristics and values relative to the European countries. One would expect,
then, the United States and Canada to have similar experiences in welfare
state development, but, in fact, they have differed significantly, especially
in the case of health insurance, the centerpiece of social policies associated with the modern welfare state. A commitment to publicly funded,
universal health insurance remains a hallmark of the Canadian health care
system, while in the United States, government involvement in insuring
health care is limited to Medicare coverage for the elderly and disabled
and insuring the costs of state-administered Medicaid programs for the
poor.

More striking still is the fact that the two countries started out from
similar settings in terms of the structure of their health care delivery systems, the opposition of powerful interests, and the reluctance of influential political leaders to address the controversial issue of health insurance.
And yet, only in the United States did the political debate culminate in
a stalemate that limited the state's role in health insurance to certain groups in society. In Canada, state responsibility was extended to
cover the "right" to health insurance and access to health care for all its
citizens.

Because of the familiarity of Canada to Americans, and because of similarities in health care delivery despite different financing arrangements,
the "Canadian model" figures prominently in debates over health care
reform in the United States as a way of evaluating the potential costs and
benefits of national health insurance.[3] Advocates of national health insurance in the United States point out that the "single-payer" model offers
valuable lessons about how to realize universal coverage and contain
health care costs; opponents of reform, meanwhile, argue that the Canadian experience is neither relevant nor appropriate for the United States,
given concerns about the quality of care and the divergent political cultures of the two countries.

Beyond the debate over the feasibility and desirability of the Canadian
model for the United States lies the more essential question: Why did the
United States and Canada end up with such different "models" of health
insurance? These two countries, who "resemble each other more than
either resembles any other nation,"[4] share integrated economies, enjoy
similar high standards of living, and participate in the world's largest bi-
lateral trade relationship. Moreover, although the impact of different
founding societies and waves of immigration must be taken into account,
Canadians and Americans today share one of the most cohesive social

---

[3] Marmor 1994, chap. 12.
[4] Lipset 1990, 212.

and cultural spheres of any two countries in the world. Why, then, did they embark on such divergent paths to health reform?

This book attempts to explain why the United States and Canada have diverged so significantly, and why the two countries have developed such very different forms of government-funded health insurance. The answer lies in a comparative historical analysis that explores the development of health reform in the two countries from the first legislative proposals of the 1930s through the passage of landmark federal health legislation in the 1960s. During these pivotal decades of the twentieth century, health care was transformed from a private relationship between doctor and patient into a complex exchange of technological and fiscal resources. In the period between the Great Depression and the Great Society, access to health care became the defining issue in the controversies surrounding the relationship between state and society. This book attempts to uncover the defining moments and decisive factors that led to the divergent paths taken by the United States and Canada on the road to health reform.

The reasons for this divergence go well beyond popular notions about different political cultures that are so prevalent in discussion of the "Canadian model" in U.S. health reform debates. The analysis in this book is rooted instead in the extensive literature on the development of the welfare state, which provides significant clues about why the two countries took such different paths to health reform. These clues include the influence of social forces, the role of state actors, and the impact of political institutions. Societal explanations concentrate on the role and influence of organized groups, examining the power of professional groups or business interests in shaping social reform.[5] Neo-Marxist explanations focus on how social policy reflects the class struggle, and demonstrate the correlation between higher social expenditures and the political strength of the working class mobilized into a social-democratic party.[6] The state-centered approach emphasizes the role of individual state actors, influential bureaucrats, and political leaders in setting the policy agenda and shaping legislation, and the state's administrative capacity to implement social reform.[7]

In order to understand why certain groups are more influential in some political settings than in others, and why policymakers are constrained in the choices that they make, scholars of the welfare state have turned their attention to the role of institutions in the political process. Political institutions represent the key components in the interaction between societal forces and the levers of state because of the way in which institutions

---

[5] Starr 1982; Naylor 1986b.

[6] Stephens 1979; Navarro 1989.

[7] Skocpol and Ikenberry 1983; Orloff and Skocpol 1984.

condition social and political activity and organization.[8] The constitutional settings that configure political institutions fashion the "rules of the game" of a political system.[9] These rules are embedded in the political institutions that impose constraints or provide opportunities for actors and groups in the policy process.[10] Thus, in political systems with multiple "veto points," incremental reform will be more prevalent than wide changes in health policy.[11] In the United States, the separation of powers and the resistance of key interests have blocked national health insurance initiatives. In Canada, by contrast, the turn toward universal and publicly financed health care can be explained by bold innovations at the provincial level and the relative cohesiveness of the parliamentary system in ensuring the passage of federal legislation.[12]

This book contributes to the theoretical debate by examining a crucial mechanism linking state and society: political parties. The analysis focuses upon how the debate over health reform was conditioned by the political institutions shaping party systems in the United States and Canada. Essentially, the argument is that the federal structure and parliamentary institutions of the Canadian political system encouraged the formation of a social-democratic third party and enhanced its efficacy in promoting health policy reform. The institutional constraints of the American political system, meanwhile, impeded the emergence and consolidation of an independent political voice for the Left, forcing health reformers toward limited strategies that could appeal to a wider coalition within the Democratic party.

This comparative historical analysis, furthermore, can contribute toward our understanding of the fate of recent health reform by informing us about the realm of the politically feasible in such debates. An important consideration in the study of health reform is to examine how policy legacies can contribute to changing the rules of the game of the political process, creating new political dynamics between actors and institutions and in turn shaping policy feedback and future reform possibilities.[13] At critical historical moments in the development of health insurance in the United States and Canada, crucial political decisions were made on the basis of past successes and failures in health reform. More significantly still, the legislative outcomes of the 1960s created very different settings for the politics of health care reform in subsequent

---

[8] Thelen and Steinmo 1992.
[9] Skocpol 1985.
[10] March and Olsen 1984.
[11] Immergut 1992, 27–28.
[12] Maioni 1997, 412–14.
[13] Heclo 1974; Pierson 1993.

decades by changing the incentives and interests of actors and groups in the policy process.

The implications of this analysis and the contributions of this book are threefold. First, the U.S.-Canada comparison can provide important insights into why the impetus for, and results of, health and social reform differ across countries. As suggested above, this study contributes to the theoretical discussion by showing how societal demands for and against social reform are profoundly transformed as they are channeled through political institutions. An examination of the dynamic impact of institutions on party systems also shows how parties fulfill their important function as intermediary between state and society in democratic political systems.

Second, this comparative analysis contributes to the rich literature on the development of the welfare state in industrialized societies and of policy development in the health care sector. There exists a vast collection of comparative historical case studies of social policies, but relatively few focus on the development of health care legislation across different countries.[14] In addition, despite the fact that the United States and Canada seem ideally suited for a close-case comparison, the study of this pair remains somewhat neglected in the welfare state literature. While there is a burgeoning interest in individual case studies of U.S. and Canadian health policy, there are very few in-depth comparative historical analyses of health policy development in the two countries.

Third, this historical comparison provides a critical component in understanding the politics of health care reform by showing how political configurations can provide opportunities and constraints in policy development. It is this analysis of how institutions shaped the politics of health reform that reveals why two countries that started off in the same direction diverged so significantly along the way. Furthermore, it also reveals why this divergence in forms of health care financing was accompanied by a relative convergence in patterns of health care delivery. Neither country was predestined to adopt the health insurance system that it has today. We cannot assume, therefore, that the future course of health insurance is cut in stone in either country. The political decisions of the past, however, have effectively transformed the nature of health politics and set the boundaries of political feasibility in policy development. Ultimately, the study of how the health care systems in the United States and Canada came about can help identify important clues about the realm of the possible in future health reform.

---

[14] These include Fox 1986; Gray 1991; Hollingsworth 1986; Immergut 1992; Jacobs 1993; Ruggie 1996; and Wilsford 1991.

HEALTH CARE IN THE UNITED STATES AND CANADA:
SIMILAR DELIVERY, DIFFERENT FINANCING

Before turning to an analysis of the reasons for divergence in health reform across the United States and Canada, it is important to understand what these two health insurance systems look like, what they have in common, and what sets them apart. Although the characteristics of health care systems vary greatly across industrialized countries, a common feature is the extent to which the public sector has come to play a dominant role in health care.[15] Despite differences in political culture or political development among these countries, there has emerged a political and social consensus around the idea of health care as a social right. In this respect, Canada resembles other industrialized societies in recognizing the need for some measure of government regulation to ensure this right.[16] Governments in Canada and other countries have sought to do so by openly confronting health care providers through the political process and treating health care as a public good.[17]

If the principles of universality, public financing and administration, and expenditure controls are integral features of health care systems throughout the industrialized world, the exception is the United States, where employer-based benefits are the norm and public insurance is limited to the elderly and disabled, and to the poor. Major government involvement is limited to a dual-tiered system of federal and state programs under Medicare and Medicaid. The latter is a social assistance program based on the means test that offers hospital and physician care to persons eligible for federal welfare benefits. Administered by the states, Medicaid plans reimburse private carriers or providers, and are jointly financed by federal and state governments. Medicare covers all elderly or disabled Americans eligible for Social Security benefits. The social insurance portion of Medicare (Part A) covers inpatient hospital care directly paid by the federal government and financed by social security taxes levied on workers. Medicare Part B offers supplementary medical insurance for physician care and outpatient hospital services. The Medicare plan is financed through monthly premiums and federal revenues. Much like the private insurance system, Medicare Part B involves substantial deductibles and co-payments (which are often covered by supplementary private insurance). In contrast to Canada and other industrialized countries, public expenditures on health care in the United States account for less than half of total spending on health. Of that

[15] For an extensive comparison, see Contandriopoulos et al. 1993.
[16] Iglehart 1986, 778.
[17] Evans 1990, 101–28.

public spending, the federal government accounts for two-thirds of the nearly $300 billion in public expenditures on health to finance Medicare and other health care programs, while the states spend one-third on the Medicaid program.[18]

Compared to this intricate patchwork, health insurance in Canada seems relatively simple, consisting of a coherent mosaic of ten provincial systems. While jurisdiction for the health system is a responsibility of the provinces, the federal government became involved in the sector through its fiscal contributions to provincial health insurance programs. In return, the provinces must adhere to five "principles": universal coverage, equal access to care, comprehensive benefits, portability across provinces, and public administration in health insurance plans. Since the passage of two key federal laws, the Hospital Insurance and Diagnostic Services Act of 1957 and the Medical Care Insurance Act of 1966, provincial insurance plans have ensured that all Canadians, regardless of age, income, place of residence, or employment status, have access to government-funded hospital and medical benefits. Each province administers a health insurance program that covers most diagnostic services, hospital care, and physician fees. Under these programs, patients generally have free choice of physicians and hospitals. Hospitals are paid through the imposition of annual global budgets by provincial governments, while physicians are reimbursed for their services according to negotiated fee schedules. These services are paid for through provincial health ministries, but the funding sources come from both provincial revenues (now about 44 percent of the total) and transfers from the federal government (26 percent). Privately insured and out-of-pocket expenses, which are growing rapidly, now account for about 28 percent of total health expenditures in Canada. These expenses are related to the cost of services not covered by provincial health insurance programs (such as specialized clinics for eye-laser surgery or in-vitro fertilization).[19]

Since the full implementation of provincial health insurance programs in the early 1970s, all Canadians are now admissible for government-funded health benefits. In the United States, meanwhile, only 40 percent of the population is covered by publicly financed hospital insurance, while 25 percent have publicly financed medical coverage. Of the Americans covered by private insurance, over 80 percent rely on benefits tied to employment. Because of the complexity and permeability of the employer-based American health insurance system, an estimated forty million Americans have no coverage, either private or public.[20] Millions more

[18] Raffel and Raffel 1997, 282; Hanson 1994, 764.
[19] Canada, Health Canada 1996, 46; Leatt and Williams 1997, 4–5.
[20] Hellander et al. 1995, 377–92.

are "underinsured," that is, insured for only part of their potential total health bill. For example, elderly Americans must pay high "out-of-pocket" expenses despite Medicare, and many opt for supplementary "medigap" coverage. In Canada, meanwhile, private insurance has been until now limited to supplemental items such as private hospital rooms or prescription drugs, and generally may not include any procedures or services covered by public health insurance.

The implementation of health insurance had a significant impact on the growth of health expenditures in the two countries. Prior to the introduction of government-funded hospital and medical insurance, the United States and Canada had similar private funding mechanisms and patterns of health care expenditures.[21] In Canada, before the full implementation of hospital insurance, total health expenditures were estimated at about 6 percent of gross domestic product (GDP) in 1960, with public expenditures representing only 43 percent of the total. By 1975, after the implementation of hospital and medical insurance in the provinces, health expenditures rose to 7 percent of GDP, of which three-quarters were spent by the public sector. In the United States, meanwhile, health expenditures started out at similar levels (5 percent of GDP in 1960), but by 1975 they accounted for more than 8 percent of GDP, with public spending (through Medicare and Medicaid) making up 42 percent of the total. Since then, the spending gap between the two countries has widened considerably. By 1994, health expenditures had risen to almost 10 percent of GDP in Canada, but represented more than 14 percent of GDP in the United States.[22] Thus, although both the United States and Canada spend relatively large amounts on health care compared to other industrialized countries, the United States still outspends Canada by a considerable margin.

The changes in expenditure patterns over time are especially noteworthy since both countries started out at relatively similar levels. The implementation of health insurance in Canada and the institutionalization of a mixed public-private system in the United States have led to significant differences in cost escalation. In the Canadian "single-payer" system, provincial governments provide the "single-tap" through which money flows into the health care system and through which costs can be contained by way of institutionalized negotiation with hospitals and doctors.[23] In the United States, the more complex "multi-payer" system, in which government regulation plays a much smaller role, has led to a much more

[21] Evans 1982, 372–74.
[22] Canada, Health Canada 1996, 42; Organisation for Economic Co-operation and Development 1995, 9–12.
[23] Naylor 1993, 38.

rapid increase in health costs, both in absolute and relative terms, despite the presence of millions of uninsured and underinsured Americans.

The divergence in financing of health benefits and in the structure and coverage of government-funded health insurance should not, however, overshadow the similarities between the two countries in terms of the delivery of health care. Historically, private fee-for-service care, the dominance of private or voluntary hospitals, charity care based on philanthropic, religious, or community care, and direct government involvement limited to public health services were essential characteristics of both countries until midcentury.[24] In both the United States and Canada, medical associations developed out of a desire to strengthen the monopoly of professional physicians and to regulate the practice of medicine.[25] Since the 1910s, medical education on both sides of the border has evolved in tandem, accreditation of medical schools falls under the same agencies, and licensing of physicians remains reciprocal across states and provinces.

Even today, the two systems of health care delivery retain important similarities. The majority of inpatient care is provided by voluntary (as opposed to government-administered) hospitals. The significant difference is that Canadian hospitals are nonprofit institutions whose operating costs are funded by provincial governments through the allocation of annual global budgets, a method that provides a strong incentive to constrain costs and tends to eliminate substantial administrative overhead. Capital expenditures for equipment and technology are subject to provincial approval and often rely on additional funding through fund-raising campaigns. Although the amount of high-technology services are in effect constrained by these budgets, they are employed subject to medical need. Nevertheless, in terms of the diffusion of technology, as with the distribution of medical care, the Canadian health care system looks more American than European.[26]

The majority of physician services are still based on private practice and fee-for-service remuneration in the two countries, and they have similar physician-to-population ratios. More Canadian doctors, however, are general and family practitioners than is the case in the United States, although a significant wage gap exists only in certain specialties. Doctors in Canada are reimbursed by a single payer (the provincial government) according to a set fee schedule, eliminating many of the administrative costs associated with fee-for-service practice in the United States. Despite

[24] Hatcher et al. 1984, 92–99.

[25] Coburn et al. 1983, 4147–18.

[26] For more detail on the structure of Canadian health care delivery in comparison with the United States, see U.S. General Accounting Office 1991. This was not the first U.S. government study of the Canadian health care system; see, for example, Hatcher 1981.

the potential constraints to physician autonomy in an era of scarce resources in Canada, and the increasing limits raised by the proliferation of managed care in the United States, doctors remain the essential "gatekeepers" of the health care system in the two countries.

The extensive similarities in health care delivery between the United States and Canada, coupled with the divergence in the costs and nature of financing and the relative success of the Canadian system, have led proponents of national health insurance in the United States to seize upon the positive features of the Canadian model. Differences in spending levels have been attributed to the setting of annual global budgets for hospitals and of uniform fee schedules negotiated between the provinces and medical associations;[27] the intensity of physician services and the greater number of "procedure-oriented" specialists;[28] the organizational structure of Canadian hospitals and the centralization of diagnostic services;[29] and the savings garnered due to the substantially lower administrative costs associated with a single-payer health care system.[30]

On the other hand, detractors of health reform have been quick to emphasize the perceived flaws of the Canadian health care system. For example, they have linked the fact that Canada spends less on health with the idea that it delivers less as well.[31] It has been argued that the universal coverage mandated in such a system would inevitably offset any administrative savings because of excessive demand and the "hidden overhead costs" from the lack of incentives to economize.[32] Beyond the question of costs are the more fundamental questions of the inevitable trade-offs between quality and access: limiting access to quality health care and free-loading off the United States for high-quality research, innovative procedures, and medical technology.[33] There is some degree of concern about the "rationing" of health care and the "queuing" for treatment associated with the control of health resources in Canada, but supporters of the system point to the fact that these occur on the basis of medical need rather than ability to pay, as is the case in private health care systems.[34]

Whatever the drawbacks of the two health care systems, public opinion polls tend to suggest that public consensus or support for the existing health care system is higher in Canada than it is in the United States. In cross-national comparisons in the late 1980s, Canadians expressed the

---

[27] Evans et al. 1989, 573–76.
[28] Fuchs and Hahn 1990, 884–90.
[29] Redelmeier and Fuchs 1993, 772–78.
[30] Woolhandler and Himmelstein 1991, 1253–1258.
[31] For a review and critique of these arguments, see Marmor 1991, 18–24.
[32] Danzon 1992, 30–38.
[33] Neuschler 1990, chap 4.
[34] Fulton 1993, chap 3.

highest satisfaction with their health care, while Americans indicated some of the weakest satisfaction rates within the industrialized countries.[35] While there is still a discrepancy among responses about the overall support of their health care system (more Canadians answer favorably to this) and the need to rebuild it (more Americans agree with this option), polls indicate a possible closing of the gap between Canadians and Americans in attitudes toward fundamental change.[36] Nevertheless, recent political debates in the two countries suggest that the main issue in Canada is how to best maintain the public health care system in an era of fiscal restraint by governments, while in the United States the focus has been on how to use government intervention to transform the existing health care system into a more cost-effective and accessible one.

OUTLINE OF THE BOOK

This book considers the emergence of health insurance in the United States and Canada in terms of a journey that leads two countries with many similar characteristics to embark on different paths on the road to health reform. Although the two countries started from comparable points in terms of the structure of their health care systems, they subsequently experienced considerable divergence in the time and nature of health reform leading to very different patterns of health care funding and coverage. What could explain this? The next chapter reviews the welfare state literature to look for insights into the U.S.-Canada comparison in health insurance, and highlights the role of institutions in establishing the conditions under which partisan politics can have a profound impact on health policy orientations.

The following chapters present the historical analysis, which spans the period between the defining moments of the welfare state in the 1930s to the definitive health insurance outcomes of the 1960s. The book concludes by reviewing the comparative historical evidence in order to address the original question of why the two countries took divergent paths in the development of health insurance. Chapter 7 evaluates the power of institutional explanations in understanding policy development and traces in a summary form the processes through which institutions influence policy outcomes. Finally, Chapter 8 addresses the contemporary relevance of the analysis. In short, the way in which health insurance legislation has emerged in the two countries has had profound consequences on the practice of health care and the interests and strategies of the players who will be involved in future battles over health reform.

[35] Blendon 1989, 2–10; Blendon et al. 1990, 2–10.

[36] Blendon et al. 1995, 220–30. About 59 percent of Canadians and 53 percent of Americans feel fundamental change of their health care system is necessary.

CHAPTER TWO

Parties and Institutions in Health Politics

A VIVID DESCRIPTION of the differences in welfare state development between the United States and Canada portrays the former as following a "big bang" trajectory of "episodic development" while the latter experienced a more incremental "steady state."[1] If this analogy is applied to health care, the U.S. case can be characterized by several major policy proposals that backfired and stalled the development of national health insurance. In Canada, meanwhile, provincial and federal initiatives led to a series of chain reactions and the gradual construction of a universal health care system.

The extensive literature on the development of the welfare state across industrialized countries provides a rich source of clues for explaining such divergent paths to health reform. This chapter outlines some of the most relevant theoretical explanations that could account for the differences in the development of health insurance in the United States and Canada and focuses upon two sets of explanations: those culled from the power resources approach, and those emphasizing the impact of political institutions. The analysis in this book underlines the importance of institutions as the locus of interaction between state and societal forces and, in particular, how the dynamics of partisan politics resulting from different institutional settings can have a profound impact on major policy orientations. Some of the pervasive elements associated with political culture and "American exceptionalism" in the U.S.-Canada comparison are also addressed at the end of the chapter.

LOGIC OF THE COMPARISON

Because the United States and Canada share many economic, political, and social attributes, the two countries seem ideal candidates for a "most-similar-systems" research design. Since common characteristics can be controlled for, it is easier to identify which explanatory variables are most relevant in understanding differences in health insurance outcomes.[2] This

---

[1] Leman 1977, 261–62.
[2] On most-similar-systems research designs, see Lijphart 1971, 682–93.

type of "controlled" comparison can help move beyond the problem of "too few cases, too many variables" in comparative welfare state studies.[3]

In examining the health reform experiences of these "similar" countries, this book relies on a case-based comparative historical analysis that allows for a richer examination of a smaller number of cases, focusing on the particular characteristics and trajectories that led to different social policy outcomes.[4] Based on John Stuart Mill's inductive logic, such historical case-based comparisons have greatly contributed to a more comprehensive understanding of welfare state development across time and space.[5] Mill's indirect method of difference is particularly relevant for a close-case comparison, such as that of the United States and Canada, because the cases are similar in many respects but differ in specific ways that are crucial in explaining differences in health policy outcomes. In addressing the question of why the United States did not develop such universal, national health insurance, "it helps to pick a comparative case that not only diverges in direction from one's own case, but that succeeded where one's own case did not."[6]

The most-similar-systems research design and the inductive logic of comparison are particularly appropriate in comparing the U.S. and Canadian experiences because the two countries resemble one another in many of the very features that have been shown to influence welfare state development. The two countries are classified as "liberal" welfare states, with similar emphasis on minimum levels of welfare effort as compared to the European nations.[7] Explanations based on economic growth and convergence, such as the earlier cross-national studies of the "logic of industrialism,"[8] are less useful in this comparison because, even though the timing and structure of Canada's economic growth differs from that of the United States, the two countries are generally considered to be among the world's more developed and prosperous economies. In addition, explanations that focus on economic openness or corporatist systems of interest intermediation between labor, business, and the state in the formation of socioeconomic policy are also less relevant, since neither country is considered to be an example of corporatism.[9] Traditional variables associated with the power of organized labor and the strength of

[3] Castles and Merrill 1989, 179.

[4] On the merits of case- versus variable-based research, see Ragin 1987, chap. 3.

[5] On the comparative historical method, see Skocpol 1984, 374–86.

[6] Amenta 1991, 186.

[7] Esping-Andersen 1990, 26–27.

[8] Cutright 1965, 537–50; Wilensky 1975.

[9] Most authors classify both countries as "weak" corporatist states, mainly due to the relative weakness of organized labor and the absence of an institutionalized mechanism for the integration of labor in policy making; see, for example, Lehmbruch 1984, 65–66.

left-wing parties have to be modified for the U.S.-Canada comparison. Indeed, the two countries are characterized by relatively weak labor movements and an absence of social-democratic government, yet labor and the Left had different experiences in the development of health insurance. Finally, although the two countries have different societal cleavages, they also share, to some extent, a historical democratic heritage as British "settler colonies"[10] and similarities in political culture that reduce the effectiveness of such explanations for understanding "American exceptionalism"; the issue of political culture will be taken up in detail at the end of this chapter.

The logic that underlies the selection of such a pair for a "close-case" comparison thus has an impact on assessing what theories can be useful for comparing health policy outcomes. The historical analysis that follows in this book attempts to integrate explanations of welfare state development from both the power resources model and the literature on state structures by tracing differences in the political articulation of societal demands through political parties. Although the distribution of power and resources among social groups can be considered the basis for the conflict surrounding the orientation of social policies, the development and outcome of social policies are conditioned by the structures of the state that present certain constraints and opportunities for the transmission of societal demands. This analysis will focus on how state structures condition the role of societal agents in transmitting demands through political parties and institutions. The possibility of third-party viability and the presence of a social-democratic party in Canada led to pressures for public, universal health insurance in Canada, while opponents were constrained in their leverage within a parliamentary system. Conversely, in the United States, the absence of an independent voice for labor and the Left forced both to act within the confines of the Democratic party. This also made it more difficult to repel opposition to universal health insurance and formulate a coherent health reform agenda.

POLITICAL RESOURCES AND GROUP POWER

The distribution of "power resources" among groups in society is an essential component in understanding the development of the welfare state.[11] Since social policies involve conflicts about redistribution of income and responsibilities, groups will attempt to organize members and pressure governments about how this redistribution should be effected, if

[10] Rueschemeyer, Stephens, and Stephens 1992, 121–35.
[11] Korpi 1983.

at all, in order to maximize their own interests. Competition among such groups can play a pivotal role in articulating social demands through political channels of influence.[12] As critics of this pluralist notion have noted, however, the influence of groups in the political system is conditioned by their financial and organizational resources, which, in the case of lobbies representing the medical profession in Canada and the United States, are considerable. The other essential features that condition group influence are the nature of the political institutions through which groups must operate and the types of coalitions they can form around policy issues: in this instance, the Canadian and American experiences are quite different.[13]

The medical profession is different from other interest groups in that much of its stature at the societal level derives from its monopoly over medical knowledge and the provision of health care, in comparison to the relative ignorance of the consumers of care.[14] Medical associations also derive much of their political power from the nonpolitical coercion they can exercise as a "professional monopoly" on doctors through access to education, licensing, and hospitals.[15] The Canadian and American medical professions also share remarkable similarities, including educational and licensing practices in addition to concerns about professional autonomy and self-interest.[16]

Medical lobbies emerged as major players in health reform debates across the industrialized world. The American Medical Association and the Canadian Medical Association, both rich in financial and organizational resources, have been actively involved in such debates. The two groups displayed, at least initially, a considerable amount of resistance toward government intervention in the health care sector. Their influence in the shaping of health policy, however, has differed because of the specific political institutions within which organized medicine must work. The American medical lobby, like other powerful interest groups in the United States, enjoys multiple levers of influence because it can engage in a wide variety of activities that affect policy development, including lobbying elected representatives and administrative agencies, and organizing public education campaigns to woo public opinion.[17] The range and access of a professional group such as the American Medical Association (AMA) in federal and state government are considerable, given the AMA's ability to build extensive networks of influence at the congressio-

[12] Truman 1951.
[13] Schattschneider 1960, chap. 2; Pross 1986, chap. 9.
[14] Rayack 1967, 5.
[15] Alford 1975; Olson 1965, 140.
[16] Coburn, Torrance, and Kaufert 1983, 418–25.
[17] Berry 1984, 6–8.

nal, executive, and agency levels.[18] The American Medical Association's organizational resources and access to legislators have also been strengthened through the use of political action committees (PACs) in contributing to individual electoral campaigns.[19] Through its effective use of these lobbying strategies, the medical profession is able to shape the public agenda for health reform in the United States and resist attempts at state intervention that would jeopardize physician autonomy.

While the medical lobby's relationship with government has been overtly adversarial in the American context, in Canada there has been more of "medical ambivalence toward the state."[20] Organized interests in Canada work within a political system that has many competing bases of legitimacy, including the federal government and provincial governments with their own spheres of power. The division of powers in Canadian federalism opens up the possibility of building "centres of resistance" to health reform initiatives in the provinces.[21] But, at the same time, the parliamentary system and party government, at the federal and provincial levels, have provided firmer resistance to the efforts of the medical profession to control the health policy agenda than does the American experience. The Canadian policy-making process is centered around the Cabinet's collective role in coordinating and formulating policy, so groups have tended to concentrate their lobbying efforts among ministers and senior civil servants.[22] While the Canadian Medical Association plays an important role as part of the "sub-government" in a health policy community, the exigencies of party discipline mean that, among individual members of Parliament, the group's reach is much more limited than in the American setting.[23]

The impact of organized medicine on the emergence of health insurance can be understood in relation to the presence of effective counterweights, namely organized labor and the influence of social-democratic politics. When it comes to comparing Canada and the United States, the power resources model is useful insofar as it informs us about the impact of the organized working class and the role of left-wing parties in the development of the welfare state. This model suggests that as the organizational strength of workers increases in the capitalist economy, this

---

[18] Gais, Peterson, and Webb 1984, 161–85.

[19] Although the jury is still out about the direct effects of PACs on legislative voting, the money raised by these organizations obviously enhances a group's access to policymakers. See Gais 1996, chap. 2; for a critique of the role of health PACs, see Ehrenreich 1970.

[20] Tuohy 1992, 118.

[21] Weir 1973, 159, 164; see also Fulton and Stanbury 1985, 269–300.

[22] Doern and Phidd 1992, 52.

[23] Pross 1992, 236.

strength can be transformed into political power as it is channeled through parties in the political system. Such studies attribute the variations in social expenditures to the organizational strength of labor movements and to the impact of left-wing partisanship. The presence of a left-wing party in power is associated with the expansion of social expenditures and the formation of a redistributive welfare state.[24] Parties of the Left can also have a positive impact when associated with center-left coalition governments or through their influence in shifting the political center leftward, based on Duverger's model of "contagion from the left."[25] In addition, labor's ability to forge alliances with other societal groups, such as farmer interests and elements of the middle class, can be crucial in consolidating its electoral power.[26] The strength of the Right, meanwhile, has been shown to have a constraining effect on welfare state expenditure and expansion, either through the presence of a right-wing party in power or through the influence of the Right on the "embourgeoisement" of the Left.[27]

Proponents of "American exceptionalism" attribute the relatively ineffectual power of the working class in the United States to the weakness of organized labor and the absence of a labor-based social-democratic party, leading to American labor's "barren marriage" with the Democratic party.[28] The fragmented nature of the American working class is reflected in the divisive history of craft versus industrial unions in the United States, and in its low levels of unionization. But the Canadian labor movement shows similar tendencies in its historical origins, as American-based international unions dominated and fragmented labor organizations in Canada until the middle of the twentieth century.[29] The labor movements in the two countries also suffered from relatively low levels of unionization; from 1930 to 1960, for example, unionization rates grew from 14 percent to 31 percent in Canada and from 11 percent to 31 percent of nonagricultural workers in the United States, while in the industrialized countries as a whole, unionization rose from 28 percent to 49 percent.[30]

If low levels of unionization and divided organization characterized both Canadian and American labor movements, what explains the differ-

---

[24] Stephens 1979, chap. 4.

[25] Korpi 1989, 313.

[26] Esping-Andersen 1985, chap.3.

[27] Castles 1982, 83–87. For a discussion of the different forms of "left contagion" and "left embourgeoisement," see Hicks and Swank 1992, 667–68.

[28] Davis 1986, chap. 2.

[29] Babcock 1974; see also Lipset 1986.

[30] Stephens 1979, 116.

ence between their respective influences in health reform? One answer lies in the linkage between labor and the Left.[31] In neither the United States nor Canada has a social-democratic party been in power at the federal level. Therefore, both countries lack one of the essential features commonly associated with a highly developed welfare state in the comparative literature. In Canada since the 1930s, however, there has been a viable social-democratic party engaged in federal and provincial politics. Consequently, we can assess the party's impact in legislative politics and the "contagion" it was able to exert within the Canadian party system. Labor had more political clout in Canada because of this third party of the Left, even before this party became formally allied with organized labor. In the United States, organized labor, particularly the craft-based leadership, avoided independent political action and coalitions with parties of the Left. When labor finally discarded its nonpartisan principles it found that, like many other social movements, it "had no place else to go" except to the Democratic party.[32] Why did labor choose different political alliances in the two countries? What explains the presence of a social-democratic third party of the Left in Canada, and to what extent did it have an impact on the politics of health reform? The answers to these questions are to be found by examining the relationship between societal groups and state structures.

STATE STRUCTURES AND POLITICAL INSTITUTIONS

As independent measures, the power and resources of groups cannot account for the different trajectories in health reform in the United States and Canada. If societal groups are the agents for social reform, whether these agents have an effective political voice depends on the political landscape in which they must perform. The most important features of this terrain are shaped by the constitutional design of the state. In the welfare state literature, comparative historical analysis has revealed four features of state structure that can affect social policy outcomes: the role of autonomous state bureaucrats, the state's administrative capacity, the design of political institutions, and the feedback effect of past policies themselves.[33]

While the comparative historical analysis in this book pays attention to the presence of reform-minded bureaucrats interested in promoting

---

[31] Swartz 1977; Navarro 1989.

[32] Schattschneider 1960, 57.

[33] Weir, Orloff, and Skocpol 1988. For examples of these variations on the state-centric approach in the welfare state literature, see, for example, Weir and Skocpol 1985; Orloff and Skocpol 1984; Heclo 1974; Pierson 1993.

health insurance and to the nature of the state's administrative capacity in the two countries, the most relevant features of the state-centric model for this comparison remain the institutional attributes of the two polities and how institutions affect political choices about reform. As Skocpol suggests, the "Tocquevillian" effect of a state's political "configuration" conditions the way bureaucratic and societal actors organize, operate, and succeed in influencing policy outcomes.[34] More recent comparative historical research has tried to show the actual processes by which constitutional structures shape political institutions and the rules of the political game.[35] For example, Immergut's work on European health insurance development traces the importance of institutional attributes in accounting for why, in certain countries, some interest groups face more "veto points" than in other countries in electoral and representational systems.[36] The U.S.-Canada comparison is an ideal extension of this analysis, given the contrast between the multiple veto points inherent to the American separation of powers and the fusion of executive and legislative powers in the Canadian political system.

Institutions perform a crucial role in "filtering" societal demands through the political process.[37] They impose the rules that guide policy choices by defining the constraints and attributes of the policy-making process that lead to the passage of legislation.[38] Institutions are important factors in the comparison between the United States and Canada because of the way in which different configurations in the two countries affected the transmission of societal interests and demands about health reform through the political system. In addition, political institutions impose constraints and provide opportunities that affect the formation and functioning of political parties. Any analysis of health reform must take into account the role of political parties, because they serve a key function as intermediary between society and the state. In effect, parties are the transmission belts that allow societal demands to be channeled through the political process. Two dimensions of the relationship between political institutions and parties are important to note: the impact of institutions on party formation and electoral success; and the impact of the formal rules on the operation of parties in representative institutions. Different political institutions, and the formal rules embedded within them, led to the emergence of an independent political voice for the Left in Canada, but not in the United States. Only in Canada was a social-democratic third party able to exert pivotal influence in the development of health

[34] Skocpol 1985, 21.
[35] Thelen and Steinmo 1992, 3–7.
[36] Immergut 1992, chap. 1.
[37] Leman 1980, chap. 1.
[38] Weaver and Rockman 1992, 445–53.

policy at both the provincial and federal levels of government. Two institutional attributes, parliamentary versus presidential government, and federalism, stand out in explaining the differences in party systems in Canada and the United States.

PARTIES AND INSTITUTIONS IN THE POLITICAL PROCESS

In both countries, political parties emerged out of competing factions in civil society. The "major" Canadian political parties emerged in the years before and after Confederation out of rival factions that opposed propertied business elites and the clerical hierarchy, who supported the Conservative party, against the antiestablishment and anticlerical reformers who formed the basis of the Liberal party.[39] Important realignments in the Canadian party system have come about as the result of regional protest by third parties, mainly in the western provinces but also in Quebec's distinctive political community, that has led to the fracturing of the two-party system at both the federal and provincial levels. In the United States, various coalitions of factions had grouped around two party labels, Republican and Democrat, by the mid-nineteenth century. During the 1930s a realignment of regional and economic interests within the two major parties consolidated into an enduring two-party system. Although third parties have acted as "protorealignment" forces in American political development, they have not had the longevity or influence of Canadian third parties.[40]

Both the United States and Canada have single-member plurality electoral systems, a situation that usually rewards larger parties but discriminates against smaller ones, and leads to the dominance of two parties.[41] In Canada, however, several regional parties have emerged to become successful third parties, profiting from the distortions of the plurality system that reward parties with concentrated support.[42] While major-party "failure" often led to the emergence of protest movements in the United States, such movements have not, at least in the twentieth century, been successful in consolidating electoral support.[43] The broad coalitions rep-

[39] Thorburn 1996, 5–12.

[40] On critical elections and realignments in the American party system, see Burnham 1970, chap. 2.

[41] As the well-known formula states, "the simple majority single-ballot system favors the two-party system." Duverger 1954, 217.

[42] Cairns 1968, 60. The Canadian anomaly led Rae to reformulate Duverger's thesis in areas "where strong local minority parties exist." Rae 1971, 95.

[43] Two twentieth-century exceptions are Theodore Roosevelt's candidacy under the Bull Moose Progressive label, which won 27 percent of the vote in 1912 and helped swing

resented under major-party labels in the United States allow them to absorb protest movements more readily, especially given the structural barriers imposed on ballot access and the primary system of candidate selection.[44]

The most obvious structural difference between the two polities is the parliamentary system of government in Canada, which contrasts with the separation of powers in the United States. The distinctive feature of parliamentary government is the fusion of executive and legislative powers. The locus of policy-making power is concentrated in a relatively small and cohesive Cabinet, and the crucial debate on issues comes before they are presented in the legislature for consideration.[45] However, the Cabinet is derived from, and responsible to, the legislature. Legislators are elected on the basis of party representation, and the party with the plurality of legislative seats forms the government. The Prime Minister is the leader of that party, and the Cabinet is chosen from among its elected members. The executive must, in formal terms, govern through the consent of the House of Commons; should important bills fail to muster legislative majorities, the government is said to have "lost the confidence" of the House and faces pressure to resign. Members of Parliament are therefore formally bound by the rules of party discipline in the House of Commons to vote with their party. This guarantees that, in the case of a majority government (i.e., when the governing party has a majority of seats in the House), government bills can be passed without "veto" from individual legislators. In the case of a minority government situation, third parties become the linchpin of this process, since they hold the "balance of power" between the government and the official opposition.

The rules of Canadian parliamentary government, in particular party discipline, also have an impact on the development and functioning of third parties.[46] The centralization of power allows party leaders to exert considerable control to reward and punish members of Parliament by the use of perks or sanctions, in addition to holding important levers over the selection of candidates and the allocation of party funds during election campaigns.[47] Given these constraints, protest groups that express consis-

---

victory to the Democratic party, and Ross Perot's capture of 19 percent of the vote in 1992. Gillespie 1993, chap. 8.

[44] On political institutions and third parties in the United States, see Key 1964, 279–81; Rosenstone, Behr, and Lazarus 1996, chap. 2.

[45] The appointed upper house in the Canadian Parliament, the Senate, has traditionally exercised only a limited role in policy making and, historically, at least, has been relatively muted in social policy matters. For a comparison of the Canadian and American Senates, see Gibbins 1993.

[46] See Lipset 1954, 175–77; and Epstein 1964, 56–57.

[47] See Pal 1988, 93–95.

tent and fundamental differences with existing parties have tended to look for political representation elsewhere rather than try to influence major parties from within. Likewise, members of Parliament unhappy with their party's record, but bound by party discipline, may choose the "exit" option to bolt to another party or attempt to assemble one of their own.[48] In the American two-party system, as Hirschman suggests, those who have "nowhere to go" must engage in political activism within the confines of the established parties.[49]

If the rules of Canadian parliamentary government make third-party formation more likely, they also offer an added incentive to third parties in that, even with little immediate chance of forming a government, they can nevertheless influence federal policy making. In a party system often characterized by two major parties acting as "brokers" between competing interests, third parties have often had "responsibility for innovation" by pushing the major parties to respond to voter discontent or pressure for social reform.[50] As issue "entrepreneurs,"[51] such parties can bring serious alternatives to the policy-making agenda and sustain them in the House of Commons. They can also pose a potential electoral threat, particularly if their support is regionally concentrated, and their platforms often serve as lightening rods for voter discontent. In addition, a minority government situation offers them an effective balance of power over the government and its policies. In the U.S. Congress, meanwhile, third parties are limited in their potential as an independent political force in light of the complex rules of the committee system controlled by the two major party caucuses. The representation of ideological dissent is submerged within the broader exigencies of party representation, such as the absorption of labor and the Left within the Democratic party.[52]

In contrast with the Canadian situation, flexibility, rather than discipline, is the keynote of the more decentralized American party system.[53] In the United States, competing bases of power make it difficult to coordinate disparate reform agendas, since there is not necessarily coordination between the executive and the legislature. The President is not

[48] Both of these tendencies are evident in current Canadian party politics: the right-wing Reform party, founded in 1987, grew out of an extraparliamentary western regional protest group, while the pro-sovereignty Bloc Québécois was originally formed by several members of Parliament from Quebec who bolted from their parties over constitutional issues in 1990. See Flanagan 1995; Noël 1994.

[49] Hirschman 1970, chap. 6.

[50] Clarke, Jenson, Le Duc, and Pammett 1996, 17.

[51] This refers to Wilson's typology of entrepreneurial politics and the way in which certain political actors can produce policies with concentrated costs but widely distributed benefits. Wilson 1973, chap. 16.

[52] Lipset 1977, 126–30.

[53] Crotty 1985, chap. 4.

responsible to the Congress but to his voting constituency, and the Congress is not bound by presidential leadership in its legislative decisions. Neither the House nor the Senate depend on party majorities in order to survive, nor does the executive formally depend on party majorities in the Congress in order to govern. The separation of powers also makes the legislative system more porous to outside demands, especially those of well-organized interest groups, since legislators are not bound by their parties in legislative voting. Party leaders often must negotiate to get compliance from legislators, and they are constrained in this by the lack of effective sanctions. Candidates for elected offices may represent the same party, but they tend to rely on independent financial and organizational resources. In effect, party members may share a common party label, but they "feel little or no compulsion to support the party for its own sake."[54] Although party affiliation is still an important determinant of voting patterns, party discipline is not a functional requirement of the U.S. political system, and the concessions necessary to build party majorities on an issue are substantial. The historical analysis shows that this can have far-reaching consequences on the shape of a policy as controversial as health insurance.

In addition to the separation of powers between the executive and the legislature, the way in which powers are distributed between levels of government is also important. Federalism is thus the second institutional attribute that stands out in the comparison between Canada and the United States. As Wheare suggests, the division of powers between competing levels of government is generally considered to complicate the policy-making process by encouraging fragmentation and discord, which makes it difficult to achieve consensus.[55] In the case of social policy, this also allows governments to "shift the burden" in taking responsibility for financing and developing social programs. Cross-national analyses have borne out this "dampening" effect of federalism on social expenditure, although, as Immergut points out, there is no "direct correlation" between federalism and health policy in the comparative evidence.[56] To understand the impact of federalism on health reform, it is important to look at the process through which the division of powers shapes the strategies of societal groups and imposes rules on political actors.

Although the United States and Canada are both federal polities, there are significant differences between the two in terms of the impact of federalism on policy outcomes. Despite the enumeration of residual powers

---

[54] Lawson 1968, 157.

[55] Wheare 1964, chap. 8.

[56] Immergut 1992, 52. On the notion that federalism constrains social spending, see, for example, Cameron 1978, 1253.

to the states in the American Constitution, and to the federal government in Canada, the Canadian federal system has evolved into a more decentralized arrangement than the one in the United States, where the relative power of the central government has been enhanced over the years.[57] In the United States, social matters are not explicitly enumerated in the Constitution. Congress has the power to tax to provide for the "general welfare" (art. I, sec. 8), while the states may be considered to have some latitude in social affairs through interpretations of the Tenth Amendment.[58] In the twentieth century, and particularly since the New Deal era, the federal government has played an increasingly important role in the direct provision of social benefits and in the cost-sharing and regulation of state-administered programs. In so doing, it has effectively shouldered the responsibility for "national" welfare and has been perceived by Americans as the primary source of social benefits.[59]

In Canada, health insurance, like most social matters, is considered to be under provincial jurisdiction through the powers of provincial legislatures to enact laws for the "Establishment, Maintenance, and Management of Hospitals" and all "Matters of a merely local or private Nature," as enumerated, respectively, in Sections 92(7) and 92(16) in the Constitution Act of 1867 (formerly the British North America Act). In the twentieth century, conflict between levels of government over power in health and social welfare grew more heated as the role of the state in these matters became much more important than originally envisioned. In effect, the federal government has considerable potential for involvement in provincial jurisdiction through its responsibility for "Peace, Order and Good Government" and its power to tax and spend in the provision of health and social services.[60] The federal government's involvement in health care has been primarily confined to the use of the federal spending power, although the "conditions" the federal government attached to the transfer of these did, in effect, have an impact on the provinces' jurisdictional capacities to design and implement health insurance programs.[61]

The presence of competing governments, each with its own complex network of state actors, can complicate considerably the policy-making process in areas of shared jurisdiction.[62] The development of social policy has indeed suffered from lack of provincial consensus, the negotiation of

[57] Smiley 1987, 36–37. On the "centrifugal" nature of American federalism as opposed to the "centripetal" forces at work in Canada, see Simeon 1995, 250.

[58] Nice 1987.

[59] Anton 1989, chap. 3. See also Page 1983, 17–18.

[60] Stevenson 1985, 80–81.

[61] For an analysis of the impact of federalism in the development of health insurance in Canada, see Tuohy 1989; and on efforts at retrenchment, see Smith 1995.

[62] Cairns 1977, 695–725.

problems over financing and control, disparities in regional demands, and the resistance of individual provinces to federal intervention. But federalism can also be regarded as having an "expansionist" potential: The decentralized nature of Canadian federalism can allow for important provincial innovations, and institutionalized federal-provincial bargaining can force compromises on social policy or expand the reform agenda.[63] In the United States, where the locus of policy debate is between competing interests at the national level, no coherent mechanism for social policy development has been institutionalized, and fragmentation has led to a situation in which the states act more frequently as regional lobbies.[64] In addition, the effects of American federalism are felt not so much in the intergovernmental arena as in the sectionalism reflected in Congress.[65]

Unlike the United States, Canada does not have a central institution that can effectively represent regional interests at the federal level, such as the U.S. Senate. The federal government generally attempts to have balanced representation from all regions in the Cabinet and party caucus, but this is not always possible.[66] Enduring regionalism and the sentiment of ineffective representation of regional interests in Ottawa have contributed to the rise of third parties and to their viability at both the federal and provincial levels. In the latter case, such parties have often supplanted the prominent role of one (or both) of the traditional major parties and reorganized the provincial partisan landscape.[67]

Given the relatively more decentralized nature of Canadian federalism, the many constitutional provisions considered to be under provincial responsibility (including health policy), and the more influential role of provincial governments in intergovernmental relations, the provinces can be said to exercise more independent power than American state governments. Thus, the election of third-party governments in the provinces can have significant implications for policy innovation. The expression of regional demands by third parties in Canada is much more pronounced than in the United States, where it can be channeled through regional blocs within the major parties. Where third parties came to power in the United States at the state level, many did so by using the machinery of existing major parties, and by usurping major-party labels in their state organization. While the influence of "radical" state-level third parties, particularly in the American Midwest in the first decades of the century, did have some impact on the major parties, those efforts were nevertheless limited by the encroachment of the federal government in the area of

[63] Banting 1987, chap. 2; Gray 1991, chap. 1.
[64] Klass 1985, 429.
[65] Bensel 1984; Quadagno 1988.
[66] Thomas 1991, 196–99.
[67] For a review of provincial party realignments, see Carty and Stewart 1996.

social policy and the ability of national parties to absorb their protest platforms.[68]

Together, these two institutional attributes, federalism and parliamentary government, provided opportunities for the rise of third parties in Canada and enhanced their potential influence on the elaboration and choice of policy alternatives. The presence of a social-democratic third party in Canada spurred universal health insurance to national prominence as a viable alternative in the health reform debate and served as a beacon for political pressure that led to the passage of legislation. By contrast, the absence of an independent voice for the Left in the United States ensured that the agenda for national health reform would be confined to the Democratic party. Political institutions also mattered because they set the rules by which interest groups played the political game. Efforts to overcome opposition to health reform were exacerbated by the multiple veto points in the American system, and this weakened attempts to achieve universal health insurance in the United States, while reformers in Canada did not face the same institutional obstacles.

THE LIMITS OF CULTURAL EXPLANATIONS

As suggested by the analysis so far, this book situates the development of health insurance in the United States and Canada within the context of how the demand for health reform was conditioned by the political institutions shaping party systems. It attempts to go beyond the "cultural" explanations for the differences in health policy outcomes that often permeate comparative analyses of the two countries. Such explanations associate the relatively low levels of welfare-state effort in the United States with an American value system based on dominant liberalism and the antistatist distrust of government.[69] This value system derives from what Hartz has defined as the synthesis of individualism and universalism, preference for limited government, and emphasis on self-reliance.[70] Canada, on the other hand, is seen as having a political culture that is rooted in the formative experience of what Lipset has called a "counterrevolution."[71] Although liberalism is a defining element of Canadian political culture, Canadian liberalism is different than its American counterpart because it

---

[68] An important example is the Democratic party in the 1930s; Lipset 1983, 273–98. Valelly's study of the Minnesota Farmer-Labor party also points to the tendency of political elites to concentrate their reform efforts in Washington; such a national power center had not yet developed in Ottawa during the 1930s. Valelly 1989, chap. 10.

[69] Rimlinger 1971, chap. 2; King 1973, 418–23.

[70] Hartz 1955, chap. 1.

[71] Lipset 1970, 55–62.

is affected by two transplanted legacies: that of a moderate absolutist ethos in French Canada and of the Loyalist experience in English Canada.[72] The impact of this counterrevolutionary experience and imperfect liberalism was to create a value system based on deference for elites, public authority, and social order, which have fostered a world view more oriented toward the collectivity. Such "communitarianism" translates into greater legitimacy accorded to government intervention, including the welfare state.[73] Another variant of this type of analysis suggests that the presence of "toryism," with its emphasis on collective values and the positive role of government, presented an alternative to liberalism and allowed for the development of socialism (and social insurance) as legitimate and acceptable.[74] Applied to the development of the welfare state, such analyses would suggest that Canada's welfare state will be more extensive and that the consensus surrounding social policies like health insurance by political and economic elites and the general public is higher in Canada than in the United States.

The political culture explanation remains unsatisfying for comparing health insurance outcomes in the United States and Canada for several reasons. First, in terms of the logic of comparison, Canadians and Americans are culturally more alike than they are different (at least when contrasted to Europeans). The two countries arguably share similar historical and democratic experiences and an emphasis on individualism derived from a common liberal heritage.[75] Moreover, it is difficult to try to establish a causal relationship between culture and political outcomes, or to build an explanatory framework based on sociocultural factors.[76] For example, aversion to government is often associated with manifestation of "republican" ideals derived from the American Revolution, but this aversion may also be related to the American political experience, in particular the excesses of patronage politics and reliance on the courts, practices that set limits on the efficacy and potential of government intervention.[77] In Canada, positive attitudes toward government intervention may have more to do with satisfaction with political institutions that deliver popular social goods. These social goods, including health care, are thus not necessarily the result of value differences, but rather such policies may have an impact on the type of consensus that emerges from competitive party politics and the translation of public demand through the political system.

[72] McRae 1964, 219–47.
[73] Lipset 1990, 137.
[74] Horowitz 1966, 150–57; Kunitz 1992, 116.
[75] Bell 1992, chap. 2.
[76] Elkins and Simeon 1979, 127–45.
[77] On the implications of this "state of courts and parties" in American political development, see Skowronek 1982, chap. 2.

Beyond evaluating the impact of culture, it is also difficult to operationalize and measure. How "different" do two societies have to be in order for this to have an impact on political ideologies or policy outcomes? If political culture is to be considered significant, then we should expect to find very different "values" reflected in the general public opinion polls in Canada and the United States about social policy and health reform. The cross-national evidence, however, does not reveal such striking differences. Polling from the 1940s and 1950s, for example, shows similar Canadian and American attitudes toward state intervention in health care.[78] Moreover, although differences between the United States and other industrialized countries in attitudes about the welfare state do exist, they "are not as consistently different as might be expected by the staunchest advocates of American exceptionalism."[79] The historical data on attitudes toward the welfare state in the United States show an enduring paradox among Americans in their views about the welfare state, their personal self-interest, and their collective concerns. For example, Free and Cantril found that from the New Deal era to the 1960s, attitudes toward social programs in the United States have been conservative at the ideological level (i.e., less favorable to the idea of "big government"), but interventionist at the operational level (i.e., that government should intervene to meet public needs).[80] More recent polling data on health reform show that "the conventional wisdom that portrays Americans as individualists and nothing more, is myopic."[81] In effect, while most Americans are satisfied with their personal health care, they are concerned with the overall condition of the system and of their fellow citizens' access to care.[82]

Empirical measurements of mass beliefs are useful insofar as such data can reveal "enduring public understandings" about issues such as the welfare state that underlie the relationship between citizens and their governments.[83] What governments do, or do not do, has a profound impact on how citizens evaluate and judge the capacity of the state to respond to their interests.[84] In the case of health reform, the initial contour of the debate was quite similar across the United States and Canada: to what extent should government play a role in ensuring access to health care for all citizens? Public preferences on this question were necessarily

[78] Coughlin 1980, 18–19.
[79] Shapiro and Young 1989, 68
[80] Free and Cantril 1967, chap. 5.
[81] Jacobs and Shapiro 1993–94, 254.
[82] Jacobs and Shapiro 1994.
[83] Jacobs 1992, 181.
[84] As Cairns suggests, the state is "embedded . . . in the society it serves." Cairns 1986, 57.

important in affecting health policy choices and outcomes.[85] What is different is the way in which public opinion and political debate around the health issue evolved in the two countries. What began as the platform of a regionally based, social-democratic party became the basis for widespread consensus around universal health insurance in Canada, while the ideological division about the role of government in health care still endures in the United States.

The next four chapters analyze the evolution of this political debate over health insurance in an attempt to trace the dynamic impact of parties and institutions on strategies for and against health reform in Canada and the United States. Chapter 3 looks at early health reform debates in the first decades of the century and introduces the major protagonists in the policy battles to follow. The focus is on the crisis politics of the Great Depression and the impact this has had on health and social reform. Here, the emphasis is on the impasse in health reform during the New Deal era in the United States, and the ineffectiveness of political leaders in Canada to respond to demands for economic and social reform. These events will have lasting implications not only on the development of health insurance but also on the configuration of political forces surrounding the health issue. Chapter 4 surveys the reconstruction period of the 1940s and the failures to enact health insurance legislation in the immediate postwar years. Despite important political and public debates on the health issue in both countries, national health insurance "failed" to be implemented in both countries, but the nature of these failures would have dramatically different consequences for the future of health insurance reform. This impact is readily apparent in Chapter 5, which deals with the political compromises of the 1950s. Here, the United States and Canada take profoundly divergent paths to health insurance, paths that were conditioned by the constraints and opportunities of political institutions and that would profoundly influence the shape of policy outcomes in the following decade. Chapter 6 examines the legislative development of these policies, pinpointing the institutional factors and societal pressures that led to the passage of federal health legislation in Canada and the more limited Medicare program in the United States. Chapters 7 and 8 attempt to summarize the historical evidence and, in addition, offer some thoughts on how past policy legacies are shaping current and future health reform debates.

---

[85] This has been shown in the comparison of public opinion in the formation of health policy in the United States and Britain; see Jacobs 1993.

CHAPTER THREE

The 1930s: Early Impasse in Health Reform

PRIOR TO THE 1930s, neither Canada nor the United States had seen any major federal government initiative in health policy, and the idea of comprehensive health insurance did not have a prominent place on the political agendas of either country. The Great Depression represented a watershed period for social legislation in the United States, culminating with the passage of the Social Security Act of 1935. While this legislation laid the groundwork of the American welfare state, health insurance was essentially left out of the picture. In Canada, meanwhile, the political upheavals of the 1930s were to have a more lasting impact than legislative innovations. In the absence of any New Deal–type legislation from the federal government, no strong foundation for a Canadian welfare state was laid during this period. Instead, the lasting legacies of this decade, stemming in part from the inaction of the major parties on social policy, were the formation of regional third parties, including one that would become a significant voice for social democracy in Canada.

SETTING THE STAGE: PRECEDENTS IN HEALTH INSURANCE REFORM

The first campaign for health insurance coincided with the waning years of the Progressive movement in the United States. By the mid-1910s, German and British precedents had convinced many social reformers and medical professionals that compulsory health insurance was "inevitable" in the United States.[1] Buoyed by the success of workmen's compensation laws, the American Association for Labor Legislation (AALL) adopted health security for workers as their next reform cause. The AALL's Model Bill on Health Insurance, which included contributory medical insurance for manual wage laborers, was introduced in several state legislatures in 1915 and 1916.[2]

---

[1] Numbers 1978, 30.

[2] The AALL's "Nine Standards for Compulsory Health Insurance" emphasized preventive care, comprehensive coverage, and an equitable private-public financing to reduce the

Health reform was supported by segments of both major parties, but was only formally endorsed by Theodore Roosevelt's Bull Moose Progressives and the American Socialist party. Socialist Representative Meyer London managed to get a version of the AALL bill onto the agenda of the House Committee on Labor in 1916.[3] Early that year, John Andrews of the AALL urged the Secretary of Labor to endorse "health insurance for wage earners," but the Democratic administration remained generally uncommited to the campaign.[4] There was support for the AALL bill in some state legislatures, in particular in California, but a referendum on compulsory health insurance was defeated in 1918, in part due to a campaign launched by the California Medical Society and insurance interests that played on wartime fears: "Made in Germany: Do you want it in California?"[5] In New York, health insurance figured prominently in Governor Alfred Smith's electoral campaign, but his attempts to act on the AALL bill were blocked by conservative Republicans.

The AALL bill also suffered from the lack of support from organized labor. The American Federation of Labor vehemently rejected the measure, and reiterated demands for wage reform as the alternative to "paternalistic" social benefits. Samuel Gompers, AFL president, was a member of the AALL but parted ways with the group in 1915 over the health issue, claiming they were "meddlers" in labor affairs.[6] Wary of government involvement in social insurance, Gompers warned "that unless the wage-earners protect themselves and establish their own devices, they will find themselves overwhelmed by state regulation and administration."[7]

There was no clear unanimity within the labor movement, however. At the national level, the United Mine Workers were the most vocal proponents of health insurance, and at the state level the New York Federation of Labor broke ranks to sponsor a succession of joint AALL-Federation bills.[8] At the 1918 AFL Convention, pressure from the rank and file led

---

economic burden of illness. For text of the draft bill, see the *American Labor Legislation Review*, June 1916, 239–68.

[3] Walker 1969, 290–304.

[4] John Andrews to William Wilson, 17 February 1916; File ¹⁶⁄₃₅₀; Box 56; DOL; RG 174; NA.

[5] Lubove 1986, 82–83.

[6] Witte 1957, 245; see also Dick 1972.

[7] Editorial, *American Federationist*, 23, no. 11 (November 1916): 1072–74.

[8] Support also came from such groups as the International Typographical Union; United Textile Workers of America; International Brotherhood of Pulp, Sulfite and Paper Mill Workers; and Brotherhood of Railway Carmen. State federations in California, Connecticut, Illinois, Minnesota, Missouri, Nebraska, New Jersey, Ohio, and Wisconsin also endorsed the AALL. Lubove 1986, 229.

to the formation of a committee to study health insurance, but the committee's report ultimately concluded it was an unnecessary measure that jeopardized trade union independence.[9]

The medical profession, meanwhile, vacillated. The American Medical Association (AMA) endorsed the AALL bill in 1915 in view of the fact that "[i]t seems to have been rather taken for granted that such compulsory sickness insurance laws would be passed."[10] The AMA stressed the necessity of cooperation in order to avoid the conflicts in recent British experience. The medical leadership had had mixed motives for joining the social reform bandwagon, however. These included the perception that health insurance was inevitable, and the attractiveness of monetary benefits associated with guaranteeing payments from low-income patients. As the debate dragged on, and doubts surfaced about professional autonomy, support for the idea waned. By 1920, the AMA had completed its about-face and went on record officially opposing "any plan embodying the system of compulsory contributory insurance against illness."[11]

In many respects, the AALL's initiative succumbed to "death by hysteria,"[12] fostered by anti-German rhetoric and fanned by private insurance and state medical interests. This first defeat of health reform showed the effectiveness of concerted campaigns with powerful symbolic messages, as well as the problems of lack of unity among the proponents of reform. Without the support of labor or the interest of the major parties, the AALL was unable to maintain a durable coalition around the issue.

Future legislative battles for health insurance would differ markedly from the AALL experience in at least three respects. First, reformers would be much more active inside the state apparatus; second, extra-parliamentary reform groups would expend much more effort in fashioning a wider reform alliance; and finally, the field of legislative conflict would move from the states to the federal arena. Although the AALL launched a nationwide health insurance campaign, its state-by-state approach proved impractical in the American federal system, both in terms of the multiplicity of veto points and because of the lack of a coordinating mechanism at the federal level. These lessons would not be lost on social reformers in the 1930s who were ready to use federal government intervention to accelerate health reform.

[9] Anderson 1968, 76–78.
[10] Fishbein 1947, 292.
[11] *JAMA* (1 May 1920), 1319; Anderson 1968, 74.
[12] Numbers 1978, 97–105.

HEALTH INSURANCE AND THE NEW DEAL IN THE UNITED STATES

After the Democratic party sweep of the White House and Congress in 1932, a "New Deal" was proposed to give workers and farmers a stronger "hand" in their relations with employers and the state. One of the most significant milestones in this New Deal era was the passage of the Social Security Act in 1935. But while it included provisions for old-age pensions, social assistance, and unemployment insurance, health insurance was left conspicuously out of the picture.

Health Insurance and the Economic Security Reform Agenda

In his historic economic security message to Congress in June 1934, President Franklin D. Roosevelt stressed "three great objectives—security of the home, the security of livelihood, and the security of social insurance."[13] Although several legislative measures dealing with social welfare had already been introduced into Congress, Roosevelt now put forward a more coordinated and comprehensive approach. The first priority in the "frontal attack" on economic insecurity was to be unemployment insurance.[14] Health insurance was not specifically mentioned in the President's address, but, from the outset, "this was a subject to which the Committee on Economic Security had to devote a great deal of attention."[15]

The Committee on Economic Security (CES) was appointed to prepare a report on economic security that would be the basis for a national social security program to be presented to Congress in early 1935. Three specifications were under study for inclusion in such a program: unemployment insurance, old-age pensions, and health insurance. The committee was chaired by the Secretary of Labor, Frances Perkins, and included several other Cabinet members.[16] Perkins named Edwin Witte, a University of Wisconsin economist, as Executive Director to coordinate

---

[13] U.S. Congress, House, *Congressional Record*, 8 June 1934.

[14] On FDR's social reform objectives, see Schlesinger 1959, 304–6.

[15] Witte 1962, 173–74. Frances Perkins quotes FDR as claiming health insurance to be "highly desirable," although unsure whether such insurance would be developed "sooner or later." Perkins 1946, 289.

[16] These included Henry Morgenthau (Secretray of the Treasury); Homer Cummings (Attorney General); Henry Wallace (Secretary of Agriculture), later a presidential candidate under the Progressive banner in 1948; and Harry Hopkins (Administrator of the Federal Emergency Relief Administration), a health insurance proponent.

and supervise the work of the Committee. Federal officials from various departments made up the Technical Board led by Assistant Secretary of Labor, Arthur Altmeyer. Eventually, this board was divided into smaller groups, including a Technical Committee on Medical Care. The CES also included the Advisory Council of experts from outside government, with separate medical, hospital, dental, and public health committees.[17]

Both Witte and Altmeyer were associated with the AALL and the so-called moderate "Wisconsin school,"[18] as opposed to more radical reformers of the era.[19] Witte's cautious approach to health insurance, however, stemmed less from his personal preferences than from the hostility of the medical profession. As unemployment insurance and old-age security became more controversial than had been anticipated, Witte carefully tried to avoid immediately committing the administration to health reform. There is, nevertheless, evidence that the CES was, at least initially, both serious about health reform and optimistic about its chances. At the first executive committee meeting of the Technical Board in September, the "committee stressed the point that the problem of medical care should not be regarded as being a third or fourth item in a general program for economic security. In its opinion this part of the program is equally important with other parts and equally feasible at this time."[20]

The CES commitment to health reform is also reflected in the recruitment to the CES of Edgar Sydenstricker and I. S. Falk, two social reformers from the Milbank Memorial Fund in New York, whose views on compulsory health insurance were well known. No one, however, had anticipated the vehement objections of the AMA and state medical societies to these appointments, protesting the lack of suitable representatives of the medical profession in the CES and accusing the Roosevelt administration of "not giving a fair deal to the opponents of health insurance."[21]

---

[17] Witte 1962, 22–25. The twenty-three-member Advisory Council was chaired by Frank Graham, president of the University of North Carolina. The labor delegation was led by AFL president William Green; business was represented by Gerard Swope, of General Electric; Marion Folsom, of Eastman Kodak; and Walter Teagle, of Standard Oil. The Medical Advisory Committee included Walter Bierring, AMA president; Robert Greenough, of the American College of Surgeons; and George Piersol, of the American College of Physicians.

[18] Altmeyer worked with the Wisconsin Industrial Commission (involved in drafting the Wisconsin unemployment plan) until his appointment to the National Recovery Administration in 1933. Witte, previously associated with the AALL, was a Commons student and expert in labor and unemployment legislation. It was Altmeyer who recommended Witte to Secretary Perkins. Altmeyer 1966, 7–8.

[19] Abraham Epstein and Isaac Rubinow, who had been the dominant force behind an AALL health insurance initiative, split with the AALL reformers over the issue of contributory pensions and unemployment insurance. Schlabach 1969, 85–87.

[20] Minutes of the Meeting of the Executive Committee, 27 September 1934; Box 1; Technical Board on Economic Security; RG 47; CES; NA.

[21] Witte to Sydenstricker, 24 October 1934; Witte VII; Box 16; CES; RG 47; NA.

From the outset, the medical lobby was at odds with the notion of compulsory health insurance and with the people advocating it. Clashes between the AMA and social reformers had arisen over the Committee on the Costs of Medical Care (CCMC), formed in 1927 as a nongovernmental research group of health professionals concerned with the escalating problems of the cost and distribution of and access to health services. The CCMC's extensive research led to a 1932 report that recommended changes in the organization of medical services through group practice and in their financing through group prepayment. An "open warfare" erupted over the report, since CCMC members like Sydenstricker and Falk felt these measures did not go far enough, while the medical lobby rejected all forms of group practice or payment, either compulsory or voluntary.[22]

In addition, the medical profession was not completely united on the issue, since several prominent physicians openly approved of health insurance in principle. In 1934, the American College of Surgeons seized FDR's message as an opportunity to propose "certain principles for the guidance of periodic prepayment plans for medical care of people of moderate means," for which the group was severely condemned by the AMA.[23] In addition to the College of Surgeons, other health professionals (such as hospital and some state medical associations) were, initially at least, more open than the AMA to health reform. More and more physicians, spurred by their personal experiences during the Depression (as would be their Canadian counterparts) and the findings of the CCMC, were expressing concern with the problems of health costs and delivery.

Reformers associated with the AALL, the Julius Rosenwald Fund, the Milbank Memorial Fund, and the Twentieth Century Fund urged these physicians to make known their dissatisfaction with the AMA's position. Many of these social reformers were friends or former associates of CES members. They lobbied the CES personally, stressing the potential weakness of the medical lobby's opposition and its highly "overrated . . . whispering campaign."[24] The AMA leadership, on the other hand, insisted that "there is no sentiment in the profession in favor of health insurance" and accused these private foundations of "trying to create sentiment for this insurance but have made very little headway."[25] But Witte

---

[22] Hirshfield 1970, 32. Representatives of organized medicine in the CCMC issued their own Minority Report expressing these views. See Starr 1982, 261–66.

[23] Franklin Martin [Director-General] to Witte, 8 September 1934; File 6; Box 40; CES; RG 47; NA; Falk 1936, 370–76.

[24] Michael M. Davis, "Some Relations between Health and Economic Security," 9 October 1934; Davis Folder; Box 18; CES; RG 47; NA.

[25] Witte, "Memorandum on the Conference with Dr. Olin West" [Secretary and General Manager of the AMA], 29 October 1934; Box 21; CES; RG 47; NA.

received indications that many individual physicians favored some kind of reform.[26] In his October progress report, Witte acknowledged that "[h]ealth insurance is causing considerable ferment among the doctors . . . A majority of the medical profession, at least as represented by the medical organizations, is unquestionably opposed to health insurance, but there is a considerable and probably growing minority which is beginning to make its voice heard in favor of this proposal."[27]

While the opposition of the AMA leadership was no secret, there is little indication that the CES thought health insurance a dead issue outright because of the reaction of the medical lobby. Altmeyer corroborates this view: "I think we were surprised at how strongly the AMA felt about even studying the question. But still up to the time of the [CES] report all of us, including the President, thought that there was a good chance of getting acceptance of a limited form of health insurance."[28]

Although organized medicine was quick to oppose these early health insurance initiatives, there was as yet no effective counterweight from organized labor. As the Depression wore on, the American Federation of Labor (AFL), under the leadership of William Green, began to reevaluate its position on social insurance. As the events of the 1910s showed, there had never been clear unanimity on health and social insurance within the labor movement. This situation was exacerbated during the 1930s, as the AFL leadership came under increasing pressure to push for legislative action on social reform. Although the industrial unions of the Congress of Industrial Organizations (CIO) would not split from the AFL until later in the decade, the strains of competition were forcing the AFL leadership to be more responsive to their rank and file.

Official manifestation of the AFL's change in attitude came at the October 1934 convention, where "whole-hearted endorsement of the general proposals for social insurance" were accepted, including support for unemployment insurance, old-age pensions, and, for the first time, sickness insurance "for all in the low income group." In addition, a resolution by the International Typographical Union to study health insurance was also unanimously adopted, the first of what were to become annual resolutions for legislative action in health reform.[29]

Social reformers hoped the AFL's shift in attitude "augurs well for health insurance proposals."[30] However, according to the CES, organized

[26] Witte to Perkins, 21 September 1934; Box 31; SEC; RG 174; NA.

[27] Committee on Economic Security, "Report on Progress of Work During October"; Box 1; CES; RG 47; NA.

[28] Altmeyer, COHC, 103.

[29] AFL, *Proceedings*, 1934, 598–602, 718. The ITU had earlier defied the AFL leadership in 1916 by endorsing health insurance and the AALL bill.

[30] *Social Security*, 8, no. 9 (November 1934): 2.

labor "didn't indicate any interest" in taking up the health reform cause during this period.[31] Health insurance ranked well below more immediate demands for unemployment insurance, and was less of a priority than the ongoing fight for collective bargaining rights. In addition, organized labor had not played an important part in Roosevelt's 1932 victory and was initially wary of the Democratic administration's initiatives. The passage of the National Industrial Recovery Act (NIRA), however, reinforced labor's confidence in the legislative process, and by 1934 many elements of the labor movement showed strong support for the administration.[32] So, too, did many groups that had taken the worst brunt of the Depression, namely the farmers and the unemployed. The success of the Democratic party in the 1934 congressional elections clearly reflected this, and gave an indication of the important electoral realignments to come in 1936.

It is hard to precisely gauge public opinion on health insurance, since no polls were conducted on this issue during the 1934–35 period.[33] However, there was a definite groundswell of support in the American public for economic reform and social insurance. Throughout the fall of 1934, Witte, Perkins, and Roosevelt received numerous letters, telegrams, and petitions from various individuals and groups concerning the work of the CES and, in particular, health reform. The voluminous mail indicated that support for health insurance came from a broad spectrum of the public, including social scientists, progressive reform organizations, insurers, public health doctors, state health officials, and many, many private citizens. Opposition to health insurance, meanwhile, came primarily from physicians and AMA-affiliated state medical societies.[34] This evidence seems to corroborate the impression that opposition to health insurance was concentrated within the well-organized medical lobby (despite dissent within the profession itself on the issue), while support was more diffused.

Part of the problem was that social reformers were now divided among themselves. The American Association for Labor Legislation, the catalyst for the 1915 model health insurance bill, was not very active in 1934. It did attempt to launch a letter-writing campaign to counteract the

[31] Altmeyer, COHC, 32.

[32] On organized labor and the FDR administration, see Galenson 1986, 53. The AFL at first opposed federal relief initiatives and supported the Black bill (for a 30-hour week) over the National Industrial Recovery Act proposals. Leuchtenburg 1963, 55–57).

[33] Data for the 1936 to 1938 period reveal generally high support for government involvement in improving access to medical and hospital care (see Schiltz 1970). A 1938 Gallup poll found 81 percent of respondents supported government responsibility for providing medical care to those unable to afford it (Gallup 1972, Vol. 1 (1935–1948), 106–107).

[34] Nine large folders of such letters were collected, under the heading "Public Opinion and Health"; Box 40; CES, RG 47; NA.

AMA's, but with little success. The American Association for Social Security, formed by Abraham Epstein after he split from the AALL, chastised the CES for its conservative approach to reform and advocated more radical social insurance measures. Epstein eventually refused to endorse the economic security bill, and his persistent attacks on the Social Security Act would prove a constant embarrassment to the administration.[35] Other more radical groups supporting health reform included the Medical League for Socialized Medicine, representing over one thousand New York City physicians. The League advocated the principle of the right to adequate medical care and embraced the idea of a publicly owned and operated health system, modeled after public education. While the League considered itself speaking for "field practitioners" and requested a place on the CES's Medical Advisory Committee, its proposals were considered too radical by the Roosevelt administration.[36]

The Social Security Act and the Fate of Health Insurance

As AMA opposition intensified in the fall of 1934, Witte wrote to Perkins in late October suggesting that "the best recommendation we can make on this subject is one of continued study," although he was careful to emphasize that he would not want to "dismiss health insurance at this time without being entirely satisfied that it can not be put into operation in a compulsory basis on the near future."[37] But health insurance was not the only potential impediment to the swift passage of an economic security bill through Congress. By the end of 1934, Roosevelt and the CES were concerned that the volatile political situation could also jeopardize other elements of the economic security program.

In November 1934, Roosevelt called the CES's Advisory Committees, including the Medical Advisory Committee, to a National Conference on Economic Security. While there was some hostility between the medical profession and the nonmedical social reformers, there was also evidence that many physicians were uneasy with the AMA's position and tactics. In fact, following the meetings, the lobby's letter-writing campaign stopped abruptly and "for some time afterward there were cordial relations" between the CES and the AMA.[38] The health issue was also overshadowed by the controversy over the design of the unemployment insurance plan,

---

[35] By December 1935, Witte was warning that "Epstein has become such a menace that he must be deflated" (Witte to Altmeyer, 23 December 1935; AASS File; CHM; RG 47; NA).

[36] Joseph Slavit to FDR, 14 November 1934; Folder 8; Box 40; RG 47; CES; NA.

[37] Witte to Perkins, 26 October 1934; Secretary's Files; Box 59; CES; RG 47; NA.

[38] Witte 1962, 180.

namely whether it was to be a national or a state plan, and whether it would involve subsidies or incorporate tax credits to employers. In addition to unemployment, old-age pensions were also becoming more controversial than expected due to the rise in popularity of alternative plans for social security, in particular the "revolving pensions" advocated by the Townsend movement.[39]

As the December 1 deadline for the CES report approached, it became obvious that the Technical Committee on Medical Care was stalled by these controversies and the difficulty in getting the Medical Advisory Committee to reach any compromise on legislative proposals. Secretary of Labor Perkins extended their deadline to March 1, indicating there would be an eventual health insurance component of the CES report, but that it would be better to deal with this after the other provisions were passed by Congress.

Thus, definitive health insurance proposals were not included in the CES's *Report of the Committee on Economic Security*, drafted in the last days of 1934, which stated, "We are not prepared at this time to make recommendations for a system of health insurance." However, Sydenstricker and Falk did prepare a section titled "Risks Arising Out of Ill Health," which included both recommendations for public health measures and a brief but specific outline of the principles for future health insurance plans. These included the exclusion of commercial insurance agents, contributory financing, and administration by the states "under a Federal law of permissive character" (similar to some of the later compromises of Canadian federal laws). The federal role was thus limited to establishing minimum standards, providing financial aid and incentives to the states to set up their own plans and to help cover medical costs of the indigent.

Many authors attribute the omission of health insurance as a turning point in the American health reform in which "the health insurance battle was lost."[40] Neither the CES nor the AMA saw it that way. According to accounts by Altmeyer and Witte, there was still a considerable amount of support for health insurance, spearheaded by relief administrator Harry Hopkins and by Secretary Perkins herself. However, the Committee appears to have agreed on a cautious strategy on health insurance based on an evaluation of the political constraints facing this and other social reform proposals.

---

[39] A former country doctor, Francis Townsend, developed the idea of compulsory retirement in exchange for monthly pensions to be financed by a national sales tax. These "revolving pensions" would have to be spent rapidly so as to recoup the money back into the economy and increase demand for goods and services. On the Townsend movement, see Schlesinger 1960, chap. 3; Leuchtenburg 1963, 103–6.

[40] Schlabach 1969, 114.

In fact, the CES report explicitly postponed rather than excluded legislative action in the health area by stating that the next step in the economic security program would be health insurance. Furthermore, the report enunciated important principles for federal involvement in health care, reflecting a certain commitment to the principle of government-funded health insurance within the Committee. Sydenstricker, who drafted these guidelines, felt that they had to be included in the report in order to keep health insurance on the public agenda and to goad the AMA to "actually sit in and work with us on the problem."[41]

Despite its limited health agenda, the CES report went far beyond what the medical lobby could accept. The AMA immediately convened a special House of Delegates meeting in February. Two significant things came out of the meeting. First, the medical lobby, conscious of public support and of divisions within the profession over health reform, eased its categorical opposition to all forms of insurance and endorsed the principle of voluntary health insurance for the first time. At the same time, however, the medical lobby also sought to close ranks within the medical profession against government intervention in health insurance and to discourage physicians from supporting the administration's health agenda. Soon after this meeting, doctors who had served on the Medical Advisory Committee and seemed sympathetic to the CES changed their attitude quite suddenly. The American College of Surgeons also abruptly withdrew its endorsement of compulsory health insurance.[42]

After having been so careful to postpone recommendations on health insurance, the CES was taken aback by this response. Sydenstricker continued to believe that "there is a strong underground opposition to the position taken by the reactionaries [in the AMA]" and urged that "the President . . . not be put in the embarrassing position of having been licked by a group of doctors."[43] Witte, however, was anxious enough not to want to deal with the controversial health issue. President Roosevelt, who was very cautiously monitoring the economic security bill's progress, could hardly be expected to volunteer any statements about health insurance.

When the economic security bill was finally introduced into Congress in January 1935, it was in fact more silent on health insurance than the CES report. While the new bill included significant increases in public health grants and new provisions for maternal, infant, and child health care through the Children's Bureau, the only reference to health insurance was found in the description of the new Social Security Board,

[41] Sydenstricker to Witte, 10 January 1935; Witte VII; Box 16; CES; RG 47; NA.
[42] Witte 1962, 184.
[43] Sydenstricker to Witte, 21 February 1935; Witte IV; Box 16; CES; RG 47; NA.

whose duties would include studying other aspects of social insurance not included in the bill, such as health.

Despite the Democratic majority in Congress, the economic security bill was far from a safe passage. Critics of the bill were divided among those who felt the President had gone too far and others who saw it as not enough. Witte succinctly summarized the political problems facing the bill:

> Our program apparently is a "middle of the road" proposal which is drawing fire from reactionary business interests and extreme conservatives on the one hand, and on the other, from the Townsendites and the advocates of the Lundeen Bill. There is one group which thinks we do not have sufficient standards and a much larger group which condemns us because we do not allow sufficient freedom to the states. This latter sentiment is particularly pronounced among the Senators from the southern states.[44]

Conservatives aligned with business interests opposed the legislation, as did southern Democrats hostile to federal intrusion in their states' economic affairs. But there was also hesitation from more liberal members supporting the rival Lundeen bill, first introduced in February 1934 by Ernest Lundeen, a Farmer-Labor party representative from Minnesota. This "Workers" bill outlined a social insurance system, financed by corporate and inheritance taxes, to provide cash compensation for workers and farmers unable to work due to sickness, maternity, accident and disability, old age, and unemployment. This program was "radically different" in that it covered all occupations, shifted the financial burden to employers, and included health services as part of the package.

As Valelly suggests, the fate of the Lundeen bill demonstrates the institutional constraints and opportunities of the American political system on third parties of the Left such as the Farmer-Labor party. On the one hand, Congress could be used as a "useful forum" for state-level radicalism; on the other hand, with a legislative system in which the "power was in numbers and in the committees," the major parties were still able to effectively control the social reform agenda.[45] Although third parties had been active at the state level in this period, they could not sufficiently influence the political agenda of Congress, even though the 1932 and 1936 elections led to the highest numbers of third-party members in Congress since the Progressive era. Resembling protest parties in the western Canadian provinces, these third-party representatives were regionally concentrated as well: the Farmer-Labor contingent from Minne-

---

[44] Witte to Frank Graham, 1 February 1935; Witte I; Box 16; CES; RG 47; NA.
[45] Valelly 1989, 168–69.

sota and the "La Follette" Progressives from Wisconsin.[46] However, there was no nationwide third-party resurgence, nor was there an official endorsement of any third-party platforms on social insurance from the labor movement, even though more than two thousand AFL locals endorsed the Lundeen bill.[47]

Although Senate filibusters later delayed the vote, the major changes to the economic security bill came in the House Ways and Means Committee, which dropped farmers and domestic workers from social insurance benefits, and relaxed standards for states to qualify for old-age-assistance grants. The committee also deleted the passing reference to the "future study" of health insurance from the legislation, which the AMA attacked during its testimony at the House hearings as a threat of federal compulsory health insurance.[48] The AMA also rejected the health provisions of the bill for the Children's Bureau, endorsing only public health grants. Apart from the introduction of a few separate health insurance bills, there was little mention of health matters during the congressional debate on the economic security bill.[49]

The administration bill was clearly facing enough trouble without adding the explosive issue of health insurance into the mix. Many members of Congress in both parties were not about to accept social insurance without a struggle. Indeed, the AMA would have been quick to find a responsive ear in Congress from those opposed to the Social Security Act. It may also be the case that supporters of the bill, and even those in Congress who favored health insurance, would have considered the situation too volatile to risk such reform at the time. This latter attitude was certainly expressed by Witte in February 1935: "Quite frankly we expected that the Economic Security Bill would be out of the way before the health insurance report was made. So long as this bill is still pending, the Committee must necessarily devote its major efforts to that bill and this may further hold up the health insurance report."[50]

The March 1 deadline for the Technical Committee's report on health insurance came and went as the administration bill faced obstacles in the

[46] On Roosevelt's New Deal electoral coalition and the failure of third parties, see Lipset 1983, 273–98.

[47] The Lundeen bill was also endorsed by the Socialist party, the Communist party, progressive farm organizations, and major urban unemployment councils and leagues (U.S. Congress, House, Subcommittee of the Committee on Labor 1935).

[48] Burrow 1963, 197.

[49] Two separate health insurance bills were introduced in Congress, one by a Democratic representative (Matthew Dunn of Pennsylvania, H.R. 5549), the other by a Republican senator (Arthur Capper of Kansas, S. 3253); neither went to hearings. Alabama's Hugo Black, a Democrat, introduced S. Res 38 to study into federal legislation for nationwide health insurance, but no action was taken.

[50] Witte to Kellogg, 28 February 1935; Witte I; Box 15; CES; RG 47; NA.

Congress. Even Sydenstricker, who had pressed firmly for immediate action on health now realized these constraints. While he still believed that once the report came out "a very large proportion of the medical men will have a different idea of what we are trying to do . . . I am not in favor, however, of getting the report out until the present economic security bill is out of the way."[51]

Despite the censure of the AMA, the Technical Committee's final report reiterated the principles set out by the CES, and proposed a health insurance system in which the federal government would establish minimum standards and provide financial incentives and subsidies for state programs. States were to determine the range of benefits and population coverage, and the report recommended that the plan be restricted to persons *under* sixty-five, earning less than $3000 per year. There was to be free choice of physician and hospital, either with a salary or a capitation fee basis for payment. The health plan deviated from the principles of the Social Security Act in that it was not an age-based entitlement, nor a program targeted at the indigent poor.

The Technical Committee felt its recommendations on health insurance were "especially conservative; but we believe that they offer a proper basis for the sound beginnings" for a comprehensive system.[52] Nevertheless, the health insurance report met with a mixed response in the CES. Harry Hopkins and representatives of Secretaries Morgenthau and Wallace had favorable reactions, but Secretary Perkins expressed some caution, while the Attorney General's office remained strongly opposed to any immediate action. Witte shared this reticence, and had been advised by FDR, through his physician, Dr. McIntyre, that "it would be very unwise to throw health insurance into the hopper while the rest of the program was still before Congress."[53] The CES was clearly under enough political pressure to consider even this limited health plan as "dynamite" because of its compulsory nature.[54] Accordingly, Secretary Perkins advised the President that the report "not be made public until the Social Security Bill, now pending before the Congress, has been enacted into law."[55]

But by the time the Social Security Act (SSA) was passed in August 1935, the CES was disbanding and there were no attempts to set an agenda for future legislation on health insurance. Instead, Perkins substituted a new letter of transmittal for the report, with one significant alter-

---

[51] Sydenstricker to Witte, 14 May 1935; Witte IV; Box 16; CES; RG 47; NA.

[52] U.S. Committee on Economic Security, *Risks to Economic Security Arising Out of Illness*, 1935.

[53] Witte 1962, 188.

[54] Altmeyer to Stephen Early, 19 August 1935; File 056.1 Health Insurance; Box 35; CHM; RG 47; NA.

[55] Perkins to FDR, 15 June 1935; Altmeyer Papers; Box 2; SHSW.

ation to the effect that "it is made clear that the Committee is not recommending immediate legislation" on health insurance.[56] In January 1936, Roosevelt sent this report to the new Social Security Board, with a request to study the health question but no mention of preparing legislation on the subject.[57] Altmeyer concedes that had Roosevelt "indicated that he wanted to press for a health insurance program, there is no doubt that the Social Security Board would have given the subject more attention."[58]

Health Insurance for Workers and the Wagner Bill

The health insurance debate reopened at the close of the decade. An Interdepartmental Committee to Coordinate Health and Welfare Activities, set up in 1937, undertook a health survey and issued a report entitled *The Need for a National Health Program* the following year. The recommendations included improved public health services, more hospitals, aid for the medically indigent, invalidity insurance, and general medical care insurance. The report was discussed more fully at the National Health Conference called by the administration in July 1938. The AMA approved all the recommendations except those dealing with medical insurance. Representatives of organized labor, meanwhile, approved the recommendations, although the CIO stressed the need for a national program of health insurance (not a state-administered program) based on general revenues (rather than payroll taxes), the type of plan that the labor movement in Canada was advocating.[59]

Although the conference received much positive attention, there was a wariness to act on its recommendations given the continued opposition of the medical lobby (the AMA held a second special meeting on health insurance in September) and because of the 1938 congressional midterm elections (in which the Democratic majority was considerably reduced in both the House and Senate). Roosevelt presented the Interdepartmental Committee's report to Congress in his 1939 address on health, but privately he indicated that "he did not want to go further at that time" on health insurance.[60]

---

[56] Perkins to CES members, 2 December 1934; File Social Security; Box 92; DOL; RG 174; NA.

[57] Roosevelt to Winant, 14 January 1936; Box 2; Altmeyer Papers; SHSW.

[58] Altmeyer 1966, 57.

[59] U.S. Interdepartmental Committee to Coordinate Health and Welfare Activities, *Proceedings of the National Health Conference*, July 18–20 1938, Washington, DC.

[60] Altmeyer 1966, 115.

Instead, in late February 1939, Senator Robert Wagner of New York introduced the National Health Bill, based on the Interdepartmental Committee's report, that emphasized public health and indigent care but also included federal grants for state medical plans. It was essentially a compromise measure to accommodate the medical lobby, by incorporating a separate indigent care program and by allowing flexibility in the administration and eligibility criteria of state programs. The AMA, however, rejected the bill as "unsound," insisting indigent care be controlled by local authorities and objecting to state medical plans, which would "pave the way for compulsory health insurance."[61]

Social reformers in and out of government felt the Wagner bill was weak, but they supported it as a "concrete program for action which could serve as a rallying point for the farm and labor organizations that wanted extensive federal health programs."[62] Although both the AFL and the CIO endorsed the bill as a compromise, it was obvious it did not satisfy all their demands.

The Senate Committee report on the Wagner bill approved the state-based approach to medical care, but postponed action until the next session.[63] Although no further action was taken (World War II intervened), these end of decade developments were significant. The emphasis on state administration of health programs and the division between indigent care and general insurance that characterized the Wagner bill would later reemerge in the 1965 Medicaid compromise. The Wagner bill also led to the first legislative hearings specifically on health insurance in which organized labor and medicine squared off for the first time. Even in the midst of internal battles that were splitting the American labor movement, health insurance remained an important legislative priority. This priority, however, remained within the confines of a social reform agenda defined by the Democratic party. In Canada, labor would also show support for health reform, but as shaped by the social-democratic principles of a third party of the Left.

THE CANADIAN SOCIAL REFORM AGENDA IN THE 1930S

Although Canadians suffered similar, if not worse, economic hardship during the Great Depression, this period did not usher in a watershed of

---

[61] Arthur Booth, AMA Board of Trustees, U.S. Congress, Senate, Committee on Education and Labor, *To Establish a National Health Program: Hearings before a Subcommittee of the Committee on Education and Labor on S. 1620*, pts. 1–3, 76th Cong., 1st sess., 5 May 1939, 152–56.

[62] Hirshfield 1970, 140.

[63] U.S. Congress, Senate, Senate Report No. 1139, 4 August 1939, 1–38.

social reform or a "New Deal" designed to alleviate the needs of workers and farmers. The political climate, however, was far from placid. Provincial governments bore the political brunt of social discontent, and regional protest movements fractured the Canadian party system.

The Absence of Federal Government Response

At the turn of the twentieth century, European developments in health insurance, particularly in Germany and Britain, incited interest and discussion in both Canada and the United States. But members of organized medicine in Canada seemed much more skeptical of these experiments than their American counterparts. The Canadian Medical Association (CMA) was harshly critical of the British system of state medicine and, from 1914 to 1917, the period in which the AMA expressed a sense of inevitability surrounding health reform, medical leaders in Canada "assumed that health insurance would be a long time coming to Canada."[64] On the other hand, from 1917 to 1920, as the AMA began to shape its opposition to health insurance, the CMA began to look more closely at the British system and the advantages of having medical professionals become "servants of the state."[65] This flurry of interest in "wartime collectivism" soon faded, however, leaving mainly uncertainty or disinterest about health insurance among Canadian medical professionals in the 1920s.[66]

Like its American counterpart, the Canadian federal government was relatively inactive in health and social reform before the 1930s. A Dominion Department of Health was established in 1919, designed mainly to coordinate federal activities in public health. In 1928, it merged with the Department of Soldiers' Civil Re-Establishment and was renamed the Department of Pensions and National Health. The Liberal government did instruct a Select Standing Committee of the House of Commons on Industrial and International Relations to study unemployment and sickness insurance; the Committee's 1929 report recommended "a comprehensive survey of public health, with special reference to a national health programme." On sickness insurance, however, it was recommended that the provinces initiate legislation, given their constitutional jurisdiction, although the federal government could enter into cost-sharing arrangements provided along the lines of the 1927 Old Age Pension Act.[67]

[64] Bothwell and English 1981, 480.
[65] See, for example, "The Medical and Allied Professions as a State Service," *Canadian Medical Association Journal* 10, no. 3 (January 1920): 71–73.
[66] Naylor 1986, 45.
[67] Canada, House of Commons, *Report of the Select Standing Committee on Industrial*

This pension legislation was the first major social legislation passed by the federal government. The federal Liberal party was the first major Canadian political party to endorse social insurance. After suffering electoral defeat in 1911, Liberal leaders were determined to begin the postwar era with a vigorous political agenda. In 1919, the party chose a new leader, William Lyon Mackenzie King and adopted a new platform that included federal-provincial cooperation toward "an adequate system of insurance against unemployment, sickness and dependence in old age."[68] King had played a key role in developing federal labor policy (as the Department of Labour's first Deputy Minister), and in 1918, published *Industry and Humanity*, a treatise that heralded the need for a larger role for the state in economic and social life. But although this proved King "could intellectualize about the need for social security protection," as Prime Minister, he failed to "convey any sense of commitment" toward social reform.[69]

King did not regard the onset of the Depression, for example, as an opportune time to consider social reform. As would be the case in many future discussions of social reform in Canada, King evoked constitutional constraints as a reason not to intrude in provincial jurisdiction over social welfare. In 1930, his government was swept out of office for failing to offer even the minimum of aid to the provinces to help deal with catastrophic unemployment. Goaded by attacks from independent labor member J. S. Woodsworth in the House of Commons on the government's insufficient relief efforts, King lashed out against the provincial governments' demands for money for "alleged unemployment purposes" and declared "I would not give them a five-cent piece."[70] This "Five-Cent Speech," one of King's rare political mistakes, cost him the 1930 election, and also contributed to the Liberal party's loss of credibility in the area of social reform.

The linkage that Roosevelt's New Deal made between economic and social renewal was not shared by King. In fact, the Liberal leader was appalled by FDR's desertion of classic liberalism, and he felt the New Deal leaned dangerously toward a planned economy.[71] King kept his public criticisms muted, however. Out of power during the worst of the De-

---

and International Relations, 1929. The Act provided for federal funds, administered by the provinces, to cover half the cost of means-tested pensions for Canadians over 70 years of age. See Bryden 1974, 61–63.

[68] Carrigan 1968, 82. On King's influence in promoting "welfare liberalism," see Campbell and Christian 1996, 77–79.

[69] Guest 1980, 66.

[70] Canada, House of Commons, *Debates*, 3 April 1930. King blamed "the hypocrisy of the Opposition & self-righteousness of Woodsworth & the Labour-Farmer group which made me speak as I did" (King Diary, 3 April 1930, quoted in Neatby 1963, 318–19).

[71] On the influence of FDR and the New Deal on the Liberal party of Canada, see McAndrew 1978, 142–43.

pression years, King could not afford to denounce the types of reforms that were proving so popular with the American public next door. In addition, many members of the Liberal party found Roosevelt's "new liberalism" politically appealing. In September 1933, these reformers organized a conference in Port Hope, Ontario, to discuss plans to rejuvenate the Liberal party, including the relevance and applicability of the New Deal for Canada. King was not convinced of this, but he could not risk alienating the progressive wing of his party, especially since a newly formed social-democratic party was popularizing the idea of government intervention as the only long-term solution to economic uncertainties.

Initially, King's successor, Conservative Prime Minister R. B. Bennett, did not have many more far-sighted ideas than his predecessor. Bennett, a corporate lawyer and "caricature capitalist," regarded the Depression as a temporary economic downswing. His government's response to the Depression was predictably limited, focusing on temporary economic stimulus through public work projects and higher tariffs. As unemployment continued to rise unabated, however, the government was forced to resort to more urgent measures, such as setting up work camps for single unemployed men in 1931 and implementing direct relief in 1932.[72]

Pressure mounted on the Conservative government, and from unlikely sources. Like the members of the communities they served, physicians in both rural and urban Canada were severely affected by the Great Depression. Middle-class families with suddenly reduced incomes found it difficult, if not impossible, to pay medical fees. The indigent medical care system, formerly financed through municipalities and charity, collapsed under the weight of drastically increased relief rolls. Although the question of unpaid service was already a problem for doctors in the 1920s, it reached crisis proportions in the 1930s. The Canadian medical profession began to realize that government intervention could be useful to offset such problems and to guarantee payment for those otherwise unable to pay for medical services. In 1933, representatives of the CMA traveled to Ottawa to press upon the Prime Minister the gravity of their situation and the need for medical relief.[73] The following year, the CMA went on record endorsing the "principle of health insurance."[74]

The Conservative government was also under increasing pressure for unemployment insurance. There was mounting unrest from both organized labor and the unemployed, especially within the work camps. A

---

[72] Thompson and Seager 1985, 261, 213–18.

[73] Bothwell and English 1981, 483–84; Naylor 1986b, 58–59.

[74] "A Plan for Health Insurance in Canada," 65th Annual Meeting of the CMA, Calgary, 18–22 June 1934, reprinted in the *CMAJ* Supplement to vol. 91 (September 1934).

deluge of resolutions from labor unions urged action on unemployment insurance, while letters flooded into the Prime Minister's office, many asking for work or financial assistance to meet medical bills.[75] The Conservative party was falling abysmally out of public favor, both at the federal level and in the provinces. By the end of 1934, Conservative governments had been swept out of office in British Columbia, Saskatchewan, Nova Scotia, and Ontario. The party was losing support not only to the Liberals but also to third parties throughout the prairie provinces.

Facing an election in 1935, Bennett finally turned to the social insurance platform that had become so important in the British and American responses to the economic crisis. During a visit to London for an Imperial Conference in 1933, Bennett met with the British Minister of Labour to discuss unemployment and health insurance; upon his return, he instructed his government to study similar types of proposals for Canada.[76] In November 1934, Canadian senior civil servants were authorized to attend Roosevelt's National Economic Conference.[77] Although Bennett had been initially quite hostile toward the New Deal, he was well aware of the enthusiasm surrounding these economic security proposals. The Canadian Minister in Washington, William Herridge, urged Bennett to "emulate . . . Roosevelt's public relations success," in order to restore economic confidence in Canada and attract electoral support from a wide variety of groups as it had in the United States.[78]

Bennett unveiled his own "New Deal" for Canada in a series of radio broadcasts in January 1935, proclaiming his commitment to "social justice" and "the end of laissez faire," and promising legislative action on minimum wages and working hours, unemployment insurance, farm support, a new old-age pensions program; even health insurance found a place in the jumble of promises. The Bennett New Deal came as a virtual surprise to everyone. The Conservative party and Cabinet, not informed previously, were stunned. So, too, were business interests, who had specifically warned Bennett against succumbing to popular demand for such measures. The Canadian Chamber of Commerce cautioned against unemployment insurance in view of efforts to reduce taxation, and the Canadian Manufacturers Association used jurisdictional arguments to voice

[75] NAC; MG 26; R. B. Bennett Papers; see also the letters reprinted in Grayson 1971.

[76] Struthers 1983, 121.

[77] W. C. Clark, Deputy Minister of Labour, was invited by the Committee on Economic Security. In accepting the invitation he noted that "it will be impossible for me to make any public statement in the meeting with regard to our own plans, as no official statement of policy has yet been given out by our Government" (Clark to Perkins, 10 November 1934; Witte III; Box 16; CES; RG 47; NA).

[78] Thompson and Seager 1985, 263; see also McConnell 1969, 33–34.

opposition against unwarranted federal action on unemployment and sickness insurance.[79] Labor perceptively labeled the effort "old wine in new bottles," comparing it to the yet unrealized 1919 Liberal platform.[80] In general, most Canadians "were almost dumbfounded to hear . . . the man widely thought of as a reactionary spokesman for big business, using the rhetoric of social revolution."[81]

The revolution did not come to pass, however. Despite the sweeping scope of Bennett's promises, the Employment and Social Insurance (ESI) Act that derived from them was not a radical program, except insofar as it treaded on provincial jurisdiction. Although Bennett's New Deal had been inspired by the success of its American namesake and modeled on British precedents in unemployment and health insurance, the ESI Act presented in 1935 was but a shadow of these initiatives. The health provisions were exceptionally vague, pledging federal cooperation for collecting health insurance data and information, or reviewing any proposed scheme with the provinces, municipalities, or private groups. Grilled by the opposition, both the Liberals and the newly formed Co-operative Commonwealth Federation (CCF), Bennett admitted that the Act "lays the foundation" for federal involvement in health insurance, but committed no real funds for that purpose.[82]

Despite opposition from business interests, the Conservative caucus voted with its leader in the House of Commons, and the ESI Act passed. Implementation was delayed, however, by the ensuing federal election in the fall of 1935. The "New Deal" was a crucial element of the Conservative party's campaign strategy, but the electoral debate focused more on the government's dismal record in office than on the promises of Bennett's "death-bed conversion."[83] With an electoral platform that boldly declared "King or Chaos," the Liberal party won over 70 percent of the seats in the House of Commons, establishing a pattern of majority rule that would persist until the late 1950s.[84]

This change in government, although a massive protest against the Conservatives, was not interpreted as a mandate for radical social reform by the Liberals. Indeed, the new government did not even implement the ESI Act. After the Supreme Court ruled the act unconstitutional because it involved infringement on provincial jurisdiction, King referred

---

[79] PAC; MG 26; R. B. Bennett Papers, for similar letters from municipal boards of trade, bank and financial officers, and other business interests.

[80] TLC, *Canadian Congress Journal* 14, no. 1 (January 1935): 8–9.

[81] Neatby 1972, 64–65.

[82] Canada, House of Commons, *Debates*, 21 February 1935, 1063–64.

[83] McConnell 1969, 37. Struthers (1983, 127) refers to the Bennett New Deal as "an act of sheer opportunism born out of political desperation."

[84] On the 1935 campaign and election, see Whitaker 1977, chap. 2.

the legislation to the Judicial Committee of the Privy Council in London; the ruling was upheld and the Act's provisions were declared *ultra vires* in 1937.[85]

Rather than launch his own New Deal, King instead appointed a Royal Commission on intergovernmental relations, with an emphasis on resolving the jurisdictional confusion that had doomed the ESI Act. Although King basically tried to continue the relief approach to the Depression, pressure for unemployment insurance was still strong, particularly in the face of rising labor militancy and the structural unemployment that plagued the Canadian economy. This debate finally came to a head in 1939–1940. With the outbreak of World War II, worker cooperation was essential to the war effort, and the provinces were amenable to agreeing to a constitutional amendment that ushered in federal unemployment legislation in 1940.

Social Reform and the Emergence of Third Parties in the 1930s

The weakness of Ottawa's response to the Depression reinforced worker and farmer dissatisfaction with the major parties, who were perceived to be in collusion with capitalist interests. These parties seemed unable and unwilling to respond to worker demands or to farmer protest, especially in the western provinces. In the United States, the New Deal attempted to respond in some measure to the economic crisis, but in Canada, no equivalent of the Wagner Act or Social Security Act was implemented by either the Liberal or Conservative government. It was the lack of such a response that helped fuel the sense of a "common foe" among protest groups: "Unlike socialist parties in the United States, where Roosevelt's New Deal became the embodiment of radicalism and thus undercut the support the American socialists had or might have gained, the CCF was seen by many Canadians to be the main fighter in legislative bodies against the Depression, and against the system itself."[86]

In vivid contrast to King or Bennett, Roosevelt deliberately sought out the leaders of political protest movements and seized their reform platforms, effectively co-opting such movements within the Democratic party coalition. As the Democratic party regrouped organized labor and the progressive Left through its commitment to social and economic reform, federal third parties of the Left (such as the Socialists or Progressives) found it more difficult to inspire widespread support. State-level third

---

[85] The decisions of the JCPC of Great Britain, which served as the final court of appeal for Canadian law until 1949, tended to interpret broadly the constitutional powers of the provinces. Manfredi 1993, 29–30.

[86] Penner 1977, 203–4.

parties (such as the Minnesota Farmer-Labor party) were facing a dual problem: in Congress, the institutional rules of the game impeded their attempts to influence the political agenda; in their home states, meanwhile, the centralizing effects of the New Deal were transforming the nature of American federalism and usurping substantial state initiative in the area of social reform.

In Canada, the regional nature of such protest movements would instead be reinforced by the political developments of the 1930s. The most important challenge facing the major parties in Canada was the emergence of regionally based third-party support, particularly in the western provinces. The first significant manifestation occurred in the 1920s, when farmer protest led to the historic results of the 1921 election in which the Conservatives were relegated to third place behind the Progressive party.[87] Sharing some of the same roots as the agrarian populist movement in the western United States,[88] the Progressives enunciated the pro–free trade stance of western Canadian farmers (as opposed to the protectionism of eastern manufacturing interests). They also tended to support the use of "state action against societal evils," including government involvement to improve the access and quality of health care.[89]

In the United States during this period, the Progressives exercised influence in state-level politics, primarily through usurping the state organization of a traditional party (e.g., the Non-Partisan League and the Republican party in North Dakota). But the real influence of the agrarian movement in the American political system during this era was felt at the federal level. By the 1920s, a western "farm bloc" was at work within both major parties, although with little independent impact.[90] In presidential races, the Progressive party, like its Populist predecessor, did influence party politics. Under the banner of Wisconsin's Robert La Follette, the Progressives won 16 percent of the vote in the 1924 presidential election by rallying labor and socialist support to agrarian dissent. The three bases of support of the Progressives (western farmer, labor, socialist) would be effectively co-opted into the emerging Democratic party realignment by the 1930s. In Canada, a coalition of these interests would lead to the formation of a third party of the Left, the Co-operative Commonwealth Federation, in 1932.

The fate of the Progressive party in Canada was conditioned by the exigencies of parliamentary politics. The dictates of party discipline forced

---

[87] On the Progressive party, see Morton 1950.

[88] The most significant parallel would be the Non-Partisan League. On the rise of agrarian reform movements and "traditions of radicalism" in western Canada and the United States, see Sharp 1948.

[89] Morton 1950, 27.

[90] Sharp 1948, 137–38.

such reform elements to seek independent representation as a third party, rather than trying to work through major-party organizations. As the case of the Progressive party shows, they also had much more potential for electoral success as a regional protest bloc in the House of Commons than did their American counterparts either in Congress or in presidential elections. However, the success of third parties, in terms of exerting a durable impact on party politics, depended on their survival as independent political entities. The Progressive party was hampered by its reluctance to abide by the rules of the game, namely, the institutional constraints of party discipline. With sixty-four seats in Parliament, the party was in a position to form the official opposition in 1921, but its members would not agree on a common leader and rejected caucus rule, making party discipline impossible. This lack of discipline, both reflecting and reinforcing the divisions within the group, meant that the electoral coalition could not survive in the legislature. By 1924, the party had split into a "Liberal" wing, effectively co-opted by the Liberal party, and the more radical "Ginger Group," which was attracted to the leadership of an independent labor member, J. S. Woodsworth.

Woodsworth was able to forge a much more effective and durable political reform coalition by embodying three pillars of protest (farmer, labor, socialist) within the Co-operative Commonwealth Federation. Although the CCF was not a direct descendant of the Progressive party, it shared some of the same roots. Woodsworth, a follower of the Social Gospel, was influenced by western populism, but his political experience was clearly labor-based and socialist, although he disagreed with both the Gomperism of the Trades and Labor Congress (TLC) and the revolutionary stance of the Socialist party in Canada.[91] In 1921, Woodsworth won a seat as the Independent Labour candidate for Winnipeg Centre, in the same protest wave that elected the Progressives.[92] By 1926, Woodsworth was joined by a second independent labor representative, A. A. Heaps of neighboring Winnipeg North. Although not the first labor representatives elected to the House of Commons,[93] the two men were the first to exercise independent political influence, such as precipitating the passage of Old Age Pension Act legislation just before the 1926 election.[94]

[91] Woodsworth was involved in social welfare reform before becoming active in the Vancouver longshoremen's union. A supporter of industrial unionism, he was arrested for sedition during the Winnipeg General Strike of 1919. See McNaught 1959.

[92] McNaught 1959, 153. The riding became Winnipeg North Centre in 1930, and Woodsworth continued to represent it until his death.

[93] Alphonse Verville (Montreal-Maisonneuve), of the TLC, was elected to Parliament in 1908 under the Parti ouvrier (labor-socialist) banner; he joined the Liberals in 1917. Lipton 1967, 121.

[94] See Bryden 1974, 69–72.

Part of this influence stemmed from the fact that they retained their independent political identity and, unlike many Progressives, would not be co-opted into the Liberal party, despite the efforts of Mackenzie King to have them join his cabinet.

Outside of Parliament, labor groups in western Canada established contacts with farmer organizations, many of which were associated with existing provincial third parties. The socialist movement in Canada, meanwhile, still faced the same ideological splits as in the United States. In contrast, however, the more moderate and noncommunist factions were moving closer toward a CCF farmer-labor coalition, a tendency that was not as successfully pursued in American national politics. Although the Depression was an important factor in bringing these groups together, the precedent of third-party politics in western Canada, and Woodsworth's leadership in uniting them into an independent alliance, were crucial to the success of the CCF.

After the 1932 Calgary Conference established the CCF, the League for Social Reconstruction (LSR) was asked to draw up an official platform for the new group. The LSR had been formed earlier that year by a group of British-educated university professors, who saw the League as the "Canadian version of the Fabian society."[95] The group was instrumental in attracting "urban radicals" to the CCF, particularly intellectuals from eastern Canada. In 1933, most of the LSR program was adopted at the CCF's first convention, forming the "Regina Manifesto," which would remain the party's political program until the late 1950s.

The Regina Manifesto attempted to define a distinctive Canadian socialism, a "mixture of Christian, Fabian, and Marxian socialism, shot through with progressive reformism."[96] As a response to the "catastrophic depression," it envisioned radical change (socialization of finance, essential industries and services, and economic planning) through nonrevolutionary methods (a broader alliance of social groups working through a political party). Social reform such as unemployment insurance and old-age pensions were to be part of a "national labor code," but the socialization of health care was the only social service singled out for attention: "Publicly organized health, hospital and medical services . . . should be made at least as freely available as are educational services."[97]

Social reform was an important issue for the new CCF in the House of Commons. In 1935, Woodsworth gave "qualified support" to Bennett's New Deal, and urged immediate constitutional amendments to allow the

[95] Underhill 1960, x–xii. The LSR was also influenced by the League for Industrial Democracy in the United States; M. J. Coldwell, Woodsworth's successor, was an active member of the latter.

[96] Young 1969, 45.

[97] Regina Manifesto, pt. 8; Young 1969, 309.

federal government more flexibility in initiating social legislation. In the debate over the health provisions of the ESI Act, Heaps offered the most concrete solution to the problem, both its social and constitutional aspect, by suggesting that the federal government "make grants to such provinces as adopt provincial schemes of health insurance," referring to initiatives developed in British Columbia and Saskatchewan.[98]

In its first federal election in 1935, the CCF faced both major parties plus two other third parties, the Social Credit and the Reconstruction parties. The latter was a Conservative splinter group that would not outlast the election, but the Social Credit became an important force in western provincial politics, particularly in Alberta and, later, British Columbia. Led by "Bible Bill" Aberhart, a radio preacher who resembled Townsend in style and tone, the party offered a populist solution to the Depression through a $25 per month "social credit" for all adults.[99]

Thus, the protest vote the CCF had hoped to capture was splintered between these groups and the newly charged Liberals. While the CCF led all third parties with 9 percent of the vote across Canada, the CCF ended up with only seven seats, in Manitoba, Saskatchewan, and British Columbia. The CCF's showing in British Columbia was especially significant, as the party won more votes than either the federal Liberals or Conservatives, echoing its success in the 1933 provincial election, when it ran second to the Liberal party.

The CCF's success in British Columbia was indicative of the strength of the labor element in the party in areas dominated by industrial unions. The relationship between independent political action and organized labor had long been subject to the same problems in Canada as in the United States and to similar disputes over the Gompers legacy, and the AFL had considerable influence in promoting nonpartisan political action in Canada.[100] There were at least two differences, however. First, interest in independent labor representation, at both the federal and provincial levels, was never completely suppressed within the Canadian labor movement, particularly among the rank and file. In 1906, the Trades and Labor Congress had approved the principle of independent political action, and in the 1920s it briefly backed a labor party. Further, radical and socialist ideals remained influential in the Canadian labor movement, as evidenced by the Winnipeg General Strike of 1919.[101] While this influence was also felt in elements of the American labor movement, it did not

[98] Canada, House of Commons, *Debates*, 21 February 1935, 1066–67; McNaught 1959, 234–35, 251–53.

[99] On the Social Credit's rise to power in Alberta, see Finkel 1989, chap. 2.

[100] On the influence of American labor on political activity in Canada, see Babcock 1974, chap. 11.

[101] Palmer 1983, 178.

exercise the same impact on labor's political agenda. Nevertheless, labor did not take center stage at the founding of the CCF. Aaron Mosher (of the All-Canadian Congress of Labour) was the only trade union representative at the party's formation at Calgary in 1932. The first official linkage with organized labor came only in 1938, when a United Mine Workers local (District 26, of Glace Bay, Nova Scotia) pledged direct affiliation with the CCF.[102]

The uncertain role of labor derived from two sources. A strained relationship existed between labor and farmer elements within the party. Although it was envisioned as a class-based party of the Left, the CCF was also a party that built on existing political entities, of which the best organized were farmer groups.[103] The regional concentration of agrarian interests coupled with the electoral exigencies of the Canadian political system meant that the CCF would be able to more readily win seats in farmer-dominated areas. Although farm and labor groups in Canada shared common social reform goals (including health insurance), they had fundamentally different economic interests, and farmer groups remained wary of labor's presence in the CCF.

The second obstacle in Canadian labor's relationship with the CCF was the clash of proclivities within the labor movement itself, between Gomperism and independent political activism. The legacy of the U.S. labor movement in promoting nonpartisan political action in Canada had a considerable impact in dampening organized labor's enthusiasm for the CCF. Although the craft-dominated Trades and Labor Congress (regrouping AFL affiliates in Canada) had previously sanctioned the nomination of independent labor candidates, the leadership rejected the party despite the overtures of the CCF and heated discussion on political action at TLC conventions throughout the 1930s. Many in the rank and file, disillusioned by the failure of the major parties to respond to economic crisis, felt the time had come to abandon a nonpartisan stand and endorse an independent third party. One particularly forceful resolution at the 1933 TLC convention stated: "Whereas President Roosevelt . . . is rapidly demonstrating what real political . . . leadership will do . . . and whereas, our two old political parties . . . have proven themselves complete failures . . . be it resolved that [this convention] endorse the new political party known as the C.C.F."[104]

Support for the CCF came from a rival labor organization, the All-Canadian Congress of Labour. The ACCL was forged out of the national unions in the Canadian Federation of Labour, which had been expelled

---

[102] Morton 1977, 13–17.
[103] On the role of agrarian movements in the CCF, see Lipset 1971, chap. 10.
[104] Resolution by the Moncton Machinists, TLC, *Proceedings*, 1933, 189.

from the American-dominated TLC in 1902, and affiliates of the Canadian Brotherhood of Railway Employees. In 1940, the Canadian affiliates of industrial-based CIO unions would join the ACCL to form the Canadian Congress of Labour (CCL). The CCL, like the CIO in the United States, was less in the thrall of the principle of nonpartisanship, and more inclined to political activism.

Just as the AFL and CIO began to converge on social reform in the United States in the 1930s, both labor organizations in Canada pressed for government action, particularly unemployment insurance. Health insurance, however, was also singled out for attention. Sickness insurance had been on the platform of the Trades and Labor Congress since 1921, and the All-Canadian Congress of Labour had supported government-financed health care since 1927. Throughout the 1930s, as in the United States, resolutions for federal health legislation were passed at labor conventions.

The pivotal role that Canadian labor and its association with the CCF would take in future health reform debates was foreshadowed by its role in the campaign for health insurance in British Columbia. Although the TLC was involved in this effort, the British Columbia labor scene was dominated by more militant industrial organizations that were, significantly, more closely aligned to the CCF in British Columbia than anywhere else in Canada.[105]

Health Insurance Efforts in the Provinces

In the absence of social insurance initiatives by the federal government, the provinces were forced to confront not only the economic consequences of the Depression, but also the protest and political instability that this produced. During the 1930s, many provincial governments began to realize the implications of what jurisdictional responsibility for social insurance would mean, and they began to examine more closely the federal-provincial relationship in these areas, including health insurance.

In contrast to the efforts of the American Association for Labor Legislation in the American states, there was no concerted effort for government-sponsored health insurance by social reformers or private philanthropic groups in the Canadian provinces. Instead, individual provinces launched some of their own initiatives in the health area, often spurred by the presence of progressive united farmer governments.

In the early twentieth century, public sector involvement was limited to

[105] Irving 1987, 168.

provincial funding for institutional care (mental illness and tuberculosis) and municipal provision of public health services, as in the United States. In the Poor Law tradition, limited care for the medically indigent was also available, often supplemented by private charities and religious institutions. Increasingly, as municipalities became overburdened by these tasks, provincial governments were compelled to take more of an interest in health care. In Saskatchewan, the Union Hospital Acts of 1916–17 set up rural area hospitals, and in 1917 the Rural Municipality Act allowed municipalities to levy taxes in order to retain rural doctors. The United Farmers of Alberta government was "ostensibly committed to implementing a state medical service," but although health insurance was passed in 1935, the new Social Credit government refused to implement the legislation, arguing that the promised social dividend would provide enough for individuals to pay for their own medical care.[106]

In the early years of the Depression, medical associations demanded government medical relief to alleviate the financial burden of nonremunerated care. Lacking a response from the federal government, medical associations took their case directly to the provinces and the municipalities. The Ontario Medical Association was in fact responsible for administering the province's medical relief plan in 1935. The most drastic action came in Manitoba, where physicians in the city of Winnipeg staged a doctor's "strike," withdrawing all but emergency services to relief recipients, to protest the absence of a medical relief policy that would offer some kind of partial payment to doctors.[107]

It was in British Columbia, however, a province wracked by militant working-class elements and the active presence of the Left in the political arena, that the question of comprehensive health insurance would be most significant during the Depression years. British Columbia had been the first province to formally study health insurance. In 1919, a Royal Commission on State Health Insurance was appointed, but its recommendations for a system of health insurance were not implemented; instead, the legislature passed a resolution urging federal action.

By the time a second Royal Commission reported in 1932, pressure for health reform was heightened by the ravages of the Depression. The report recommended compulsory health insurance for lower-income workers, with voluntary participation for all other residents.[108] The Conservative government did not act on this or other social insurance measures, and, like King's and Bennett's experiences at the federal level, this inac-

---

[106] J. J. Heagerty, "Health Insurance in Canada"; NAC; RG 29; Box 1063; File 502–1-1, pt. 6.

[107] On Canada's "first" doctor's strike, see Naylor 1986, 151–80.

[108] British Columbia, *Final Report of the Royal Commission on State Health Insurance and Maternity Benefits*, 1932.

tion was rewarded by a decisive electoral defeat in 1933. The new Liberal premier, Thomas "Duff" Pattullo, won election on a New Deal platform for "Work and Wages." Pattullo had no qualms about being associated with Roosevelt's liberalism and considered government intervention necessary to alleviate the economic ills of the Depression. In British Columbia, a province that had developed the most radical blend of protest politics and labor militancy in Canada, Pattullo was encouraged to take this position out of political necessity. The 1933 election was the first campaign of the newly formed CCF, and the party's more radical provincial wing in British Columbia won the support of industrial labor organizations and gained a significant part of the working-class vote. The CCF won 31 percent of the vote at the polls, and although this translated into only seven seats, the CCF nevertheless became the official opposition in the British Columbia legislature.

Pattullo's strategy was aimed at convincing the federal government to assist the province out of its economic crisis through financial loans, unemployment insurance, and public works projects. Pattullo also emphasized the need for federal assistance in order to implement provincial innovations in social insurance, of which the most important was the commitment to implement the health insurance recommendations of the 1932 Royal Commission.[109]

While the public seemed generally in favor of health insurance, there was a clear split in opinion along ideological and class lines over the issue: labor, the CCF, progressive Liberals, and lower-income workers against business, organized medicine, and conservative Liberals. Many members of Pattullo's Cabinet were certainly not as committed to reform as he was. In addition, the lack of financial guarantees from Ottawa to help finance the program posed serious problems. Although Pattullo tried to convince King that increased public spending was the only way to rid the Liberal party of the CCF threat, the Prime Minister refused to commit himself. In the meantime, business voiced opposition to the contributions required by employers to finance health insurance. Business opposition included boards of trade, chambers of commerce, and the powerful British Columbia Loggers' Association, who feared the higher taxes associated with the health plan would give competitors elsewhere a market advantage.

The medical profession in British Columbia had participated in the drafting of the health legislation, and it had initially supported the plan because it covered the indigent and limited compulsory insurance to low-wage earners.[110] Doctors in British Columbia, reeling from the economic

---

[109] Fisher 1991; and Ormsby 1962, 277–97.
[110] British Columbia, *A Plan for Health Insurance for British Columbia*, 1935.

impact of the Depression, could be assured payment from higher-risk economic groups. In addition, they could now get compensation for the unpaid care they were often obliged to provide: "So long as doctors could expect the measure of government control to be modest, they could contemplate it with equanimity, and could see their acceptance of control as a new altruism replacing the direct financial sacrifice inherent in their traditional provision of unpaid service."[111]

But serious financial constraints, including the federal government's reluctance to commit any funding, and the opposition of business to higher taxes, forced the Pattullo government to modify the plan, notably by eliminating coverage for the indigent. With the primary economic incentive removed, doctors began to express reservations about the rest of the arrangement, particularly the sweeping powers of the proposed British Columbia Health Commission and the "state control" over the physicians' autonomy in fee setting.

The health insurance bill passed in April 1936, and although the CCF found the plan too limited, the opposition party voted with the government party in the legislature. Lacking the committed support of the medical profession, implementation was postponed. By 1937, another provincial election was called, coinciding with a referendum on health care that found that 59 percent of residents supported comprehensive health insurance.[112] However, with the election safely won, an economic recovery in the air, and CCF fortunes waning, the social reform agenda was postponed. Pattullo's initial enthusiasm for health insurance was rooted in the political saliency of the issue and its importance in attracting electoral support away from the CCF in the midst of the Depression. The fiscal requirements of the plan, and the federal government's reticence to assist the province, combined with opposition from medical and business interests, led to the loss of the issue's political luster. Borrowing a useful tactic from Prime Minister King, Pattullo suspended implementation until jurisdictional issues could be resolved with the federal government.

These health insurance debates in British Columbia served as a warning to the medical profession across Canada about how far such proposed public intervention could intrude on professional autonomy, and they impressed upon the medical lobby the need to carefully monitor government initiatives. The British Columbia health plan was the topic of considerable discussion about the dangers of "socialized medicine" at the 1936 CMA meetings. The following year, the association published a statement on health insurance that underlined the need for government responsibility for care of the indigent and the importance of professional

---

[111] Andrews 1983, 129–41, 135.
[112] Fisher 1991, 308; Naylor, 1986a, 79–86.

autonomy in setting fees and administering any proposed plan.[113] The British Columbia experience also demonstrated the extent to which concerted opposition from the medical lobby, with support from powerful allies (such as business interests), could heat up political controversy over health reform.

CONCLUSION

By the end of the 1930s, neither the United States nor Canada had implemented health insurance, but their reform agendas had already diverged considerably. In the United States, the health reform debate coincided with the Roosevelt administration's response to the Great Depression. The controversy surrounding the Social Security Act set the limits of social reform, including health insurance. The decision to drop health insurance from the legislative proposals was a politically mandated, rather than a bureaucrat-driven, choice on the part of Roosevelt and his administration. Many senior bureaucrats in the administration were in favor of health reform, but political circumstances, and the more pressing demands for unemployment and old-age security, stymied legislative initiatives in this potentially treacherous and already controversial area.

The scope and shape of the Social Security Act were based on both the constraints and opportunities in American political institutions. Despite the broad mandate given the Roosevelt administration after the 1932 election, considerable divisions persisted between the executive and Congress, and the Democratic party itself remained divided on social and economic reform. In contrast to the Canadian experience, however, significant opportunities existed. The most striking was the ability of the national government in the United States to enact sweeping legislation and effectively cement federal dominance in the area of social policy. In Canada, such bold initiatives were more problematic, given the reticence of the major parties to embark on social reform and the jurisdictional problems that plagued federal efforts.

The absence of social reform in Canada during this watershed era would have significant consequences. First, neither labor nor the Left was "appeased" to the same extent as in the United States. The absence of efforts toward labor relations legislation made organized labor wary of both major parties in Canada. In addition, the potential of class-based party politics and the possibility of a farmer-labor alliance were beginning to materialize with the formation of a third party of the Left. Although

[113] "Report of the Committee on Economics," *CMAJ* Supplement to vol. 37 (September 1937).

working-class voters did not desert en masse, both major parties would be forced to modify their social reform platforms in the 1940s as a result of the persistence of the CCF threat.

The absence of a viable third party of the Left in the United States during the 1930s was due more to institutional and political factors than to cultural and value differences. Progressive and left-wing political movements were very much in evidence during the 1920s and 1930s. Roosevelt and the Democratic party were able to co-opt more moderate currents and effectively marginalize more radical ones. This was due, in part, to the success of the social reform initiatives, but also to the flexibility of the two-party system in American politics. As the Democratic party regrouped labor and the Left behind the commitment to social and economic reform, third parties of the Left became unable to inspire widespread support. At the same time, this reform agenda would have to accommodate the broad political coalitions represented by the Democratic party itself, particularly the presence of a strong conservative southern wing.

Just as the reform agenda could be used to refashion political coalitions within the Democratic party in the United States, the absence of such an agenda in Canada encouraged the formation of a farm-labor-Left alliance outside the major parties. Similar currents of protest were as evident in the Canadian West as in the American Midwest, but they were effectively excluded from the major parties due to the relatively more closed nature of party coalitions and the requirements of party discipline. In the wake of the economic crisis and the failure of the federal government to respond to it, protest movements forged independent political identities as third parties within the parliamentary system, at both the federal and provincial levels.

In both countries, labor began to take an interest in social legislation, despite widening divisions within the trade union movement. But American labor leaders accepted the social reform agenda set by the Social Security Act and would be compelled to accept the Democratic party's leadership in future debates, including the legislative compromises surrounding health insurance. In Canada, proponents of national health insurance would be able instead to coalesce around the social-democratic platform of the CCF.

The other principal interest group in the health debate, organized medicine, began to flex its political muscle in the 1930s, foreshadowing its central role in future battles against health reform. The medical lobbies in the two countries expressed concern over protecting physician autonomy and professional interests, but they had different political agendas and playing fields. The AMA became very visible as a well-organized, mobilized lobby ready to do battle on the health issue, the perfect example of a single-interest group that can wield considerable power in the American political process. Roosevelt did not consider health insurance a necessary attraction for his strong, if diffuse, New Deal coalition; rather, he feared such a controversial issue might lead to confrontation with the medical lobby and jeopardize the entire economic security bill.

Canadian physicians actively lobbied government for medical relief and were aware, at least initially, of the potential of state intervention to serve their own interests. When the implications for professional autonomy were raised, organized medicine took a more cautious tone. The British Columbia experience indicated the limits to medical cooperation when faced with government initiatives that did not reflect their interests and reminded the Canadian medical lobby to be vigilant in protecting its professional interests in the face of governments under pressure for reform.

In summary, the 1930s represented a time of "impasse" in the development of health insurance both in Canada and in the United States. It was an impasse rather than a decisive defeat because the issue was not definitely resolved. However, several clues emerge as to the shape of future health battles in the two countries. In the United States, the Democratic administration became the champion of social insurance as defined by the limits of the Social Security Act and the divisions within the party itself. In Canada, meanwhile, in the absence of policy precedents, the stage was set for provincial initiatives and the potential influence of a social-democratic third party.

CHAPTER FOUR

The 1940s: False Starts and Failures of Postwar Health Insurance Proposals

HEALTH INSURANCE was one of the most important social reforms on the immediate postwar agenda in both Canada and the United States, but, in spite of growing public demand, health insurance initiatives were not translated into legislative outcomes. These initiatives failed for different reasons, however, and their defeat would profoundly influence the political struggle for health reform in the two countries. The legacy of health insurance debates in the 1940s eventually opened the door to future reform in Canada, but it closed the window of opportunity for national health insurance in the United States.

HEALTH REFORM AND PARTISAN STRATEGIES IN CANADA

The Liberal Government and Health Reform

The jurisdictional uncertainties that had plagued health and social welfare initiatives in the 1930s were addressed by the Royal Commission on Dominion-Provincial Relations, appointed by Prime Minister King in 1937. The 1940 report (also known by the names of its co-chairs as the Rowell-Sirois Report) emphasized that regional variations in economic and social conditions precluded the imposition of a centralized health insurance plan by the federal government and confirmed that "provincial responsibilities in health matters should be considered basic and residual"; however, the report also maintained that such responsibility posed a heavy financial and administrative burden on the provinces that could be alleviated by use of the federal spending power or by the provinces' delegating authority to the federal government.[1]

Since the late 1930s, officials in the Department of Pensions and National Health (DPNH) had been studying health insurance and gathering information on provincial initiatives in social security. The Department's

---

[1] Canada, Royal Commission on Dominion-Provincial Relations, *Final Report*, Book 2: *Recommendations* (Ottawa: King's Printer, 1940), 34–35, 42–43.

minister, Ian Mackenzie, a member of Parliament from Vancouver, had at least two political motives for promoting such activity. After having been removed from his position as Minister of National Defence at the outbreak of war in 1939 and put in charge of what was seen as a minor department, Mackenzie could use the social reform agenda to regain status in King's Cabinet.[2] In addition, the minister was conscious of public support for health insurance in his home province, and of its prominence in B.C. labor demands and the CCF platform. Since the B.C. experience had shown firsthand the difficulty of implementing effective health reform in the face of financial constraints and resistance from organized medicine, Mackenzie was convinced of the need for federal cooperation (through financial support of provincial plans) or initiative (through a federal act that would require a constitutional amendment) in formulating a national health insurance program.

Within the DPNH, the main bureaucratic actor in the health debate of the 1940s was J. J. Heagerty. As the Director of Public Health Services (and himself a public health doctor), by 1940 Heagerty was convinced that "the time is not long distant" when public health insurance would be enacted by the provinces.[3] Mackenzie appointed Heagerty to head an internal Committee on Health Insurance that drafted three model bills: a provincial plan, a federal plan necessitating constitutional amendment, and an enabling act for the provinces.[4] In September 1941, Mackenzie approached Prime Minister King, suggesting that national health insurance could be the foundation of a postwar reconstruction program. Mackenzie emphasized the precedent of unemployment insurance in 1940 and the growing demand for such health insurance (particularly from organized labor). King, however, remained noncommittal, agreeing in principle that "National Health Insurance is most desirable and necessary to complete our programme of social insurance," but also pointing out that neither the provinces nor the federal treasury were ready to confront such a challenge.[5]

Despite King's hesitation, Mackenzie allowed the bureaucratic wheels to keep turning. He convinced a reluctant Cabinet to set up an interdepartmental Advisory Committee on Health Insurance, chaired by Heagerty, to "continue the study of health insurance with a view to for-

[2] Bothwell 1978, 193.

[3] Heagerty to R. E. Wodehouse [deputy minister] NAC; RG 29; Vol. 1063; 2 December 1940.

[4] J. J. Heagerty, Ross Millar, and F. S. Burke to R. E. Wodehouse NAC; RG 29; Vol. 1063; File 502-1-1, Pt. 1; 7 January 1941.

[5] NAC; MG 26-J; King Papers; Vol. 310; Mackenzie to King, 22 and 29 September 1941; King to Mackenzie, 24 September 1941; see also MG 27 III B-5; Mackenzie Papers; Vol. 79; File 567–27.

mulating a health insurance plan."[6] The Committee began to research its report by soliciting the opinions of relevant interest groups on the draft health insurance bills. As rumors of this government activity leaked out, a flood of inquiries and requests for information inundated the DPNH, forcing Mackenzie to impose a gag rule on Committee members to avoid inciting public expectations or provoking controversy over the issue.[7]

By December 1942, the Advisory Council's revised draft bills were completed, one an enabling act authorizing federal contributions to fund provincial health insurance plans (supplemented by contributions from the individual insured), the other a model bill for the provinces.[8] In January 1943, Mackenzie presented these proposals to the Cabinet, but his colleagues remained divided on legislative action, again raising the jurisdictional problem and the financial costs of the program.[9]

The Prime Minister, however, was by now more conscious than before of the popularity of health insurance. The sacrifices of the war effort galvanized public interest in social security matters, as did Lord Beveridge's highly publicized visit to Canada to promote the ideals of postwar reconstruction. Opinion polls showed considerable support for health and other social insurance measures: by 1943, 75 percent were favorable to a program of health insurance, while 71 percent supported the idea of "postwar reform."[10] Still hesitant, King compromised by appointing a Special Committee on Social Security of the House of Commons to review the proposals.[11] Although this effectively stalled immediate legislative action on the matter, it set the stage for the first public debate on health insurance in Canada.

The opening of the hearings of the Special Committee on Social Security in March 1943 coincided with the public release of both the Advisory Council proposals (drafted by Heagerty) and the report of the Advisory Committee on Post-War Reconstruction, a government-appointed committee composed of representatives from academics, business, and labor and chaired by F. Cyril James, the principal of McGill University. The committee's mandate had been to examine plans for demobilization and the "economic and social implications of the transition from war to

[6] Order-in-Council P. C. 836, 5 February 1942, in NAC; RG 29; Vol. 1063; File 502-1-1, Pt. 7.

[7] See NAC; RG 29; Vol. 1125; File 504-4-1, Pt. 3.

[8] These provisions closely resembled the original draft, except that coverage was universal, and a new system of federal public health grants was introduced. NAC; RG 29; Vol. 1125; "Brief Summary of the Draft Bill," January 1943.

[9] On Cabinet considerations, see Taylor 1987, 19.

[10] Sanders 1944, 527–28.

[11] Canada, House of Commons, *Debates*, 28 January 1943, 1–2.

peace," but in the end its report produced a comprehensive plan for post-war social security.[12] Drafted by Leonard Marsh, a student of Beveridge, a former president of the League for Social Reconstruction, and an active member of the CCF, the report reinforced the idea that the federal government was responsible for reconstructing a postwar order that would extend beyond physical defense to the provision of social security, including universal health insurance. In sharp contrast with the Heagerty report, Marsh insisted on federal—rather than provincial—administration and financing, and he argued that the jurisdictional problem should be solved by a constitutional amendment.[13]

The House of Commons Special Committee on Social Security heard testimony from federal bureaucrats, provincial health ministers, health professionals, business, labor, and other societal groups.[14] Many of these groups had already been solicited by the Advisory Council on Health Insurance in the drafting of the health insurance bills. Most prominent in this regard was the Canadian Medical Association.

Initially, the CMA executive enjoyed a cordial relationship with Heagerty and other officials in the DPNH, who were "at great pains to maintain the friendliest relations with them."[15] The CMA contributed to the Advisory Council's draft proposals, and many of the revisions, such as the fee-for-service payment and the inclusion of indigents, had been formally requested by the CMA.[16] Heagerty was conscious of the need to assuage a CMA leadership that remained "fearful that a plan of health insurance in which they [were] not in agreement [might] be foisted upon them."[17] During the drafting of the bill, Ian Mackenzie had warned Heagerty that the plan had to meet public approval, particularly among the working class: "This proposal," he wrote in a letter to Heagerty, "is developing into a doctor's bill. I definitely do not want this to be the case. I want this to be a people's act. The great interest in this measure will be among the working people of Canada."[18]

Although the general consensus in government circles was that Heag-

[12] Guest 1980, 109–17.

[13] Marsh 1975, xiii–xxvii. Marsh was also a member of the Advisory Committee on Health Insurance, but Heagerty soon demanded Marsh's resignation, accusing him of publicly contradicting the Council's views. NAC; RG 29; Vol. 1125; File 504-1-1, Pt. 4; Heagerty to Marsh; 1 November 1943.

[14] Canada, House of Commons, Special Committee on Social Security, *Minutes of Proceedings and Evidence*, Nos. 1–26, March–July 1943.

[15] NAC; RG 29; Vol. 1111; File 504-2-4, Pt. 1; Heagerty to Mackenzie; 9 April 1942.

[16] NAC; RG 29; Vol. 1111; File 504-1-1; Heagerty to Mackenzie; 17 October 1941.

[17] NAC; RG 29; Vol. 1111; File 504-2-4; Heagerty to Mackenzie; 9 April 1942.

[18] NAC; MG 27 III B–5; Mackenzie Papers; Vol. 79; File 567–27; Mackenzie to Heagerty; 12 August 1942.

erty "gave the doctors everything they wanted," the CMA did not specifically support these proposals.[19] At a special meeting in January 1943, the CMA endorsed the principle of health insurance and indicated it would favor a plan that would "be fair both to the insured and to all those rendering the services." At the Special Committee hearings, the CMA presented much the same position, reiterating its wish that the compulsory plan be limited to low-income people and the indigent.[20] This was consistent with the medical lobby's support for government intervention to cover economic losses incurred by caring for high-risk income groups. Although medical representatives pledged their continuing cooperation, there was no explicit indication that the medical profession would accept government-financed universal and compulsory health insurance in Canada.

By the end of the hearings, the CMA was expressing considerable uneasiness over the government proposals. The lobby began circulating memos to members criticizing the lack of guarantees for medical representation in an independent Health Insurance Commission to control the implementation of the proposed plan. In addition, questions began to arise over the complacency of the CMA toward health insurance, especially as compared to the overt hostility the AMA was expressing against such measures in the United States.[21] By 1949, the CMA revised its principles to effectively drop any support of compulsory government health insurance and instead endorsed prepaid voluntary health insurance, relegating the government's role to care of the indigent.[22]

While many other health professionals (dentists, optometrists, pharmacists, and nurses) were generally favorable to the health insurance plan, the medical lobby found allies in the health and business sectors. Like the CMA, the Canadian Hospital Council approved of health insurance in principle but did not endorse the draft bill, nor the idea of a compulsory program, preferring the Blue Cross alternatives that were emerging in Canada. The Catholic Hospital Council was even more adamant in promoting voluntary alternatives and in limiting government involvement (particularly federal) to the barest minimum.[23] Although the Canadian Life Insurance Officers Association did not come out against the plan, its

[19] Bothwell and English 1981, 488.

[20] "Resolution re Health Insurance" *CMAJ* 48, no. 2 (February 1943); "The Medical Profession and Health Insurance," Submission of the CMA to the Special Committee on Social Security, *Minutes of Proceedings and Evidence*, 6 April 1943.

[21] NAC; RG 29, Vol. 1111; File 504-2-4, Pt. 1; T. C. Routley to CMA members; 6 August 1943; see also Bothwell and English 1981, 491.

[22] Text in Blishen 1969, 182–83.

[23] Canada, House of Commons, Special Committee on Social Security, *Minutes of the Proceedings*, 9 April 1943; 11 June 1943.

suggestion that a separate means-tested plan be set up for those unable to pay regular contributions for health insurance was rejected by Heagerty as "illogical and unsound."[24]

The Canadian Manufacturers Association had been solicited on several occasions during revisions to the draft bill. The association did not publicly comment nor present a brief to the Special Committee, but elsewhere Heagerty noted that "from private information received it is understood that it may oppose" the health insurance proposals.[25] Another group that did not testify at the hearings was the Canadian Pharmaceutical Manufacturers Association. The absence of a direct response from these groups in the 1940s is noteworthy, as they would play a major role in opposing medical insurance in the 1960s. Significantly, at the same time that the hearings were taking place on health insurance, members of the business community and the pharmaceutical industry were involved in promoting anti-CCF campaigns that attacked the party's "socialistic" platform.[26]

Although the Advisory Council had attempted to involve labor organizations in the drafting of the health insurance proposals, labor leaders were wary of the Liberal government's health plan. As Ian Mackenzie had feared, they questioned the extent to which the proposed health proposals colluded with the interests of provider groups. In addition, like their counterparts in the United States, Canadian labor leaders preferred a federally administered public health insurance plan, in order to ensure control of equal standards and conditions for workers across the country and to reduce the administrative control of provincial medical associations.

Because of the labor movement's generally positive stance toward social reform issues, Heagerty felt that "this organization is in favour and will not make strong objection" to the government proposals.[27] Nevertheless, at the Special Committee hearings, the Trades and Labor Congress of Canada president Percy Bengough denounced the plan as a "complete closed shop agreement between the governments and the union of medical practitioners . . . the Act must be entirely reconstituted

[24] Canada, House of Commons, Special Committee on Social Security, *Minutes of the Proceedings*, 8 June 1943; NAC; RG 29; Vol. 1113; File 504-2-10, Canadian Life Insurance Officers Association.

[25] NAC; MG 27 III B–5; Mackenzie Papers; Vol 40; File G-25(3); "Views of Committees," 7–8; and NAC; RG 29; Vol. 1125; File 504-4-1, Pt. 3; CPMA to Heagerty, 10 May 1943.

[26] Caplan 1973, 158–63.

[27] "Views of Committees," 6–7; and NAC; RG 29; Vol. 1401; File 504-1-4; "Comment by a Committee of the Trades and Labor Congress of Canada on the Tentative Draft Act Respecting Health Insurance," 28 February 1942.

to take control away from the medical profession and place it in the hands of the contributors."[28]

The Canadian Congress of Labour expressed the same suspicions before the Special Committee. The CCL brief (prepared by Research Director Eugene Forsey, Leonard Marsh's colleague and a member of the Co-operative Commonwealth Federation) expressed a preference for a national health insurance plan with general revenue financing that would ensure the same standards of health care delivery across Canada, essentially the type of system suggested in the Marsh Report rather than in the Heagerty proposals.[29] There was also an important letter-writing campaign, supporting public health insurance, directed at the federal government during the course of the hearings from CCL member unions, mainly in British Columbia.[30]

By the 1940s, as its union membership increased dramatically, the CCL's political strategy had shifted toward more direct action. In 1942, a political action committee was formed, along the lines of the CIO's Political Action Committee in the United States. The Trades and Labor Congress eventually also formed a PAC, but, like its AFL counterpart, it still refused to endorse a particular party. In contrast to both the TLC in Canada and labor organizations in the United States, the CCL's PAC publicly endorsed the CCF and the social-democratic party's platform, including health and social security reform.[31]

The other group that shared labor's wariness toward the federal government proposals was the Canadian Federation of Agriculture (CFA). The Canadian farm movement was not divided to the same extent as were American agricultural interests between the progressive National Farmer's Union in the Midwest and the conservative American Farm Bureau Federation, with its important power base in the South. And, unlike their American counterparts, Canadian farmers continued to regard the major parties with suspicion, particularly in the western provinces, where agrarian organizations formed the backbone of CCF membership. The CFA preferred the CCF's social reform over the Liberal government's plan and urged a universal, compulsory national health insurance system,

---

[28] Trades and Labor Congress, *Proceedings*, 1943, 291–92; Canada, House of Commons, Special Committee on Social Security, *Minutes of the Proceedings*, 18 May 1943. The same sentiment was frequently expressed in the editorial pages of the *Trades and Labor Congress Journal*; for example, in warning against the similarities between the Canadian and American medical lobbies, see "Menace of Medicine Men," *Trades and Labor Congress Journal* 24, no. 4 (April 1945): 9–10.

[29] Canada, House of Commons, Special Committee on Social Security, *Minutes of the Proceedings*, 31 March 1944

[30] NAC; RG 29; Vol. 1064; File 502-1-4, Pts. 1–2; "Health Insurance Resolutions."

[31] Young 1969, 82–83.

rigidly controlled by independent commissions so as to curb the power of the medical profession.[32]

The CCF and the Social Reform Agenda

The Special Committee finally recommended against legislative action on the health insurance proposals until "financial and constitutional questions" were resolved, a view implicitly shared by the Prime Minister and most of the Cabinet.[33] Nevertheless, the Liberal government was still preoccupied with the issue because of political pressures.

Although support for the Co-operative Commonwealth Federation was concentrated in agrarian sectors, the party was broadening its political appeal in urban centers and central Canada, shaking King's conviction that the working class was the "natural constituency" of the Liberal party. The surprise of the CCF's upset of former Conservative Prime Minister Arthur Meighen in a 1942 Toronto-area by-election clearly worried both the Liberal and Conservative parties.[34] Public opinion polls at the federal level confirmed the CCF's soaring popularity. A startling poll in September 1943 even put the CCF slightly ahead of both major parties.[35]

In provincial politics, the CCF faced considerable antisocialist rhetoric from the major parties and their allies, and those who painted it as a communist movement. Nevertheless, CCF fortunes rose precipitously in many provinces. The CCF became the Official Opposition in the Ontario legislature in 1943, relegating the former Liberal government to third-party status. British Columbia premier Duff Pattullo was forced out of office in late 1941 by a Liberal-Conservative coalition government. Created to offset electoral gains by the CCF, this "free enterprise" coalition effectively shut the party out of power in the province.[36] Despite its virulent attacks against "socialism and dictatorship," the Liberal government

[32] "Health on the March," Submission of the CFA, Canada, House of Commons, Special Committee on Social Security, *Minutes of the Proceedings*, 14 May 1943.

[33] Canada, House of Commons, Special Committee on Social Security, *Minutes of the Proceedings*, 23 July 1943.

[34] No Liberal candidate even ran in York South, as King was convinced the Conservative candidate, former Prime Minister Meighen, would win in "the strongest Tory riding in all of Canada" (King diaries, in Pickersgill 1960, 348). The Conservatives had won 46 percent of the vote in the riding in 1940 election; in 1942, the CCF candidate, Joseph Noseworthy, a local schoolteacher, won by 4,500 votes (Scarrow 1962, 113).

[35] CCF support was estimated at 29 percent, the support for Liberals and Conservatives at 28 percent each. While this support was still concentrated in the West rather than in Ontario, 42 percent of labor respondents across Canada chose the CCF (Caplan 1973, 110–11).

[36] Young 1983, pp. 85–87.

in Saskatchewan was routed by the CCF in the 1944 provincial election, which was dominated by the health reform issue. The CCF won 53 percent of the Saskatchewan vote and forty-seven of the fifty-two seats in the legislature, ushering in "the first 'socialist' government in the United States or Canada."[37]

The substance of these political developments was that the CCF had become a player in Canadian politics and that its message would need to be addressed by the major parties. The Conservative party, struggling to regain national prominence, was already in the process of restructuring its platform with a new "Progressive Conservative" label.[38] After Meighen's defeat to the CCF, the party appointed a new leader, John Bracken, who had served as premier of Manitoba under United Farmer and Liberal-Progressive governments. Despite the misgivings of the Conservative old guard, Bracken was considered "the only man who could beat the C.C.F." in western Canada and rural Ontario, and the new Progressive Conservative platform was designed to attract his potential followers to the party. This new platform was designed as an alternative to the "state socialism" of the CCF and emphasized traditional "Tory" values about the state's role in responding to social needs, including a national system of medical care "to be delivered by free enterprise, with government help if needed."[39]

The potential appeal of the rejuvenated Progressive Conservative in western Canada and the growing popularity of the CCF in urban areas raised concern within the Liberal party. King was haunted by the specter of the British Liberal party, squeezed between the Conservatives and the Labour challengers, and he became convinced that "the loss of labor's support was the greatest threat to the chances of the Liberal party winning the next election."[40] Social reform promises would thus have to be designed to fight off challenges on two fronts: the "superficial liberalism" of the Tories and the "socialist menace" of the CCF.[41]

Health Insurance and the Politics of Postwar Reconstruction

It is no coincidence that the Liberal government began to publicly take an interest in health and social insurance. While King took heed from his

---

[37] Lipset 1971, 153.

[38] On the conversion to the Progressive Conservative label, see Campbell and Christian 1996, 37–38.

[39] Granatstein 1967, 134.

[40] King diaries, in Pickersgill 1960, 572.

[41] NAC; MG 27 III B–5; Mackenzie Papers; Vol. 79; File 567–27; "The Progressive-Conservative Platform", analysis prepared by C. S. Senior for Ian Mackenzie, n.d.

Cabinet that they should not try to "outdo the C.C.F.," he certainly appreciated the strategic relevance of social reform.[42] Highlighting a commitment to postwar reconstruction seemed the logical answer to "rounding out" King's political career as well as attracting working-class voters and absorbing the moderate wing of the political Left.

The government's 1944 Throne Speech reflected this strategy, emphasizing social security as the primary domestic objective of the Liberal government. A "comprehensive national scheme" including health insurance was mentioned, but the government signaled its intention to wait for the approbation of the provinces before acting. Health insurance was thus submerged within a broader program of postwar economic and social reform dependent upon provincial initiative, giving the federal government some breathing space on the issue. In the meantime, the federal government introduced direct family allowance payments, addressing the immediate need of labor's acceptance of postwar wage and price controls.[43] The Progressive Conservatives, despite their name change, reacted with traditional aversion, horrified that "the Prime Minister has promised everything but the kitchen sink," and expressing fears about the "socializing of medicine." CCF leader M. J. Coldwell, meanwhile, criticized the jettison of the health insurance issue back to the provinces once more as "a prize example of passing the buck."[44]

Before the next election was called, the federal government released a set of "Green Book" proposals, or reference papers describing the government's blueprint for postwar social reform. These proposals were prominently featured in the 1945 election campaign, one that represented a crucial "contest for labour" between the Liberals and the CCF.[45] Both the Progressive Conservative and Liberal parties engaged in substantial antisocialist discourse to discredit the CCF, but the real campaign against the left-wing party was waged by business allies. These included the Canadian Chamber of Commerce and powerful corporations such as Algoma Steel and Canadian Pacific Railways, which faced militant labor unions associated with the CCF. Although the "socialized medicine" epithet was in use, this attack was not waged by the medical lobby against specific individuals, but was part of the broader attack aimed at the CCF and its influence in the labor movement. The federal CCF also suffered from the intense antisocialist campaign in the Ontario provincial election, held just one week before federal polling, which resulted in the decimation of the Ontario CCF.

[42] Pickersgill 1960, 635.

[43] Canada, House of Commons, *Debates*, 27 January 1944, 1–2; Kitchen 1987, 235–38.

[44] Canada, House of Commons, *Debates*, 27 January 1944, 1–3; 31 January 1944, 49–50; 3 February 1944, 157–59.

[45] Brodie and Jenson, 1988, 201–211.

Although the antisocialist rhetoric may have contributed to the third party's failure to make a widespread breakthrough, the CCF's representation in the House of Commons jumped from eight to twenty-eight seats, mainly at the expense of the Liberal party. King's government barely survived the June 1945 election, which reduced the Liberals' majority to five seats. It is difficult to decipher precisely the impact of health and social insurance on the election results, but King clearly felt that his fears about the CCF and the labor vote had been justified: "It is the CCF vote that has done the damage," he reflected, including the loss of his own seat in the CCF sweep of Saskatchewan.[46] In addition, vote tallies revealed that the CCF effectively swung victory from the Liberals to the Tories in thirty-three contests, most significantly in urban Ontario.[47]

Once the election was won, preparations began for a Dominion-Provincial Conference on Reconstruction to discuss the "Green Book" proposals for social programs. In addition to extending old-age pensions and social assistance, the federal government proposed unconditional grants to assist the organization and implementation of health insurance programs, public health, and hospital construction in the provinces. The implementation of the health program, however, was contingent upon the continuation of wartime tax rental agreements (by which the federal government collected taxes for the provinces).[48]

Several provincial governments had already voiced concerns about the financial burden health insurance would impose on provincial treasuries, and the jurisdictional problems surrounding federal involvement in the program, but it was the lack of consensus on the tax rentals that doomed the discussions.[49] The opposition came from the two largest provinces, Ontario and Quebec. Ontario's Conservative premier George Drew and Quebec's Union Nationale premier Maurice Duplessis (both political foes of the Liberal Prime Minister) resisted the intrusion of the federal government and its refusal to relinquish taxation control. The conference ended in deadlock, and, as health insurance was tied to the plan's fiscal arrangements, the proposals for health reform expired along with the conference.

The provinces were not the only sticking point at this juncture. The Liberal party still remained divided on health reform, and the CCF no

    [46] King diaries, in Pickersgill and Forster 1968, 417.

    [47] The CCF increased its support in Ontario almost fourfold, although it lost its only seat there. Scarrow 1962, 118–29.

    [48] Canada, Dominion-Provincial Conference on Reconstruction, 1945, *Proposals of the Government of Canada.*

    [49] NAC; RG 29; Vol. 1125, "Meeting of Provincial Ministers and Minister of Pensions and National Health," 21 September 1942; and NAC; RG 29; Vol. 1131; "Report of Conference on Health Insurance." See also Guest 1980, 133–41.

longer seemed as imminent a threat now that the election had been won and the CCF had not made the electoral breakthrough that many Liberals had feared. Privately, King worried that "we were going far too rapidly with some of our social legislation."[50] Although the health insurance proposals were shelved once federal-provincial negotiations broke down, however, the federal government could not remain inactive on health altogether. The expectations raised by the 1945 proposals were kept alive by the CCF, both in the House of Commons and in the Saskatchewan legislature. Despite the federal stalemate on health reform, in 1947 the province of Saskatchewan inaugurated the first government-financed hospital insurance program in Canada, an initiative that would bolster public demand for health insurance across the country.

Paul Martin, the new Minister of National Health and Welfare, was aware of the potential of the Liberal party in continuing to influence the public debate over health insurance, particularly since he represented a heavily unionized area of southern Ontario where Liberals vied with the CCF for the labor vote. By 1948, Martin was convinced that the government had to "keep faith" with its promises and quell criticism that it was once again using the provinces as excuses for inaction. He proposed that instead of dealing with the entire health insurance package at once, the government could inaugurate "preparatory steps" through a program of National Health Grants to the provinces. These had been part of the original Heagerty proposals, providing federal grants for public health services and hospital construction. Proclaimed as the first step in the "ultimate goal of Health Insurance," it was also a practical way of saving face on health reform.[51] Although some Cabinet members remained hesitant, Martin used the CCF threat to convince them of the continued demand for some kind of health care initiative among voters and the more left-wing members of the Liberal caucus.[52]

King, close to retirement, was responsive to the idea. He saw it as a way to "round out the policy of a national minimum of employment and security which I have sought" as well the more pragmatic reason "that this program will probably ensure the return of the Liberal party at the

[50] King diaries, in Pickersgill and Forster 1970, 207; on the CCF threat and the Liberal party, see Swartz 1977, 321.

[51] NAC; RG 29; Vol. 1063; File 502-1-1, Pt. 11; Martin to King, 5 January 1948; and NAC; MG 32 B-12; Martin Papers; Vol. 29; File Health Insurance: National Health Programs; "Memo for Cabinet Consideration of Health Insurance," May 1948; see also Paul Martin 1985, chap. 2.

[52] NAC; MG 32 B-12; Martin Papers; Vol. 110; File National Health Plan July–Sept 1948; Martin to Davidson, 19 December 1947. The memo was attached to the clipping, "CCF Will Press Ottawa to Implement Health Plan," *Toronto Daily Star*, 19 December 1947.

next election."[53] His predictions turned out to be correct. The National Health Grants program enjoyed wide approval, including sanction from the Canadian Medical Association. The Liberal party, even without Mackenzie King, was reelected with a stunning majority in 1949.

The health reform issue, however, would not go away for long. Despite the passage of the 1948 program, the CCF party continued to keep national health insurance system at the center of the political agenda. And despite the federal stalemate in implementing this system, the CCF government in Saskatchewan inaugurated its own government-financed hospital insurance program that served to encourage other provincial action and bolstered public demand for health insurance.

THE DECISIVE FAILURE OF HEALTH REFORM IN THE UNITED STATES

Reformist Bureaucrats and the Fair Deal Leadership

As in Canada, discussions of postwar reconstruction in the United States heightened debate over the role of the state in ensuring social security for its citizens. Although the Social Security Act of 1935 had already fashioned this role for the federal government, health insurance remained the "unfinished business" of the New Deal. Veteran bureaucrats who had been involved in the Committee on Economic Security (such as Arthur Altmeyer, now chairman of the Social Security Board, and Isidore Falk, head of the Board's Bureau of Research and Statistics) began to take a greater interest in developing a national program of health insurance, rather than implementing federal grants for state plans. This federal approach seemed warranted because of the problems being encountered in state-administered unemployment insurance plans, and also because state-level initiatives in health care remained sporadic and limited.[54] The California Medical Association launched a successful public-relations campaign in 1945 against Governor Earl Warren's proposals for state-administered contributory health insurance. Several health insurance bills were introduced in other state legislatures, but no public plans were implemented. The absence of effective reform at the state level convinced SSB reformers that the most effective way to implement health insurance would be as a federally administered program.

The response was in the form of an omnibus bill, introduced in 1943, that proposed centralizing social insurance functions and adding a new

---

[53] King diaries, in Pickersgill and Forster 1970, 287–88, 291.

[54] The only legislative action of the decade was in cash sickness benefits, implemented in Rhode Island in 1942 and in California in 1945 (*Congressional Digest*, 1946, 199).

program of national medical and hospitalization care. This bill (S. 1161, H.R. 2861) was dubbed the Wagner-Murray-Dingell (WMD) bill after its congressional sponsors. Inside the Social Security Board, the proposal was known more informally as the "AFL bill." Although the proposals were designed by senior bureaucrats, as they had been in the Canadian case, their main support came from organized labor and prolabor legislators, particularly Senator Robert Wagner of New York, the sponsor of the 1939 health insurance bill.

Despite evidence of public support for national health insurance the bill did not reach the hearings stage, nor did it receive official administration approval.[55] Although Roosevelt was intrigued by the Beveridge Report and felt, in much the same way that Mackenzie King had, that it reflected his own vision for the postwar era, he was cautious about translating this vision into legislation.[56] It was not until his fourth-term reelection bid, in the midst of the final months of World War II, that Roosevelt took an active interest in promoting postwar social security. The 1944 presidential campaign focused on an "Economic Bill of Rights," including the right to medical care. Neither the campaign nor the subsequent 1945 State of the Union address, however, outlined any specific legislation. Nevertheless, within the Social Security Board, a revised WMD bill was in preparation, designed to embody the President's postwar social security agenda with a national health program as its centerpiece.

When Harry Truman became President in 1945, after the death of Franklin Roosevelt, he took a personal interest in social policy, and he seemed willing to make health insurance a primary domestic policy objective. While Truman was impressed with the advanced progress in the Social Security Board, and may have been swayed by reformist bureaucrats, the new President's interest in social reform was not without precedent.[57] The former senator had been a straight-ticket New Dealer, and he demonstrated a sympathetic attitude toward social insurance generally. In addition, Truman had an obligation to maintain New Deal programs, both to highlight the continuity in leadership with the Roosevelt administration and to carve out his own reform legacy. As a politician, Truman was prepared to forge ahead despite the controversy surrounding health

---

[55] Health insurance (through expansion of the Social Security Act) was favored by 59 percent of Americans in 1943 and 68 percent in 1944. Erksine 1975, 128–43, 135.

[56] Secretary of Labor Frances Perkins credits FDR with coining the term "cradle-to-grave" and recounts his dismay at Beveridge stealing his thunder. Perkins 1946, 283.

[57] There is much debate among Truman scholars on this point: the "fair dealer" school argues that Truman enacted a myriad of social legislation despite the enactment of Taft-Hartley and the failure of the National Health Program; "new left" revisionists paint Truman as a classic liberal who could not do battle with Congress. For a review of the debate, see Hamby 1972; Neustadt 1954.

insurance: "He didn't realize all of the opposition. . . . And if he did, he didn't give a damn, as he would say."[58]

On November 19, 1945, Truman presented a historic message to Congress on health insurance, the first President ever to do so. The text outlined a comprehensive federal health insurance plan that consisted of five major programs (hospital construction, public health, medical education and research, cash payments for the disabled, and compulsory prepaid medical care).[59] The same day, a bill outlining this plan was introduced by the sponsors of the former WMD bill, Robert Wagner of New York and James Murray of Montana in the Senate (S. 1606) and John Dingell of Michigan in the House (H.R. 4730). While the 1943 WMD bill had been an omnibus measure that included several other amendments to the Social Security Act, the new bill focused on health insurance. This channeled the bill to the Senate Education and Labor Committee, chaired by one of the bill's sponsors, James Murray, rather than to the Finance Committee, a stronghold of powerful southern Democrats that had blocked hearings on the WMD in 1943.[60]

The new bill described a far more centralized national health insurance system than had been contemplated by the Roosevelt administration in the 1930s or by the Liberal government in Canada. The "National Health Program" had two major components: a federal insurance program covering medical, hospital, and dental care for workers and their families, funded by payroll tax revenues that would reimburse health professionals; and federal grants to the states to fund public health services and to cover the costs of medical care for "needy persons" (i.e., the unemployed, elderly, and indigent). In the Federal Security Agency, work began immediately on the logistics of implementing the program.[61] Disputes within the administration on how this was to be realized prompted President Truman to make a personal appeal for unity on the issue in an attempt to broaden the promotion of health insurance. He urged the FSA Administrator "to mobilize all the resources necessary with the Federal Security Agency for vigorous and united action directed toward achieving public understanding of the need for a National Health Pro-

---

[58] Altmeyer, COHC, 37.

[59] U.S. President, *Public Papers of the Presidents*, Harry S. Truman, 1945, 19 November 1945, 475–94. The text was prepared primarily by Altmeyer, Falk, and Judge Sam Rosenman, formerly FDR's special counsel and speech writer. Poen 1979, 39–40, 62–63.

[60] Murray had been elected in the Democrats' 1934 sweep. The Senate Finance Committee was chaired by Walter George of Georgia. The bill was also kept out of Ways and Means (presided over by Robert Doughton, D-N.C.); it eventually went to Interstate and Foreign Commerce, but no hearings were held (*Congressional Directory*, 1939, 1178–79; and 1945, 180–81).

[61] "Agency Information Activities Implementing the President's Health Message," 28 November 1945; Vol. 11; File 011.4; FSA; RG 47; NA.

gram. . . . I am asking the Secretary of Agriculture, the Secretary of Labor and the Administrator of Veterans Affairs . . . to assist in every possible way in this effort."[62]

Group Positions on the Truman Health Plan

The 1946 hearings on S. 1606 extended over four months and three thousand pages of testimony, and indicated the battle lines that had formed around health reform. It was clear from the outset that the campaign against the Truman plan would be led by the American Medical Association. Like its counterpart in Canada, the U.S. medical profession had been worried by rumors of government intervention in the health care sector, particularly after the outbreak of war.[63] But the initially cordial relationship that existed between the medical lobby and senior bureaucrats in Canada was noticeably absent here. In its place was personal bitterness and overt hostility between the AMA and the Social Security Board, in part due to the legacies of past battles over the 1935 economic security bill and the 1939 Wagner bill.

In response to Truman's health message, the AMA House of Delegates adopted a "Fourteen-Point Platform" and released its own health insurance program in February 1946. This new alternative, presented at the 1946 hearings, emphasized individual responsibility and free enterprise in the health sector, with government involvement limited to local services for public health and maternal and child care. The AMA also voiced its approval of voluntary prepayment systems for hospital care through the expansion of Blue Cross, for medical care through state and county medical society plans under Blue Shield, and for private insurance plans that complied with AMA standards and administrative criteria.[64] This emphasis on voluntary insurance as a suitable alternative to compulsory plans was a significant shift from the AMA's earlier position in the 1930s, which had opposed the interference of any third party in the delivery of medical care. It was influenced by growing public interest in prepayment plans and increasing evidence of rifts within the medical community on the issue of health insurance.

As early as 1934, several physicians, mainly in the public health field, had begun to vocalize their dissatisfaction with the status quo and the AMA leadership. By 1946, there existed three physician groups that sup-

[62] Harry Truman to Watson Miller, 19 March 1946; File 011.4; Vol. 8; FSA; RG 47; NA.

[63] AMA leaders even expressed their concern to FSA officials about these rumors; see Olin West to Paul McNutt, 27 June 1941; File 056.1; Vol. 60; CEN; RG 47; NA.

[64] U.S. Congress, Senate, Committee on Education and Labor, *National Health Program: Hearings on S. 1606*, 79th Cong., 2d sess., 17 April 1946, 551–604.

ported government intervention in the health care sector and formally endorsed the Truman plan: the Physician's Forum, set up in 1939 (numbering one thousand members); the Committee of Physicians for the Improvement of Medical Care (with thirty-odd members); and the National Medical Association (representing black doctors). Although the AMA's voice was by far the strongest in terms of professional strength, these groups accused the lobby's elite leadership of misrepresentation, challenging the AMA's claim that 95 percent of American doctors opposed the bill. They also denounced the scare tactics of the National Physician's Committee for the Extension of Medical Service, the AMA's lobbying arm.[65]

Organized medicine nevertheless did have allies in the health care community. The Association of American Physicians and Surgeons was even more emphatic than the AMA in its support of voluntary insurance, and, although this was not mentioned in its hearings testimony, the AAPS had threatened to boycott services and to refuse its participation in the administration's plan.[66] The American Hospital Association, the Blue Cross Commission, and both the Protestant and Catholic Hospital Associations all testified against the bill and encouraged the use of voluntary hospital insurance plans instead. Except for a group of dissenting dentists, the American Dental Association also opposed compulsory action. The American Nurses Association, meanwhile, remained noncommittal on the proposals.[67]

As in Canada, pharmaceutical groups (both retail druggists and manufacturers, even though the latter subsidized the National Physicians' Committee) and commercial insurance carriers did not take a public stance in the health reform debate. (The Actuarial Society of America did, however, present a harsh critique of the plan's "dictatorial control.") The National Association of Manufacturers was also absent at the hearings. The United States Chamber of Commerce made a brief appearance, represented by Andrew Court, a labor economist at General Motors, who attempted to disprove the existence of economic barriers to health care.[68]

The most vocal public endorsement of the Truman plan came from labor representatives. Despite the internal splits in organization, both the AFL and the CIO converged in their emphatic support of national health

[65] Lowell Goin, head of the California Physicians Service made this claim while being questioned by Senator Murray; earlier in the day, R. L. Sensenich of the AMA had denied all knowledge of or association with the NPC. U.S. Congress, Senate, 18 April 1946, 735–73, 787–94; and 26 June 1946, 2649–65.

[66] *Congressional Quarterly* 2, no. 4 (1946): 622.

[67] U.S. Congress, Senate, 22 April 1946, 929–65; 23 April 1946, 1018–37; 24 April 1946, 1082–86.

[68] U.S. Congress, Senate, Pt. 4, 22 May 1946, 1924; and 20 June 1946, 2338–48.

insurance.[69] Testifying at the 1946 hearings on the administration bill, AFL president William Green commented that Gompers, too, would have changed with the times:

> I submit that there is great significance in the fact that our organization has not always supported this position. . . . Some of the enemies of this program have attempted to taunt us by quoting my predecessor, Samuel Gompers, in opposition to health insurance. . . . I knew Gompers as a progressive leader—one willing and ready to change his views with the changing times. True to this tradition, the American Federation of Labor . . . has changed its position regarding health insurance to meet the changed conditions of our times.[70]

The AFL president went on to stress that, given the unpredictability of illness and the rising costs of treatment, in addition to the deficiencies of most private insurance plans, workers needed to be assured of access to quality health care through government funding of a national health insurance plan. James Carey, the CIO representative, reiterated these points and also added that public demand for health reform was growing. Testimony was heard from individual labor organizations as well, including representatives of textile and railway workers, who had successfully developed their own worker health plans but recognized the need for federal legislation.

Although both Canadian and American labor organizations supported national health insurance, they had different positions on government proposals for health reform. American labor leaders had much more input into drafting the administration bill—which incorporated many of labor's preferences in the delivery and financing of health care—than did Canada's Trades and Labor Congress. Indeed, this Canadian labor organization expressed serious reservations, claiming that the Canadian government proposals reflected the preferences of medical interests rather than those of workers.[71]

In addition to labor, another source of support in the U.S. case was the National Farmers' Union (NFU), representing the progressive agrarian movement in the American Midwest. Unlike the Canadian experience, U.S. farming interests were divided between the pro-reform NFU and the American Farm Bureau Federation (AFBF, the largest farm organiza-

[69] AFL, *Weekly News Service*, 20 November 1945; and CIO, Statement by Philip Murray, 20 November 1945; both reprinted in the *Congressional Record Appendix*, 26 November 1945, A5097–A5098.

[70] U.S. Congress, Senate, 16 April 1946, 464–65.

[71] On the relationship between organized labor and reformers on the Social Security Board and in the Democratic party, see Derthick 1979, chap. 5.

tion in the United States), which vehemently opposed the administration's bill.[72]

Both labor and farmer groups were essential components of the public education campaign for the Truman health plan spearheaded by the Committee for the Nation's Health. The CNH, which had no real equivalent in Canada, was an umbrella organization of over two hundred progressive interest groups, social reformers, philanthropists, and influential private citizens that worked together as advocates for the Truman plan. The CNH's goal was to counterbalance the AMA by "correcting misinformation" and encouraging "widespread discussion of the issues" in the media and general public.[73] While many senior bureaucrats in the Federal Security Agency had felt an official "all-out" public education campaign was necessary, others, like Surgeon General Parran, had urged delegating this role to a "grass roots" organization such as the CNH that would be better able to engage in a longer-term public education campaign.[74]

The Senate hearings ended in June, but the four months of political fireworks had precluded any legislative action. Pro–health insurance activists, both in the Congress and in the CNH, decided to retreat and revise the proposed legislation for the next session of Congress.[75] By November, midterm elections brought a Republican majority in the Congress, making the likelihood of action on health insurance more remote than ever. The only legislative action on Truman's health proposals was the 1946 Hill-Burton Act, a bipartisan measure directed at increasing the supply of health resources by providing federal funds to the states for hospital construction. Far from being considered the "first step" toward national health insurance, as the 1948 National Health Grants in Canada had been, this measure was designed to reinforce the voluntary nature of health care delivery and limit the federal government to a more peripheral role in health care for the time being.[76]

---

[72] U.S. Congress, Senate, 26 June 1946 (CNH, 2649–2705); 26 April 1946 (NFU, 1211–66); 30 April 1946 (AFBF, 1383–1400).

[73] Committee for the Nation's Health to Members, 2 April 1946; Truman to Fotheringham [CNH Chairman], 25 March 1946 (Witte Papers; File 1945; Vol. 210; SHSW). Both William Green and Philip Murray were honorary vice-presidents of the CNH; others included Eleanor Roosevelt and Gerald Swope, former president of General Electric, who testified on behalf of the CNH at the hearings.

[74] Zipha Franklin to Watson Miller (FSA Administrator), 7 March 1946; and Mary Switzer to the Administrator (Miller), 11 March 1946; File 011.4; Vol. 10; FSA; RG 47; NA.

[75] Committee on the Nation's Health, "Confidential: Revisions of the National Health Insurance Bill," 15 October 1946; File 011.4; Vol. 8; FSA; RG 235; NA. I. S. Falk, "1947 Legislative Prospects," 25 October 1946; File 011.1; Vol. 4; DRS; NA.

[76] Significantly, the Hill-Burton program was directed by the U.S. Public Health Service

Postwar Cleavages in American Health Politics

The Eightieth Congress, the first Republican Congress since the Hoover administration, culminated in an anti-Democrat backlash that had been steadily growing since the 1938 congressional elections, intensified by dissatisfaction with Truman's postwar economic performance and the rising tide of worker militancy. Republican leaders in Congress perceived their victory as a mandate to reject the excess of the New Deal and as a repudiation of organized labor. These two issues, social reform and labor, were intimately related and would become, in turn, the focus of attempts to link health insurance, labor militancy, and the Truman administration with socialist subversion in the context of the nascent Cold War.

The campaigns against health insurance and labor were led by Senator Robert Taft, the Republican chairman of the Senate Labor and Public Welfare Committee (formerly called Education and Labor Committee). Taft sponsored both the Taft-Hartley labor relations bill (S. 1126, H.R. 3020) and an alternative health bill (S. 545) for state-administered, means-tested medical care plans for the indigent. The AMA had clearly influenced the latter bill, particularly the requirements for physician administration of the state plans. The singling out of the indigent also addressed AMA concerns about unpaid health care services.

Both the Taft bill and the revised administration bill (S. 1320, introduced by Senator Murray) were debated at the same hearings in 1947 and early 1948.[77] Apart from the often bitter exchange of hostilities, these hearings held little interest. In the absence of any real possibility that legislation would be enacted, Taft and his Republican colleagues "were far more interested in discrediting the Truman administrations' health forces than in promoting their own health package."[78]

President Truman decided to face the opposition head on.[79] He appointed Oscar Ewing, a health insurance advocate, as Federal Security

---

rather than the Social Security Board. The sponsors of the bill included a southern Democrat (Lister Hill) and a Republican senator (Harold Burton) who had the support of both conservative Democrats and influential Republicans such as Robert Taft. Stevens 1989, 216–19.

[77] U.S. Congress, Senate, Committee on Labor and Public Welfare, *National Health Program: Hearings on S.545 and S.1320*, Pts. 1–4, 80th Cong., 1st and 2d sess., May–July 1947 and January 1948.

[78] Poen 1979, 101; see "Blueprint for the Nationalization of Medicine," prepared by Marjorie Shearon, U.S. Congress, Senate, 23 July 1947, 1706–7. In the House, Forest Harness (R-Ind.) tried to associate I. S. Falk with communist-front organizations; an FBI investigation actually ensued, but charges were dropped. Poen 1979, 104–5.

[79] "That was Harry Truman for you," remarked Altmeyer. "He wasn't going to let any AMA tell him where to get off at; he was going to tell them." Altmeyer, COHC, 133.

Administrator with the mandate to prioritize the health issue. He continued to emphasize health reform in a Message to Congress on health insurance in May 1947 and in the 1948 State of the Union address.[80] Truman also made health insurance an issue in the 1948 presidential election campaign that was fought more against the "do-nothing" Eightieth Congress than against the Republican presidential candidate, Thomas Dewey. For his part, Dewey was relatively silent on the health issue even though his running mate, Governor Earl Warren of California, had experienced legislative defeat on health insurance in 1945.

Truman's embrace of health reform was also motivated by political strategy. As the southern "Dixiecrats" had defected from the Democratic fold in the 1948 election, Truman was anxious to attract the "labor-liberal" vote.[81] This vote may have seemed precarious given the disastrous Taft-Hartley legislation and the presence of a third party candidate, Henry Wallace, running under the Progressive label. Wallace, a former Cabinet member under Roosevelt and a staunch supporter of the Wagner-Murray-Dingell bill initiatives in the 1940s, made national health insurance a prominent campaign pledge and berated both parties for inaction on the measure.

Nevertheless, organized labor, in the process of embracing postwar liberalism and purging its membership of more radical elements, did not support Wallace (who was perceived to have communist leanings). In fact, independent political action through a third party option held only limited appeal for American labor; at the same time, an officially nonpartisan stance was no longer viable. The CIO had already established its Political Action Committee in 1943 and had pledged to "abstain from and discourage any move" toward third-party formation that would "only serve to divide labor and the progressive forces and assure the election of our political enemies."[82] After the calamitous experience of the Eightieth Congress, the AFL finally dropped its nonpartisan stance to form Labor's League for Political Education in 1947. Both political action committees directed their efforts toward electing pro-labor Democrats rather than third-party candidates. In doing so, American labor organizations institutionalized their political alliance with the Democratic party.

Even though there was skepticism in some labor circles about Tru-

---

[80] U.S. President, *Public Papers of the Presidents*, 1947, 17 May 1947, 250–52. For an example of "do-nothing" rhetoric on health insurance, see Truman's address in Los Angeles, 23 September 1948, in U.S. President, *Public Papers of the Presidents*, 1948, 557. On health insurance in Truman's campaign strategy, see Poen 1979, 99.

[81] Lichtenstein 1989, 134–35.

[82] Resolution No. 9, Statement on Political Action (formation of the CIO-PAC), CIO, *Proceedings*, 1943, 239–41. On labor and the formation of political action committees, see Lichtenstein 1989, 138–39; Rayback 1966, 398–400; Davis 1986, 82–87.

man's leadership and the Democratic party's ability to represent labor interests, there was also a growing consensus that the Democratic party, especially its "labor-liberal" wing, represented the only viable political vehicle for American labor. Whatever the actual depth of his commitment to such reform, Truman's "liberal . . . rhetoric and gestures did serve a crucial political purpose, for they returned labor securely and energetically to the Democratic fold and denied a big dominant issue to a possible third-party movement."[83] The fight to repeal and stem the antilabor backlash in Congress necessitated a Democratic victory, while the continued hostility of southern Dixiecrats made it imperative to bolster support from the progressive wing of the Democratic party.

Despite the Democratic party's 1948 electoral victories, the Truman administration was no more successful in reaching legislative consensus on the issue with the Democratic-controlled Eighty-first Congress than it had been with the Republican Eightieth Congress. Although the absence of the "Dixiecrats" in Truman's coalition had made the party attractive to labor, the conservative Southern members soon returned to the Democratic fold after the election. A "conservative coalition" between Republicans and southern Democrats effectively continued to block the administration's initiatives, particularly the Taft-Hartley repeal and national health insurance. In contrast to the situation in Canada, the Democratic party faced a political power struggle in which the main threat came from the conservative Right. Compromise on issues like health insurance would have to make reform palatable to the Right, while in Canada, meanwhile, the Liberal party had to contend with pressure from the Left.

Health reform remained on the legislative front burner in Truman's 1949 State of the Union address and in his third (and final) message to Congress on national health insurance.[84] These proposals were embodied in a new bill (S. 1679), which enunciated the same principles as earlier proposals, except that it was deliberately more vague on coverage and scope of benefits. In response to anti-health insurance rhetoric and hostility in Congress, some senior bureaucrats had even considered replacing comprehensive benefits and universal coverage with a "staging" mechanism to gradually introduce various benefits. The intense discussion in the Federal Security Agency and Social Security Board on these strategies marked a widening split between the reform "purists" and the growing number of political "realists" in these agencies.[85]

[83] Hartmann 1971, 90.

[84] U.S. President, *Public Papers of the Presidents*, 1949, 5 January 1949, 1–7; 22 April 1949, 226–30.

[85] "Summary of Meeting on Health Insurance," 11 February 1949; File 011.4; Vol. 5; FSA; RG 235; NA. See also Barkev Sanders to Falk, 26 January 1949; Ida Merriam to Falk,

Senate hearings on the new bill were brief, but intense, and they included the discussion of three other health bills, including an AMA measure (S. 1581, sponsored by Taft) for voluntary health insurance plus federal funding for state and local aid to the poor and unemployed. For the first time, House hearings were also held on the President's measure (H.R. 4312 and 4313), sponsored by Andrew Biemiller of Wisconsin and John Dingell of Michigan.[86]

While senior bureaucrats might have doubted the chances of finally implementing a national health insurance program, the AMA was convinced that the administration's renewed commitment to health reform signaled that "Armageddon had come."[87] The AMA's response was to underwrite a "blitzkrieg" campaign to annihilate national health insurance.[88] Over $2 million was spent over the next two years in what would become "one of the most sensational and dramatic campaigns that an organization ever conducted."[89]

This "National Education Campaign" of the AMA was directed by Whitaker and Baxter, the public relations agency that had successfully blocked health insurance initiatives in California. The agency was charged with a dual mission: to turn the public against "compulsory" health insurance and "further to destroy the credibility of its spokesmen."[90] A barrage of publicity was aimed at convincing citizens instead that "The Voluntary Way is the American Way." An immense drive was launched to encourage state, local, and national organizations to publicly endorse the AMA. By the end of 1949, almost two thousand such endorsements were on record, including those from the National Economic Council, the American Farm Bureau, Catholic Charities, the American Hospital Association, the American Dental Association, the National Association of Life Insurance Agents, and the Chamber of Commerce. In addition, doctors were encouraged to campaign in their communities, and Congress members' personal doctors were encouraged to seek out the critical legislative support of their patients.

Although the "socialized medicine" label had been used to designate government health insurance in both Canada and the United States, it was now used to link supporters of health insurance to communist infil-

---

27 January 1949; and Falk to Murray, 31 March 1949; File 011.1; Vol. 2; DRS; RG 47; NA.

[86] U.S. Congress, Senate, Committee on Labor and Public Welfare, *National Health Program, 1949: Hearings on S. 1106, S. 1456, S. 1581, and S. 1679*, Pt. 1, 81st Cong., 1st sess., May-June 1948; U.S. Congress, House, Committee on Interstate and Foreign Commerce, *Hearings on H.R. 4312 and H.R. 4313*, May-June 1949.

[87] Starr 1982, 284–85.

[88] On the AMA's association with Whitaker and Baxter, and its 1949 campaign, see Kelley 1956; and Kennedy et al. 1954: 938–1022.

[89] Burrow 1963, 362.

[90] Kelley 1956, 74.

tration and threats to American national security. Antisocialist rhetoric in Canada had also been directed at the CCF and, by association, at the social reforms they proposed, but "only in America was growing anti-communism channeled into opposition to health insurance."[91] The AMA's message was particularly menacing for Democratic legislators facing mid-term elections in 1950. The AMA's National Education Campaign launched in October specifically targeted several health reformers: Andrew Biemiller, sponsor of Truman's 1949 bill in the House, was targeted by Wisconsin doctors' "Physicians for Freedom" campaign; his co-sponsor, Senator Elbert Thomas of Utah was also defeated, as was Senator Claude Pepper of Florida, whose support of compulsory health insurance was portrayed as symptomatic of his "pro-Communist leanings."[92]

While the AMA could devote its undivided attention to defeating health legislation, organized labor was distracted by other pressing legis-lative matters, such as attempts to repeal the Taft-Hartley Act. The labor press (particularly the CIO's) kept up a publicity campaign for health insurance, as did the Committee for the Nation's Health, but the pro-reform forces were clearly overwhelmed by the AMA and its allies.[93] The battle for public opinion also proved difficult to sustain. Polls showed growing opposition to the Truman plan, and more support for the AMA's voluntary insurance alternatives. While 58 percent of Americans had supported Truman's health initiatives in 1945, by the end of 1949 this figure had dropped to 36 percent.[94]

After 1950, concern with the potential political fallout made health reform an untenable issue for Democrats. The party refrained from en-dorsing health insurance and tried unsuccessfully to ignore the contro-versy, even though Truman continued to champion reform throughout his last year in office, blasting the AMA at every opportunity, and embar-rassing Democratic presidential candidate Adlai Stevenson in the process.[95] Republicans, meanwhile, prominently opposed "socialized medicine" in the 1952 elections. After the crushing defeat of Truman's health reform initiative, Eisenhower's victory effectively sounded the deathknell for na-tional health insurance.

[91] Starr 1982, 289.

[92] Pepper with Gorey 1987, chap. 7. On the AMA and these elections, see Kelley 1956, chap. 3.

[93] They were financially eclipsed by the AMA. In the first half of 1952, the AMA, the AFL, and the CNH all made the "top 26" reported spenders list, but the CNH was 26th and the AFL 12th, while the AMA was the second highest spender. *Congressional Quarterly Almanac*, 1952, 434.

[94] Gallup 1972, Vol. 2, 801–3; 886; Schiltz 1970, 129–31. Most of the support for the AMA alternative came from professionals, white-collar workers, and farmers; blue-collar workers were evenly split.

[95] Poen 1979, 199–200; 202–4. In Altmeyer's words, "Mr. Stevenson didn't want to touch it [the health insurance issue] with a ten-foot pole." Altmeyer, COHC, 135.

CONCLUSION

Despite the fervor of postwar reconstruction, initial public support for health reform, and the political saliency of the issue, by the end of the 1940s the only legislation that had been enacted was limited to grants-in-aid to help finance hospital construction. Nevertheless, that decade represented a watershed era for health reform in Canada and the United States. It was in the 1940s that the federal governments in the two countries put forward the first tangible proposals for health insurance. Although these proposals were not implemented, the future health reform agendas of the two countries were set.

In the United States, senior bureaucrats committed to health reform were unable to formulate a successful strategy to enact a national health insurance program. By the end of the decade, confronted with the structural constraints of the political system, including the presence of an intransigent Congress and the inability to forge a legislative and public consensus around the Truman proposals, many reformers seemed ready to concede defeat on the issue and retreat to a more feasible health reform strategy.

Harry Truman and Mackenzie King took up social reform as a key element in their plans for postwar reconstruction. President Truman's championing of health reform was an important milestone: a tangible attempt to forge a link with the Roosevelt legacy and, at the same time, a political vehicle that contributed to the 1948 election victory. Such energetic executive leadership, however, did not result in legislative action on health insurance, regardless of the party composition in Congress. In Canada, meanwhile, Prime Minister King understood that health and social insurance promises could be useful as a counterweight to deflect the political appeal of the CCF's social-democratic message among working-class voters.

There is no question that the intensity of opposition from the medical lobby was greater in the United States than in Canada. This was due in part to the fact that the stakes were much higher in the United States, since the AMA faced an administration ready to legislate a health program for which the input of the medical profession had been minimal. In addition, the AMA was also able to exploit its power within a political system in which groups with concerted interests and financial resources could exert considerable influence over public opinion and individual legislators. In Canada, such groups had less leeway over individual legislators bound by party discipline. The belligerent attitude of the AMA toward the Truman administration stands in contrast to the relatively less confrontational relationship between the CMA and the Liberal government. The absence of acrimonious memories (unlike those between the

AMA and New Deal reformers) may have made such cooperation easier, but the CMA's attitude may also have been due to the fact that the Liberal government, despite its rhetoric, remained divided over the health insurance issue and reluctant to enact such a program.

In both countries, organized labor emerged as a principal advocate for health insurance. Social reform, including health care, was a central element in the contest for working-class votes in Canada, and in consolidating labor's position within the Democratic coalition in the United States. Given the structural constraints facing third-party formation in the American political system, labor chose the Democratic party as its political vehicle. And even though American labor was much more involved in formulating health legislation, it faced a more hostile legislative environment. The political options of the Canadian labor movement, by contrast, were considerably expanded by the presence of a social-democratic party that effectively enunciated many of labor's social insurance demands. In the United States, health and social insurance were submerged within the Democratic party's broader platform, making electoral promises for health insurance easier to put off after they were decisively blocked in Congress. In Canada, these reform issues occupied a prominent place in the CCF's social-democratic program at a time when the third party was beginning to occupy a more important position in Canadian politics, at both the federal and provincial levels. The presence of the CCF ensured that health insurance would remain on the political agenda and that social-democratic principles, such as universality and equal access, would be the foundations of any federal legislation.

Federalism provided both opportunities and constraints in health reform in the two countries. Instead of serving as a laboratory of innovation, the states were the testing ground of campaigns against health insurance, such as the California experience in 1945. In the place of state experimentation, the Truman plan proposed a truly "national" health insurance system centralized at the federal level . The positions of the states on health reform were not given as much attention as were the provinces in the Canadian setting. In a sense, regional blocs in Congress acted as more effective checks on the federal government than did the actions of individual states.

In Canada, federal proposals were explicitly designed to accommodate provincial health plans. But jurisdictional wrangling, in particular over fiscal agreements, doomed these proposals. At the same time, however, the considerable autonomy of the provinces in the sphere of social insurance would provide an opportunity for a CCF government to embark on a social-democratic experiment in health reform that would spur other provincial innovation and make "national" health insurance a politically feasible option in Canada.

CHAPTER FIVE

The 1950s: Diverging Paths to
Health Reform

THE DEMOCRATIC PARTY entered the 1950s deeply divided over the health reform issue. The Truman administration's proposals had suffered a decisive defeat at the hands of both the AMA and the conservative coalition in Congress. Activists in the party, allied with labor and other social reform interests, were faced with the opposition of more conservative members and with the specter of the AMA's influence in the electoral arena and in setting the tone of the public debate on the issue. In the context of such constraints, reformers were forced to retreat to more feasible legislative compromises.

The health insurance debate in Canada evolved differently. Entering the 1950s, the federal government was still divided on health reform, but its margin for maneuver was limited by the pressures of the provinces, and of the CCF and its allies in the labor movement, in defining the legislative agenda and the public debate on health insurance. In Canada, a step-by-step process of reform would be adopted, in which federal government involvement in the financing of health care proceeded through stages, the first of which was the passage of hospital insurance legislation in 1957.

PROVINCIAL IMPETUS AND FEDERAL HESITATION IN
HOSPITAL INSURANCE

Alternatives to Federal Legislation in Health Care

With the failure to enact government health insurance legislation in the 1940s, private health insurance rapidly developed to cover the costs of hospital and medical care in Canada. The most important development in medical services coverage came after the official approval by the Canadian Medical Association of physician participation in voluntary health plans in 1949. In 1951, the CMA inaugurated Trans-Canada Medical Services, a coordinating body that included seven insurance plans in the provinces, sponsored by the provincial divisions of the CMA. By 1955, there were two million subscribers to plans operating in all ten provinces; and by

1959, almost 23 percent of Canadians were covered by these physician-sponsored nonprofit medical insurance plans.[1]

By 1956, 43 percent of Canadians had some form of nonprofit or commercial hospital insurance, and 37 percent were covered for medical benefits. There were, however, important variations according to region or urban center, and this insurance did not come cheaply, especially for single-rate subscribers, and premiums were not based on ability to pay. In addition, these voluntary plans did not offer comprehensive coverage; Canadians were still paying half of the costs of hospitalization and two-thirds of the costs of medical care out of their own pockets.[2]

But private health insurance was not the only alternative available to Canadians. The Saskatchewan Hospital Services Plan provided the catalyst for government involvement in hospital insurance. Despite the breakdown of federal-provincial discussion on the issue in 1945, the CCF government decided to "go it alone" and introduced a hospital insurance plan that went into operation in 1947.[3] Initiating health reform through hospital insurance made sense, given the rural character of the province and the fact that municipal arrangements for doctors' services were already in effect in many regions. More importantly, this form of intervention avoided immediate conflict with health providers, since the medical profession had already rejected the CCF's plan for salaried doctors and public control of medical services.[4]

The Saskatchewan hospital program, while modest in scope, was a momentous step since "no other jurisdiction in North America had committed itself to government planning in the health field."[5] Very soon, however, other western provinces would also experiment with hospital insurance. In British Columbia, the Liberal-Conservative coalition government was under acute pressure from both the CCF opposition and organized labor. A plan for hospital coverage (with government paying premiums for residents out of tax revenues) was introduced in 1948, but

[1] On these insurance initiatives, see Shillington 1972, chap. 11; and Naylor 1986b, 160.

[2] NAC; MG 32 B-12; Martin Papers; Vol. 30; File 1; Departmental Seminar, 1 March 1957.

[3] Taylor 1987, 105. Premier Tommy Douglas (who simultaneously served as Minister of Health) had asked Henry Sigerist, a professor in history of medicine (including of the Soviet Union) at Johns Hopkins University, to rapidly survey the province's health needs. He recommended "gradual socialization of services," focusing on the hospital benefits first and experiments with medical services in one or two "health regions" in the province. Naylor 1986b, 138–39.

[4] Nevertheless, the CCF did initiate an experiment to cover both hospital and medical benefits in the Swift Current health region. After protests from the Saskatchewan medical lobby, and the CMA, the government agreed to reimburse doctors on a fee-for-service basis. Naylor 1986b, 140–42; Lipset 1971, 290–93.

[5] McLeod 1971, 86.

the program was plagued by administrative and financial problems; in 1954, the new Social Credit government turned to sales-tax financing. In Alberta, the Social Credit gradually set up hospital insurance from 1949 to 1953 through a municipal hospital plan in which patients contributed through daily deductible fees.[6] By 1955, Ontario, Canada's most populous province, was also moving toward hospital insurance.

The Federal Government's Vacillation

Despite these provincial developments, the successor of Mackenzie King as prime minister, Louis St. Laurent, favored voluntary insurance through the expansion of private initiatives in the health sector. He supported the medical profession's involvement in sponsoring health plans and underlined the federal government's willingness to help the CMA "carry out this undertaking under their autonomous powers."[7]

St. Laurent was conscious of the Quebec government's objection to federal intrusion in provincial jurisdiction. Accordingly, the prime minister retreated from postwar promises of health reform by emphasizing provincial responsibility in health.[8] During the 1953 election campaign, St. Laurent insisted that the provinces "have to take the initiative" in the health insurance field, "which should, as far as possible, be left to Provincial administration."[9] His party's electoral platform spelled this out succinctly: "The Liberal party is committed to support a policy of contributory health insurance to be administered by the provinces when most of the provincial governments are ready to join in a nationwide scheme."[10] By 1955, it appeared that most provinces were ready for "nationwide" hospital insurance. The success of the Saskatchewan plan and other provincial initiatives, coupled with the demands of the Ontario government, led to pressure on the federal government to coordinate and help finance provincial hospital insurance.

Paul Martin, the Minister of National Health and Welfare, understood the political importance of the health issue for the Liberal party and continued to champion this program despite St. Laurent's reticence and the

---

[6] The other province with government insurance in this period was Newfoundland: its Cottage Hospital and Medical Care plan, based on voluntary premiums to finance care in government-owned hospitals, dated from 1935. See Canada, *Report of the Royal Commission on Health Services* 1964, 408–10.

[7] Canada, House of Commons, *Debates*, 20 June 1951, 4349.

[8] Taylor 1987, 108.

[9] Statement by St. Laurent, broadcast on the CBC, 9 July 1953; reprinted in Canada, House of Commons, *Debates*, 19 June 1954, 6302.

[10] Carrigan 1968, 209.

"rearguard actions" of his Cabinet colleagues.[11] Martin was well aware that provincial leaders, organized labor, and the CCF were increasingly restless with the limits of the health grants program. He warned that federal commitment was necessary to "keep alive the faith" of Canadians in the health and social reform promises of the Liberal party.[12]

Senior civil servants within the Department of National Health and Welfare endeavored to keep health insurance "a live issue"[13] by studying different strategies for the next step in health insurance legislation. The idea of "staging" benefit coverage had been discussed as early as 1950, when an Interdepartmental Working Committee on Health Insurance reported that the first stage of federal grants to the provincial health plans "should begin with basic hospital services."[14] Although there was general consensus that the staging of benefits was a workable mechanism for introducing health insurance, there was initial disagreement about which services should be targeted first. The director of Health Services, F. W. Jackson, favored the provision of insurance for general-practitioner services as the logical first step that would cover the most Canadians and reduce the initial costs of the program as much possible.[15] This view may have been influenced by the opinion of American bureaucrats in the Federal Security Agency with whom Jackson corresponded. Isidore Falk, a veteran of the 1940s health reform debates, expressed his pessimism about the staging of benefits, particularly if hospital services were the first step. Based on previous battles with the AMA, Falk feared that this would allow the medical lobby more time to organize its efforts to undermine future expansion to medical benefits.[16]

[11] Martin 1985, chap. 7.

[12] NAC; RG 29; Vol. 1061; 500-3-2, Pt. 1; Paul Martin to Louis St. Laurent, 8 October 1952; and Vol. 28; File 1; Martin to Walter Harris (Minister of Finance), 1 September 1955.

[13] NAC; RG 29; Vol. 1061; File 300-3-4; Cameron to Martin, 27 November 1950.

[14] NAC; RG 29; Vol. 1061; 500-3-4, Pt. 1 ("Confidential"); "Working Committee on Health Insurance of the Interdepartmental Committee on Social Security: Final Draft of Report," 14 February 1950. For more on staging discussions, see NAC; MG 32 B–12; Martin Papers; Vol 29; File 2.

[15] NAC; RG 29; Vol. 1372; 1–1; Confidential memo, "A Suggested Method of Implementing Health Insurance in Canada," 20 February 1952; and NAC; RG 29; Vol 1061; "Confidential File," 300-3-4, Pt. 2; F.W. Jackson, "Priorities in a Health Insurance Plan," 2 September 1955.

[16] NAC; RG 29; Vol. 1095; 502-5-1, Pt. 4; Joseph Willard [Research Officer] to F. W. Jackson, "American Thinking on Problems of Implementation and Priority," 16 March 1950. Falk had been monitoring the Canadian situation and was interested to "learn of further developments in this field of program planning and legislation in Canada"; NAC; RG 29; Vol. 1095; 502-5-1, Pt 3; , I. S. Falk to J. L. Little [Health Studies, DNHW], 16 May 1947. This exchange of information between senior bureaucrats, while never really formalized, had been going on since the 1930s.

Although Jackson continued to champion the idea of medical benefits, the department moved toward preparing hospital insurance legislation.[17] This was partly due to the existence of provincial precedents, in Saskatchewan and elsewhere, but the move also was a response to the more pressing need for hospital services and funding. Furthermore, this approach was appealing because it would be easier to administer and finance and would avoid direct confrontation with organized medicine. Finally, and this was no small consideration, this incremental approach represented the "easier route" to get the backing of reticent Cabinet members and the Prime Minister.[18]

The notion of targeting benefits to specific groups in the population, which was being discussed in the United States, was not given as much attention in Canada. Significantly, in the Canadian case, this discussion did not revolve around the aged, but rather around workers and their dependents, and it was thought that Canadian labor would be "100% in favour" of this option.[19] Organized labor, however, continued to champion the idea of a universal health insurance program for all Canadians. This universality principle was also the centerpiece of the federal CCF's platform for health insurance: a national, general-revenue-financed plan that would offer comprehensive health care coverage for all Canadians.

The Medical Lobby's Wary Reaction

The medical lobby was cautious in its reaction to government initiatives in hospital insurance. In a 1949 policy statement, the Canadian Medical Association reiterated its approval of "the principle of health insurance," but only in terms of the "practical application of this principle in the establishment of voluntary prepaid medical care plans."[20] Even though the CMA supported the staging of hospital benefits, it preferred that government intervention be limited to covering the costs of premiums for individuals unable to afford such insurance.

Although the medical lobby in Canada had been more conciliatory toward government proposals for health insurance than the AMA, by the 1950s the CMA recognized the utility of voluntary health insurance alternatives. With the development of consumer-controlled group plans

[17] For an indication of the differences of opinion between Jackson and Cameron [deputy minister] see 1955 memoranda in NAC; RG 29; Vol. 1372; 1–1.

[18] Martin 1985, 226.

[19] NAC; RG 29, Vol. 1372; 1–1; "Confidential Draft No. II, A Plan for Partial Health Insurance in Canada," 1 February 1952.

[20] "Statement of Policy Adopted by the General Council of the Canadian Medical Association, 1949," in Blishen 1969, 182–83.

and cooperatives in the medical field, the adoption of hospital insurance initiatives in Saskatchewan and other provinces, and the growing public interest in health care delivery, CMA leaders realized the importance of supporting a viable alternative to government-sponsored health insurance. As in the United States, the answer was to encourage voluntary health insurance plans and physician-sponsored plans that would retain fee-for-service practice and professional autonomy.[21] With its policy thus defined, the CMA concentrated its efforts on expanding enrollment in Blue Cross and physician-sponsored schemes, which "politically . . . were in a race with public demand and possible government responses."[22]

Accordingly, the Canadian Medical Association increased its efforts to keep abreast of political developments in the health sector. The association's membership fees doubled in 1952, the first increase in thirty years, due in part to the fact that "Canadian citizens, including politicians, are, in increasing numbers, taking more than a casual interest in . . . our business."[23] As the CCF made health insurance an issue in the 1953 electoral campaign, the CMA reaffirmed it would fight against "socialized medicine" and "not stand idly by and allow CMA standards to be jeopardized because of political expediency."[24]

The message was not lost on doctors. That same year, the CMA general council voted against universal and compulsory hospital insurance. In 1955, a definitive health insurance policy was accepted by the general council, highlighting voluntary prepayment plans as the way to ensure health insurance for all Canadians.[25] Although, as Naylor points out, "the issue of state-administered hospital insurance was less clear-cut than medical services insurance," the CMA was not necessarily amenable to either type of program; indeed, the CMA rejected the federal government's hospital insurance proposals in 1956 because of the universal and compulsory nature of the plan.[26] When the federal government outlined its

---

[21] As early as 1947, some Ontario doctors were proclaiming prepaid medical care "a medical weapon" to guarantee free enterprise in the health field, but one that could be developed through governmental encouragement of voluntary health insurance. *CMAJ*, May 1947, 574.

[22] Naylor 1986, 149. Unlike the AMA, the CMA did not do legal battle with consumer-controlled group medical plans. In the cooperative heartland of Saskatchewan, for example, the profession instead amalgamated the Regina cooperative into its own group plan; and in Saskatoon, it chose to compete directly for cooperative subscribers (and succeeded). See Naylor 1986b, 148–50.

[23] NAC; RG 29; Vol. 1111; 504-2-4, Pt. 3; T. C Routley to CMA Members, 15 July 1952.

[24] CMA President Charles Burns, quoted in the *Toronto Star*, 18 June 1953.

[25] "The Canadian Medical Association, Statement of Principles and Policies on Health Insurance in Canada, 1955," in Blishen 1969, 184–86.

[26] Quoted in Naylor 1986b, 164; see also Taylor 1987, 219–20.

hospital insurance proposals in 1956, the CMA debated but ultimately rejected them, mainly because of the compulsory and universal nature of the plan.

The Canadian Hospital Council shared the view that government intervention should be limited to helping low-income individuals meet the costs of Blue Cross premiums or other voluntary insurance. The CHC had its own ax to grind with the federal government in terms of the shortcomings of hospital construction grants and the council's preoccupation with maintaining independent administration of hospitals. This latter concern was of paramount importance to the Catholic Hospital Conference, which did not welcome government involvement, particularly federal interference in hospitals in Quebec, preferring provincial health plans and private enterprise.[27] This group was potentially much more influential than its American counterpart, the Catholic Hospital Association, given its regional concentration, and the fact that the prime minister and his Quebec caucus shared these opinions.

The network of opposition widened outside the health sector during the 1950s. For example, the Canadian Chamber of Commerce took a strong and visible position on the issue of health insurance, criticizing compulsory "state medicine" and endorsing the voluntary insurance approach. The Canadian Pharmaceutical Manufacturers Association also began to publicize its opposition to government involvement, supporting the CMA in promoting voluntary health insurance.[28] The rapid rise of private health insurance gave the Canadian Life Insurance Officers Association (CLIOA) an incentive for reevaluating its 1940s position on health insurance and taking a firm opposition to widespread government involvement. The insurance industry emphasized the success of private insurance and declared that government's role should be to facilitate the purchase of such insurance, either through subsidies to lower-income individuals (the "hopeless risks") or through American-style tax exemptions. This approach was "highly consistent with the personal philosophy of Prime Minister St. Laurent"[29] and of many Cabinet members as well. Indeed, a chief spokesperson for the insurance industry was former Cabinet member Brooke Claxton, who had been responsible for drafting the federal government's social insurance proposals in 1945. Now an executive for Metropolitan Life Insurance Company, Claxton reformulated his ideas about the role of government in the health care sector, declaring,

[27] Taylor 1987, 192–94.

[28] The CPMA's "Health Insurance" bulletins followed the activities of the CMA and kept readers abreast of government insurance initiatives in Canada and abroad. NAC; RG 29; Vol. 1063; 502-1-1, Pt. 11; "Health Insurance," May 1950; and NAC; MG 32 B-12; Martin Papers; Vol 30; File 2.

[29] Taylor 1987, 196.

"If government action is needed, it should supplement, not supplant, private insurance."[30]

The Pressure from Organized Labor

Although both the Trades and Labor Congress (associated with AFL affiliates) and the Canadian Congress of Labour (which included CIO-affiliated unions) had been wary of federal proposals for health reform in the 1940s, both organizations now pushed the Liberal government to act on its postwar social reform promises. The two major points stressed by labor were the inadequacies of the voluntary approach and the need for federal participation in any health insurance program. Canadian labor leaders had experienced firsthand the struggle for adequate health coverage through collective bargaining, and they were aware of the significant gaps in coverage and the high costs of private insurance. Federal action was considered necessary to nudge recalcitrant provinces into action, to provide adequate financing of the program, and to ensure national standards that would guarantee adequate health benefits for workers and their families in every province. Although the staging of benefits was not ruled out, the Canadian labor movement placed the emphasis on providing benefits for working Canadians, rather than the poor or the elderly.

During the 1950s, organized labor publicized health reform with increasing frequency, and sharply criticized the political impasse on the issue. A resolution on national health insurance at the 1955 CCL convention declared that "this Convention strongly urge the Federal Government to enact a proper health plan which will provide adequate medical, surgical, optical, dental and hospital treatment for the people of Canada, in conformity with the requests of organized Labour and other broadly representative citizen groups."[31]

The TLC passed similar resolutions, deploring the federal government's procrastination and urging that "every member of every local union . . . take up this matter directly with his Member of Parliament."[32]

The question of political action as a means of securing health and other social reform was hotly debated within the Canadian labor movement. The Canadian Congress of Labour continued to support the Cooperative Commonwealth Federation, while the Trades and Labor Congress formally retained a nonpartisan position. There was no unanimity

---

[30] NAC; MG 32 B-12; Martin Papers; Vol. 30; File 2; Summary of CLIOA memorandum, 9 October 1956.

[31] Resolution No. 107, CCL, *Proceedings*, 1955, 56.

[32] "Government's Reply to Memorandum," *Trades and Labor Congress Journal*, December 1953, 9.

on the subject in either organization. Although the CCL executive stressed the need for loyalty to the CCF (and farmer-labor cooperation), some members were skeptical about the "political apostles" in the CCF, preferring "honest-to-God labour men."[33] In the TLC, meanwhile, members were expressing impatience with the nonpartisan tradition and questioning its relevance for labor in the Canadian political process:

> Now, the question of rewarding your friends and defeating your enemies may have some purpose in the United States . . . Congress and the Senate [where] there is a certain liberty given to the members. Now, this doesn't obtain in Canada. If you belong to a political party, no matter what your private thoughts may be, when the whip goes down in the House of Commons, you vote the party line or you stay away. . . . If you are going to have any kind of political action in Canada then you have got to support a political party.[34]

When the TLC and CCL merged to form the Canadian Labour Congress in 1956, the political action question was not yet resolved. A CLC Political Action Committee was charged with initiating discussions with farm groups, cooperative movements, and the CCF "or other political parties pledged to support the legislative programme of the Canadian Labour Congress."[35] Controversy still reigned as to whether the CLC could "dictate" the choice of a political party to its members, and whether the CCF in fact represented the ideal of a Canadian labor party. On one issue, however, organized labor stood united and supported the CCF: health insurance as part of a national social insurance system. The CLC platform emphasized health reform as "the No. 1 aim" of the new organization.[36]

The CCF in the House of Commons

In an attempt to expand its political base nationally and to revive its sagging electoral fortunes, the Co-operative Commonwealth Federation had begun to move closer to organized labor, particularly after the 1956 merger of the CCL and TLC. The CCF also attempted to galvanize public attention and support through its attacks on the federal government's inaction on the health insurance issue. More than ever convinced

---

[33] From debate on the motion to endorse the CCF as the political arm of labor. CCL, *Proceedings*, 1954, 13–20.

[34] Delegate W. L. Hood, from debate on the motion for nonpartisan political action. TLC, *Proceedings*, 1955, 205.

[35] Substitute Resolutions on Political Education and Action. CLC, *Report of the Proceedings of the 1st Constitutional Convention*, Toronto, 23–27 April 1956, 49.

[36] Donald Swartz 1977, 323.

that the Liberals would not act "unless they are shoved," the CCF resolved to carry on a "process of jolting and jabbing" the government for health legislation.[37] Stanley Knowles, the CCF party whip and social reform critic, lost few opportunities to underline the success of hospital insurance in Saskatchewan and the unfulfilled promises of the federal government.[38] In the early 1950s, the CCF focused on the absence of a response by the federal government to launch debates on the issue in the House of Commons. The most forceful opposition to the CCF came from members of Parliament who were also physicians (particularly Liberals from the province of Quebec). The right-wing Social Credit party also rejected government involvement in "socialized medicine" and emphasized individual responsibility for health and health care costs. The Conservatives, meanwhile, mocked the CCF's "obsession" with health insurance, suggesting the CCF "should consider changing its name to the health insurance party [since] this subject now appears to have become the *raison d'être* of the party."[39]

Through its efforts in the House of Commons, the CCF publicized health insurance in a highly visible, public forum. The virtues of universal health insurance, and of the Saskatchewan model of hospital insurance, were extolled before a national audience, and these attempts were not lost on federal politicians. A weary Paul Martin wryly remarked that Stanley Knowles—"that constant thorn in my side"—was making good on his threat to "push and prod me on every occasion—and he has resorted to almost every occasion—to try to get me to pronounce the government's policy on health insurance."[40] Martin, who was having a hard time selling health reform to the Cabinet, made good use of the CCF threat in "convincing the doubters" of the political saliency of such measures.[41]

The CCF's campaign also compelled other opposition parties, individual MPs, and interested groups to express their positions, intensifying the debate over health reform and hospital insurance. In effect, the CCF acted as a lightning rod for societal groups that supported universal health insurance in Canada, especially farm and labor groups that had strong ties with the social-democratic movement.

[37] Stanley Knowles, Canada, House of Commons, *Debates*, 1 December 1952, 339; and 23 November 1953, 258.

[38] Active in both the cooperative and labor movements in Manitoba, Knowles occupied J. S. Woodsworth's former seat of Winnipeg North Centre after 1942. Trofimenkoff 1982, chap. 5. Other CCFers active in the health debate were party leader M. J. Coldwell; Joseph Noseworthy, the 1942 York South victor; and Angus MacInnis and H. W. Herridge from British Columbia.

[39] Owen Trainor (physician and Conservative M.P. from Winnipeg South), Canada, House of Commons, *Debates*, 1 December 1953, 522.

[40] Martin 1985, 223; Canada, House of Commons, *Debates*, 20 January 1954, 1298.

[41] Martin 1985, 227.

The Hospital Insurance and Diagnostic Services Act of 1957

Despite the Liberal government's hesitancy on health insurance, increasing pressure from the CCF in the House of Commons and from the newly unified labor movement was raising the political stakes of the issue. Public opinion polls showed that a substantial majority of Canadians were in favor of government-financed hospital insurance, "even if it meant higher taxes."[42]

The opposition parties continued to beleaguer the Liberal government during the preparations for the October 1955 Federal-Provincial Conference. Along with the CCF, the Conservative party, despite its past contradictions on the issue, now demanded federal action. Even the right-wing Social Credit party agreed that it would be ready to support a plausible plan.[43]

Most provincial governments were also pressuring the federal government to alleviate some of the financial burden of putting hospital plans into operation. Developments in Ontario were particularly significant. Leslie Frost's Conservative government was under considerable pressure from organized labor and from the provincial CCF to introduce hospital insurance in Ontario.[44] As Paul Martin, the federal health minister noted: "Frost did not have an ideological commitment to health insurance, but as the head of a large, industrial province, he was shrewd enough to support it." The premier's advisers, meanwhile, agreed that Frost "would sooner leave things as they are and do nothing about health insurance but felt this was an untenable position and that something probably had to be done about it."[45] The Conservative government in Ontario, however, was not prepared to experiment alone as Saskatchewan had. Frost wanted federal cost-sharing guarantees before implementing a province-wide hospital insurance plan.

The pressure from Premier Frost, and insistence from minister Paul

[42] Sixty-two percent of Canadians responded positively to an April 1956 Gallup Poll that asked: "Would you favor, or oppose, a government-operated plan whereby any hospital expenses you incurred would be paid for out of taxes—even if it meant higher taxes?" (NAC; RG 29; Vol. 1372; 1–1 [from The *Montreal Star*, 18 April 1956]). By September, this margin had grown to 72 percent (PAC; MG 32; Martin Papers; Vol. 28; File 2 [from the *Toronto Daily Star*, 5 September 1956]).

[43] On the Conservative health insurance amendment, see Canada, House of Commons, *Debates*, 10 January 1955, 30–34; and Canada, Social Credit, House of Commons, *Debates*, 15 July 1955, 6240.

[44] Swartz 1975, 323.

[45] Martin 1985, 220; NAC; RG 29; Vol. 1372; File 1–1; G. F. Davidson (Deputy Minister, Welfare) to Paul Martin, Memo on "Health Insurance and Ontario," 5 August 1955. On Leslie Frost and hospital insurance in Ontario, see Taylor 1987, chap. 3.

Martin, forced St. Laurent to place hospital insurance on the agenda of the next Federal-Provincial Conference, scheduled for October 1955. At the conference, the prime minister publicly endorsed hospital insurance, and the following January he signaled a formal commitment to a federal-provincial plan for hospital insurance and diagnostic services.[46] The proposal indicated that the federal government was prepared to share one-half of the costs of hospital and diagnostic services in the provinces, provided that the services were available to all residents of the province, without excessive "deterrent" fees. There was, however, an important prerequisite: "a majority of the provincial governments, representing a majority of the people of Canada," would first have to agree to put their provincial plans into effect.[47]

Essentially, the proposal still embodied the Liberal government's 1953 position on health reform that declared federal action would depend on provincial initiative. In this case, a majority of provinces, including one of the most populous provinces—Ontario or Quebec, would have to institute their own hospital insurance plans before the federal government would set up a cost-sharing program. Given the explicitly noninterventionist attitude of the Duplessis government in Quebec, the actual timing of the hospital insurance plan remained highly uncertain. In Ontario, Premier Frost's enthusiasm had cooled substantially after the Conservative party was re-elected. Only three provinces seemed in a position to negotiate with the federal government: British Columbia, Alberta, and Saskatchewan. While the CCF government in Saskatchewan was eager for federal contributions and national standards, the Social Credit in Alberta and British Columbia insisted that any federal grants should be free of conditions.[48]

Both organized labor and the CCF were quick to criticize the federal proposals. The Canadian Labour Congress wryly noted: "We can hardly hail the Dominion proposal as the health insurance millennium. . . . [It] is at best a first and halting step in the direction of health insurance."[49]

---

[46] Prime Minister's statement on health insurance, 6 October 1955. NAC; RG 29; Vol. 1372; 1–1; C. A. Roberts (Health Insurance Studies) to Cameron (Deputy Minister, Health), 17 January 1956; and NAC; RG 29; Vol. 1372; 1–2. Diagnostic services, including laboratory and radiology services, were already being subsidized to some extent by the National Health Grants Program.

[47] Statement by Prime Minister on Health Insurance, Canada, House of Commons, *Debates*, 26 January 1956, 555–556; and NAC; RG 29; Vol. 1372; 6-1-1; "Secret" Memorandum re Health Insurance Policy, 20 January 1956. For a summary of the proposal, see Taylor 1987, 217.

[48] Canada, Federal-Provincial Conference, *Proceedings*, Ottawa, 3 October 1965; and NAC; RG 29; Vol. 1372; Canada, Dominion-Provincial Conference, 1955; "Record of a Meeting of the Federal-Provincial Committee on Health," 6 October 1955.

[49] "Health Insurance?" *Trades and Labor Congress Journal* 35, no. 2 (February 1956): 10.

Although the CLC was willing to compromise on provincial administration of health insurance and the staging of services, its major criticism was that the timetable of the staging did not conform to the goals of a national health insurance program. Labor continued to press for a national plan financed from federal general revenues under provincial administration, the type of plan that Department of National Health and Welfare (DNHW) officials felt "could [not] be accepted by any government except one which is frankly and totally socialist in philosophy."[50]

For its part, the CCF was now faced with a dual agenda: to make sure that these legislative proposals were acted on, by insisting that the Liberal government follow through with the passage and implementation of hospital insurance; and, at the same time, to ensure that the proposed plan would be but the first step in a broader program of universal health insurance. In the House of Commons, Knowles chided the Liberals for their "least common denominator" approach to health insurance and urged the federal government to "talk turkey" with the provinces in order to get their approval of the hospital plan as quickly as possible.[51]

Uncertainty about hospital insurance continued, as no legislation was introduced in 1956 or mentioned in the Liberal government's 1957 Throne Speech. With the majority province agreement formula, the plan had become a "political football," and the CCF took every opportunity to question the government on provincial reactions to the plan.[52] An important obstacle was Ontario; Premier Frost, who had insisted on federal action, now objected to the universal and compulsory nature of the plan, preferring a voluntary approach. Frost "finally caved in" in early March to public and political pressure, particularly from the CCF in Ontario, led by labor executive Donald MacDonald.[53]

With the approval of Ontario and four other provinces, hospital insurance legislation (Bill 320) was introduced on March 25 in the House of Commons. Debate on the matter began on April 4. On April 10, 1957, the House unanimously passed the Hospital Insurance and Diagnostic Services Act (HIDS), 165 to nil.[54] The unanimous vote is noteworthy. The real political struggle over hospital insurance had already taken place before the bill was introduced: in the House led by the CCF attrition campaign; in the Cabinet, where the Prime Minister and several members were still reluctant about reform; and in the federal-provincial arena in

---

[50] NAC; RG 29; Vol 1401; 504-1-4; Memorandum from Cameron (Deputy Minister, Health) to the Minister, 26 September 1956.

[51] Canada, House of Commons, *Debates*, 26 January 1956, 404; 26 July 1956, 6559.

[52] M. J. Coldwell, Canada, House of Commons, *Debates*, 9 January 1957, 39.

[53] Martin 1985, 244.

[54] Canada, House of Commons, *Debates*, 25 March 1957, 2642 (first reading); 4 April 1957, 3096 (second reading); 10 April 1957, 3366 (third reading); 3393–94 (roll call).

negotiations with the premiers. With party discipline in force, the swift passage of the act through Parliament was assured by a majority government, since the Liberal caucus was bound to vote with the party in the House. The unanimous vote was also a sign of the political stakes the issue had engendered, including those of the Progressive Conservative party, which had expressed some objections during the debate on the details of the bill, but which was careful to support the measure, particularly in the face of the upcoming election. It was, in fact, the CCF that quibbled most strongly with the bill, disputing the partial nature of benefits, and the six-province requirement for implementation.

The timing of passage is also significant. Only two days later Parliament was dissolved, and a federal election was called. The political pressure on the Liberal government had risen precipitously, making legislative action on health insurance a compelling preelectoral strategy. Nevertheless, the passage of hospital insurance proved a "futile bid to stave off electoral defeat."[55] In June 1957, the Liberal party's twenty-two-year tenure in government ended. Although the campaign was fought on several issues, the victorious Progressive Conservative party reaped important profits from its leader's populist commitment to social reform.[56]

When Parliament reconvened, hospital insurance was still on the agenda. The CCF charged the new Prime Minister, John Diefenbaker, with stalling the implementation of the legislation, and reiterated demands to amend the provincial approval formula and set a definite starting date.[57] The CCF went so far as to threaten a vote on the issue, a serious matter since the Conservatives were in a minority-government situation. Prime Minister Diefenbaker could not afford to face criticism on the health issue in the next election, which was sure to be fairly soon. After the November 1957 Federal-Provincial Conference, Diefenbaker removed the majority-province rule, enabling federal participation in hospital insurance to begin July 1, 1958. It proved to be a shrewd political move that contributed to the Conservative's landslide election victory in March 1958.

Although the Hospital Insurance and Diagnostic Services Act contradicted the CMA's idea of limited government involvement in health insurance, there is little evidence that the CMA used electoral tactics against health reform proponents. The medical lobby (and their allies) did express their grievances to the Cabinet, but once legislation was introduced, it passed easily. Nor did the CMA mount a major campaign

[55] Swartz 1987, 257.

[56] In fact, the Liberals obtained a higher percentage of the popular vote than the Conservatives (41 to 39), but they lost 65 seats, for a total of 105. The Conservatives picked up 61 to obtain 112, while the CCF gained 2 (to 25) and the Social Credit 4 (to 19).

[57] Knowles, Canada, House of Commons, *Debates*, 18 November 1957, 1235.

against the federal hospital plan in the way the AMA would against a limited hospital insurance plan for the aged. Instead, the CMA strategy shifted to one of containment: to keep hospital insurance from becoming the first stage in a comprehensive health insurance system.

THE SEARCH FOR POLITICALLY FEASIBLE HEALTH REFORM IN THE UNITED STATES

By the time control of the White House and Congress had changed hands in 1953 from the Democrats to the Republicans, under President Eisenhower, national health insurance had effectively become a moribund issue for both the Democratic and Republican leadership in the United States. Nevertheless, as Sundquist suggests, "If the 1952 campaign saw a bipartisan repudiation of national health insurance, it also saw a bipartisan acknowledgment that a problem did exist."[58] The basic problem, as in Canada, was how to ensure that health care remained accessible and affordable. Both major parties would proffer solutions during the 1950s, but neither would embrace the idea of public, universal coverage for all Americans.

Filling the Gaps in the Insurance Market: Health Reinsurance

As in Canada, there was a tremendous growth in private health insurance in the United States during the 1950s. Particularly influential in this respect was the medical profession, which had definitively shed its former objections to insurance and encouraged private and nonprofit hospital and medical plans (although it continued to oppose prepaid group medical services).[59] Although Blue Cross and Blue Shield had existed since the 1930s, they now expanded rapidly, followed by commercial carriers that began to offer health insurance. Whereas in 1940 only 9 percent of Americans purchased hospital insurance coverage, by 1950 the figure had soared to 61 percent; and by 1960, 68 percent of Americans were covered, half by nonprofit plans.[60] In 1948, only 6 percent of private expen-

---

[58] Sundquist 1968, 291.

[59] Much like their Canadian counterparts, American physicians were suspicious of group prepayment that threatened choice, autonomy, and fee-setting controls. Despite AMA campaigns against such plans (e.g., against the Kaiser Foundation Health Plan in the Pacific states), they continued to grow in urban centers (e.g., Health Insurance Plan of Greater New York, the Group Health Cooperative of Puget Sound). Stevens 1971, 422–23.

[60] Stevens 1989, 259.

ditures for physicians' services were met by insurance; by 1960, private insurance covered 32 percent of the cost of such care.[61]

The expanding network of nonprofit, commercial, group, and union-sponsored health plans, Starr suggests, "provided enough protection for groups that held influence in America," and this forestalled "any great agitation for national health insurance in the 1950s."[62] Nevertheless, as gaps in private health insurance became visible, the political saliency of health reform remained apparent.

In effect, out-of-pocket expenses were still high, and insurance premiums rose as health costs soared. The rise in competition and costs contributed to the exclusion of vulnerable groups, such as lower-income workers, the poor, and the aged, from the private insurance market. Elderly Americans were especially affected by the "experience rating" system of groups that was used by commercial carriers in order to remain competitive and to avoid being saddled with uninsurables.

Like Prime Minister St. Laurent in Canada, President Eisenhower favored the voluntary approach to health insurance. However, both leaders also understood that this approach had serious gaps. The Liberal government in Canada had left these gaps for the provinces to deal with, until mounting political pressure forced a federal response. The Republican administration, on the other hand, did not turn to the states. Instead, it attempted to implement a voluntary prepayment program of health reinsurance through which the federal government would broaden the coverage, both of subscribers and services, of nonprofit and private health insurers by assuming part of their liability for high-risk groups.[63]

Despite the strong backing of the administration, hearings on the plan in 1954 revealed a lack of support from all sides.[64] The supporters of national health insurance in the 1940s balked at the use of public funds to subsidize the inadequacies of private insurance, although the AFL leadership did not reject the principle of reinsurance outright.[65] Oppo-

[61] Reed 1961, 3–11, 10–11.

[62] Starr 1982, 334.

[63] "The Health Problem—Message from the President of the United States," 18 January 1954, *Congressional Record*, 379–81. Reinsurance was a common practice in the commercial insurance market, and proposals had already been introduced in Congress as early as 1950, by Republican Charles Wolverton, of New Jersey. See Stevens 1971, 429–31; Anderson 1968, 140–45.

[64] Hearings on S. 3114/H.R. 8356 were held in the Senate Labor and Public Welfare Committee and in the House Interstate and Foreign Commerce committees. For a summary of testimony, see *Congressional Quarterly Almanac*, 1954, 215–19.

[65] The AFL criticized the plan for the lack of standards and safeguards and for lack of assistance for those unable to afford commercial premiums (AFL, Report of the Executive Council, *Proceedings*, 1954, 296–98). The CIO, meanwhile, termed reinsurance "the pa-

nents of national health insurance, including medical, business, and insurance lobbies, denounced even this limited intrusion of the federal government as a first step toward "socialized medicine." The only support came from the American Hospital Association and its Blue Cross Commission, who welcomed the protection against significant losses incurred from insuring and treating society's uninsurables.

Eisenhower continued to champion reinsurance, but his proposals were not enacted.[66] The failure of reinsurance suggested a bipartisan recognition of the deficiencies of the private market in health insurance in the United States, but it also reminded political actors that even a plan anchored in the market approach had met with opposition from the medical lobby and their allies in business and insurance. The reinsurance debate also revealed evidence of an initial rupture between the AMA and hospital organizations, and between private and nonprofit insurers, over the role of the federal government in regulation of health care. Finally, the reinsurance proposals moved the health insurance debate, beyond the all or nothing face-off between compulsory and voluntary health insurance, toward the idea of partial reform, without greatly expanding the role of the state in health care delivery.

Modifying the Debate over Health Reform: Targeting the Aged

Evidence of the "politics of incrementalism" was already apparent during the battle over the Truman health plan.[67] Senior bureaucrats in the Social Security Administration contended that there "was never a decision to drop" national health insurance, but rather that the agency began to explore "specific beginnings such as hospital benefits."[68] The staging idea had in fact been discussed as early as 1941–42, and was revived after the comprehensive approach failed in 1949–50.[69] Aware of the controversy

---

thetic offspring of reliance on private plans and unwillingness to spend money for people's welfare" (CIO, *Proceedings*, 1954, 185).

[66] The bill was reported favorably out of committee, but it was recommitted by a wide margin (75R-162D vs. 120R-14D) and died in the House (*Congressional Record*, 13 July 1954, 10425). Eisenhower launched the reinsurance idea again the following year, but no further action was taken in Congress.

[67] On the emergence of this incrementalism, see Marmor 1973, 14; and Jacobs 1993, 88–91.

[68] Altmeyer 1966, 39.

[69] Falk had studied the idea of including hospital benefits under OASI in 1941, in which all covered workers and their dependents would be eligible for benefits similar to those offered by voluntary nonprofit plans. Memo from I. S. Falk to Wilbur Cohen, 11 June 1941; Cohen Papers; Folder 4; SHSW. On the limited-approach precedents, see Poen 1979, 190–91.

surrounding health reform, reformers in the SSA "realized that we could only get a very limited beginning and so we looked for the sort of beginning that would be attractive, enough to overcome the opposition of the AMA," or, more bluntly, something that they could "rescue from the wreckage" of Truman's failed health initiative.[70]

Isidore Falk had opposed the idea of staging, fearing such an approach would "freeze in" partial services rather than build toward a comprehensive health insurance system. The biggest danger, according to Falk, was that if the process began with hospital insurance, the AMA would seize the delay in order to effectively preclude the inclusion of medical benefits at a later date. Most of his colleagues, however, sensing that sweeping reform was beyond the realm of the politically possible, were open to alternative measures, even if this meant a partial rather than a comprehensive approach.[71]

By 1950, the blockade of a national health program gave rise to alternative proposals within the Federal Security Agency. Senior officials, including Oscar Ewing, were already discussing a "line of retreat," most notably a voluntary alternative and the possibility of staging benefits.[72] At a strategy session early in 1950 it was noted: "The Agency's general position on S.1679 [Truman plan] should be maintained since retreat or major compromise would confuse and alienate advocates without winning over opponents. . . . Approval might later be given to a more limited program, such as compulsory hospital insurance or insurance against catastrophic illness, however, if there were reasonable chances of adoption."[73]

The "reasonable chances" refrain was to become the guiding principle of health reformers both in and out of government throughout the 1950s. The strategy was to build a politically feasible alternative to national health insurance, combining the staging principle with the existing social insurance system. Concentrating on hospital insurance could deflect some of the fears of an AMA backlash, and using the popular social security program that targeted the aged could build consensus for reform.[74]

In June 1951, Ewing publicly outlined a limited plan that offered sixty

---

[70] Altmeyer, COHC, 41, 138.

[71] Milton Roemer (Department of Public Health, Yale), for one, explicitly warned against targeting groups, suggesting that the success of the Saskatchewan and UAW plans "illustrated the value" of the staging-of-benefits approach (Roemer to Falk; 5 January 1950; File 056.1 1950 (#40); Box 25; DRS; NA).

[72] Memo from Cornelius A. Wood (FSA Health Insurance Committee) to Oscar Ewing, 20 January 1950; File 011.4; Box 7; FSA; NA.

[73] "Position on Compulsory Health Insurance" [n.d.]; File 011.4; Box 7; FSA; NA. The participants included Ewing, Altmeyer, and Falk.

[74] Marmor 1973, 15, 17.

days of hospital care per year to all Social Security beneficiaries. Although this proposal did not attract much attention at the time (in the midst of the AMA blitz against "socialized medicine"), the genesis of the 1960s Medicare system was beginning to take shape. Through this mixed compromise of partial benefits (hospitalization only) and limited group coverage (Old-Age and Survivors' Insurance recipients), health reformers believed they had found the perfect "wedge" to open the door to national health insurance: "We looked at it as a small way of starting something big."[75]

Age-based entitlement would thus emerge as a logical political choice to reanimate the health insurance debate. The Social Security Act had created an important clientele group of older Americans, whose lives were already greatly affected by state intervention. Higher life expectancy and exposure to modern diseases made them especially vulnerable to the gaps in the private insurance market system. The aged represented the greatest high-risk group, both in medical and in economic terms, but at the same time they "commanded public sympathy" as those "about whom the moralistic arguments of self-help did not apply."[76]

The absence of this kind of targeting of the aged was one of the most important distinguishing features of the Canadian hospital insurance plan being formulated at the same time. The Social Security Act had set the precedent for age-based cleavages in the American welfare state and had reinforced the idea of "deserving" social groups. In Canada, no such precedent had been firmly institutionalized. Rather, the health reform debate focused on universal eligibility, reinforced by the demands of the CCF and labor, and by the precedent set by the CCF government in Saskatchewan in 1947. In addition, the race card, an important element in the power of conservative southern legislators in the United States, was absent in the Canadian context, where societal cleavages were regional and linguistic, and where the federal government tended to use the welfare state as a unifying rather than a divisive force.[77]

Party and Group Politics in the Health Insurance Debate

Sundquist notes that, in its role as the "out-party" during the 1950s, the Democratic party moved toward consensus, acting more like a "responsi-

---

[75] Wilbur Cohen (then assistant to SSA commissioner Altmeyer), quoted in Harris 1966, 55. The original proposals extended coverage to all beneficiaries of OASI, including the aged, dependent children, widows, and orphans. For more detail on the "Ewing Proposal," see Myers 1970, 33–34.

[76] Marmor and Morone 1983, 137.

[77] Myles and Quadagno 1994, 62.

ble party," after the disastrous divisiveness of the Truman years.[78] In the case of health reform, however, this divisiveness was still very apparent: between "liberal" reformers and the Democratic leadership in Congress, and between Congress and activists within the Democratic Advisory Committee.

Senator James Murray and Representative John Dingell, the sponsors of national health insurance in the 1940s, introduced bills based on the Ewing proposals to extend hospital coverage to OASI beneficiaries in 1952 and 1953.[79] With Republican control of the Congress and presidency, no legislative action was taken on the measures. The Democratic party regained control of the Congress in 1956, but this did not immediately facilitate health reform. In 1955 and 1956, Congressional debate centered around extending OASI to include disability insurance, an initiative that demonstrated that even in the face of AMA opposition, targeting aid to a "deserving" group (i.e., the disabled) could help win over congressional reluctance.[80]

In 1957, Nelson Cruikshank (the AFL-CIO's Director of Social Security) and Andrew Biemiller (the former House member and now the organization's Director of Legislation) approached influential Democrats on the Ways and Means Committee with a new health insurance plan based on the 1952 Murray-Dingell bill.[81] They had little success with the committee's powerful southern Democrats, particularly the committee's chairman, Wilbur Mills. After much persuasion, the fourth-ranking Democrat on the committee, Aimé Forand of Rhode Island, reluctantly agreed to be sponsor, although he was not particularly interested in social insurance, nor was he optimistic about the bill's chances. The Forand bill was introduced on August 27, 1957, just before the 1957 session of Congress ended, and hearings were held the following year. No legislative action was taken, but by the time Forand reintroduced the measure in 1959, these proposals for health insurance for the aged had taken on a

---

[78] Sundquist 1968, 389–415. The American Political Science Association organized the Committee on Political Parties, under E. E. Schattschneider, in 1946; their report, *Toward a More Responsible Two-Party System*, was published in 1950. The theme of intraparty cohesion for effective party government is emphasized in Schattschneider 1948.

[79] The companion bills (S. 3001/H.R. 7484) called for increased Social Security premiums to finance sixty days of hospital care per year. Dingell reintroduced a version of the bill in the House in 1955 and 1956; similar bills were sponsored by Rep. Emanuel Cellar of New York.

[80] Disability insurance was first recommended as part of the Wagner bill proposals in 1939 and had been an important legislative priority of the SSA since 1949. On disability as a prelude to health insurance, see Derthick 1979, 319–20.

[81] The new plan was drafted with the help of Wilbur Cohen, I. S. Falk and Robert Ball. Accounts by these participants are found in Derthick 1979, 320–23; Sundquist 1968, 296–308, 391–92; and Harris 1966, chap. 13.

momentum of their own, spurred on by an all-out campaign led by organized labor.

With the Democratic party still divided, and the major bureaucratic
veterans of health reform now dispersed,[82] the impetus for health insurance for the aged came primarily from reformers outside government,
most notably from organized labor. Since the mid-1940s, labor unions,
especially within the CIO, had been pursuing an aggressive strategy to
include health benefits under collective bargaining, and, in particular, industrial unions had fought for negotiated health plans under joint worker
and management control.[83] As union-sponsored and company health
plans began to cover a larger portion of workers and their families, these
work-related benefits developed into a "functional substitute for social
insurance."[84] With access to health insurance increasingly becoming tied
to employment and income, it seemed logical for health reformers to
focus on the groups shut out of the active labor market, such as the
elderly and the poor.

In the same way that the creation of the CLC mobilized labor pressure
for hospital insurance in Canada, the merger of the AFL and CIO in
1955 re-energized the campaign for health reform in the United States.
While unity made the AFL-CIO a more effective political messenger, it
also hastened the adoption of a more pragmatic position on health reform. The new legislative agenda gave central prominence to "national
health insurance," but more specifically to hospitalization insurance under OASI.[85] A Social Security department was set up under Nelson
Cruikshank, and it soon took over the duties of the Committee for the
Nation's Health, effectively becoming the national clearinghouse for information and the center of the public campaign for health reform. Al-

---

[82] When the Federal Security Agency was replaced by the new Department of Health,
Education, and Welfare (DHEW) in 1953, Altmeyer's retirement was hastened and Isidore
Falk moved on to Yale. Wilbur Cohen replaced Falk as Director of Research and Statistics
in the Social Security Administration, before leaving for the University of Michigan in 1956
(he became Assistant Secretary at the DHEW in 1961). Robert Ball was the exception; he
stayed in the SSA (eventually taking over its leadership in 1962). See Derthick 1979, 18–
19, 64–65.

[83] In 1948, 2.7 million workers were covered by such plans; by 1950, the figure had
skyrocketed to 7 million, and in 1954 to 12 million. Starr 1982, 313. CIO unions in the
clothing, coal, and steel sectors had originated these programs under worker control. See
Goldmann 1948, 91–92, and Munts 1967, chap. 1.

[84] Starr 1982, 311.

[85] AFL-CIO, 1st Constitutional Convention, *Proceedings*, New York, 1–2 December
1955, 84–85. The AFL had endorsed the proposal for hospitalization coverage under
OASI since 1951. AFL Report of the Executive Council, *Proceedings*, 1951, 182–89, 531–
32.

though Cruikshank had the support of the AFL-CIO leadership, there was dissension on his "feasible" approach from more progressive members of the committee and from the rank and file.[86]

The political effort of the AFL-CIO on behalf of health insurance for the elderly reflects, on the one hand, "the extent of the entire labor movement's break with Gompers' voluntarism" as unions fought for an issue that held "little immediate organizational interest."[87] On the other hand, this represented the strategic acceptance of an ideology of "conservative social insurance,"[88] particularly in comparison with the Canadian labor movement, which was able to maintain a much different position on health reform rooted in principles of public control and universal access. Different political constraints conditioned the adoption of a more limited strategy in the United States. Labor leaders had suffered the bitter lesson of the defeat of Truman's national health plan, and they were cognizant of the intransigence of the medical lobby and the enduring divisions in Congress on the issue. Whether labor perceived this legislative strategy of targeting health insurance to the aged as a means to an end or as an end in itself is debatable, but it is clear that it provided an immediate and pragmatic political alternative. In addition, as Derthick points out, organized labor's "programmatic" alliance with reformers in the Social Security Administration and its "partisan" alliance with the liberal wing of the Democratic party forced labor to adhere to a limited vision of health reform.[89] Within the two-party political system, organized labor was in effect forced to transmit its reform agenda through the Democratic party and was thus impelled to seek the type of reform that could break through the party's conservative resistance.

Joining the AFL-CIO's campaign for health insurance for the aged were several former supporters of national health insurance, including the National Farmers' Union, the American Public Health Association, and the National Association of Social Workers. Lobbying efforts also came from newly mobilized seniors' groups (discussed in the following chapter). In addition to reformers in the Physicians Forum and the National Medical Association, a new ally was found in the American Nurses' Association, which broke with the AMA and came out strongly in favor of the

---

[86] Derthick 1979, 122; Derthick notes that surgical benefits, for example, were included to appease such "progressive" members; probably more militant CIO unions, such as the UAW. In 1955, the UAW had negotiated a generous package of hospital insurance that included 120 days of care, and all in-patient diagnostic, surgical, and medical care (UAW-CIO, *Social Security Reporter*, November, 1955).

[87] Greenstone 1969, 337.

[88] Cates 1983, 142.

[89] Derthick 1979, 117–18.

Forand bill. The American Hospital Association, while preferring the private approach, expressed concern over health care for the aged and the eventual need for reform through Social Security.[90]

After spending millions of dollars on its campaign against "socialized medicine" in the 1940s, organized medicine may have felt the health insurance war had been won and that "less draconian measures" were now required.[91] Nevertheless, extending health insurance to the aged still represented "the thin end of the ever-present wedge" toward a renewed effort for compulsory health insurance.[92] As the labor movement revived the debate over the Forand bill, the medical lobby began a renewed campaign against health reform. By 1958, the AMA had increased its lobbying budget, hired a new public relations firm, and put doctors and state medical societies on "legislative alert" in time for the midterm elections.

As the lobby had learned during the debate over disability benefits in 1956, however, it was difficult to counter reform targeted at a group that elicited public sympathy. It would prove difficult to employ the theme of "socialized medicine" against a measure that health reformers had framed as a way to alleviate the problems of the aged. Accordingly, the AMA turned to two other tactics. The first was directed at discrediting the Forand message by insisting that the aged were not in such dire straits, neither medically nor financially, as to warrant government intervention. In 1958, the AMA organized the Joint Council to Improve the Health Care of the Aged with other health professions to publicize this idea, but the venture was not very successful. Nurses' and hospital groups did not entirely support the AMA's position, and the aged themselves remained unconvinced. The second AMA tactic involved killing the messenger, by branding the labor movement and its Democratic allies as political grandstanders exploiting the aged and their problems.

The AMA's campaign against the Forand proposals set the tone for its efforts against Medicare in the 1960s. It also presaged the AMA's changing alliances in the fight against health insurance reform by revealing, on the one hand, the growing cracks in the AMA coalition with the rest of the health profession and, on the other, the consolidation of its ties with business and insurance interests. The U.S. Chamber of Commerce had been associated with the AMA in opposition to health insurance in the

---

[90] U.S. Congress, House, Committee on Ways and Means, *Hospital, Nursing Home, and Surgical Benefits for OASI Beneficiaries: Hearings on H.R. 4700*, 86th Cong., 1st sess., 13–17 July 1959. For a list of groups in favor or opposed, see the *Congressional Quarterly Almanac 1960*, 164; for more on the AHA's position, see Stevens 1989, 269.

[91] Stevens 1971, 426. In both 1949 and 1950, the AMA had spent over $1 million in lobbying; in 1953, this had fallen to $100,000; by 1957, down to about $50,000 (lobby spending reports in *Congressional Quarterly Almanac*, 1950 through 1958).

[92] Stevens 1971, 434.

1940s, and now the National Association of Manufacturers also became more vocal. While private insurers had not actively participated in the 1940s debates, the industry had since experienced a phenomenal growth in the lucrative health business, and it did not want to see this jeopardized by government interference, particularly if health insurance were later to be extended to the rest of the population.[93] Industry's main argument echoed the AMA theme that voluntary insurance could adequately cover the health needs of the aged.

The Legislative Outcome (Kerr-Mills) and Nonoutcome (Forand)

Hearings on the Forand bill in 1958 and 1959 unleashed a torrent of debate on health insurance for the aged. These hearings also forced the interested parties to redefine their positions on health insurance, and drew the battle lines for the future debate on Medicare. In addition, they revealed the extent of partisan confusion on the issue: as one observer commented, "The jerseys were so muddied that you couldn't tell who was on which team."[94] Opposition came from the Republican administration, but also from the Democratic leadership in both the House and Senate; at the same time, pockets of support for the measure grew in both parties as the 1960 electoral year approached.

The decisive defeat of the Forand bill in committee vote in March 1960 reflected the enduring strength of the bipartisan "conservative coalition" in Congress and the opposition of Democratic leaders, particularly the Ways and Means Committee chair Wilbur Mills and House Speaker Sam Rayburn.[95] It also showed that, despite the high-profile campaign led by AFL-CIO in favor of the proposals, in the South "the influence of doctors and insurance agents far outweighed the influence of organized labor."[96]

Nevertheless, despite the absence of legislative action, the Forand bill became a major domestic policy issue in the 1960 presidential campaign, as neither party could ignore the significance of the "rocking-chair" vote.

[93] The Life Insurance Association of America and the Health Insurance Association of America testified together against the Forand bill (U.S. Congress, House, 16 July 1959, 434). On the industry's attitude toward social insurance, and the decline of its progressive wing, see Derthick 1979, 136–42.

[94] Quoted in Harris 1966, 88.

[95] The vote was 17–8; led by Mills, seven southern Democrats joined the Republicans (*Congressional Quarterly Almanac*, 1960, 154). The "conservative coalition" is the alliance of Republicans and southern Democrats (see "CQ Fact Sheet on Conservative Coalition," *Congressional Quarterly Almanac*, 1959, 141).

[96] Sundquist 1968, 306.

Senator John Kennedy was particularly alert to this. In January 1960, he introduced his own version of the Forand bill (S. 2915), which specified that hospital benefits (dropping in-patient surgical services) would be available only to *aged* Old-Age, Survivors', and Disability Insurance recipients (those 68 years and over), thus cutting right to the heart of the political potency of the issue.[97] The Democratic party had officially endorsed the Forand bill since 1958, but after Kennedy's nomination the Democratic platform embraced health insurance for the first time since 1948. The "right to adequate medical care," defined as health insurance for the aged, was a prominent feature of the Democratic platform in 1960. Despite the divisions among congressional Democrats, health insurance for the aged became identified with the Democratic party at the national level.

Pressured to launch a counteroffensive, the Republican administration unveiled a health insurance plan in May 1960, designed to provide matching federal funds to the states to cover the medically indigent aged. The plan was the first legislative recognition of medical indigence, and it greatly expanded the federal role in state health provision.[98] It also illustrated an antithesis to the social insurance approach embodied in the Forand bill by limiting eligibility through the means test.[99] Above all, the administration bill represented an effective legislative compromise: a measure designed to attract public recognition by helping the needy aged, introduced by a Republican administration and cosponsored by two powerful southern Democrats, Senator Robert Kerr and Representative Wilbur Mills.[100] The AMA, after initial hesitation over the extent of government interference, eventually backed the bill as preferable to the Forand-type alternatives being discussed in the Senate. Once these were defeated, the Kerr-Mills proposal quickly passed as part of the omnibus Social Security amendments bill (H.R. 12580) that was signed into law in September in the midst of the presidential campaign.[101]

[97] The first bill to focus only on the aged under OASDI was introduced by Rep. Lee Metcalf of Montana in 1959 (H.R. 12418). The Kennedy changes to Forand were also included in the Anderson amendment on health to H.R. 12580, which was cosponsored by another candidate, Hubert Humphrey. Lyndon Johnson also ended up supporting the principle of health insurance through social security, but he avoided the Forand label.

[98] The medically indigent included non-OAA (old-age assistance) recipients whose incomes were insufficient to pay for the costs of health care; the Kerr-Mills program was designed to cover the costs of both hospital and medical services (Myers 1970, 40–41). Stevens (1971, 436) traces the legislative origins of the measure to Senator Taft's proposals against the Truman plan (e.g., S. 545 in 1947).

[99] See Marmor 1973, 35.

[100] The bill was also designed by Wilbur Cohen, a drafter of the Forand bill, who envisioned this as a "step up the ladder," with the Forand plan as the next step (Harris 1966, 110–12).

[101] Mills and Rayburn speeded the bill's passage through the House in June; in the Sen-

This new program of medical assistance for the aged did little to quench demands for hospital insurance along the lines of the Forand approach. Instead, the momentum engendered by the Forand bill, and public support for it, would frame the future terms of reference for health reform. The focus had shifted from universal, comprehensive benefits to targeted, limited health insurance for the aged, but the battles over a social insurance versus a means-tested approach, and over compulsory versus voluntary insurance, were not yet resolved.

CONCLUSION

The 1950s marked a transition period in the health reform debate both in Canada and in the United States. The experiences of the two countries were shaped by past legacies, but at the same time they portended the eventual legislative outcomes of the 1960s. In the United States, there was a definitive rupture with the failed drive for national health insurance, but at the same time there was a certain continuity with past success, such as the Social Security Act, which served as a precedent for targeted coverage of limited benefits for certain groups. These two legacies were absent in the Canadian context. The campaign for national health insurance had not been decisively defeated, and the legacies that affected the development of health insurance derived from provincial innovations, including those of a social-democratic government.

There was also a certain institutional momentum at work in Canada, as federal government officials were still working within the parameters of an agenda set by the 1945 reconstruction proposals. In the United States, bureaucrats were influential in keeping health reform alive during the Republican administration, but important too were the contributions of former officials to the health agenda through their exchanges with labor leaders and liberal Democrats in Congress. The decision to narrow down this agenda was shaped by the important lessons learned about the feasibility of federal health legislation.

In the two countries the medical profession encouraged the private approach to health insurance and felt government intervention should be limited to coverage of the indigent. The Canadian Medical Association, however, had a more measured opposition, and Canadian doctors may not have felt their immediate interests were in danger as hospital insurance was implemented in the provinces. The American Medical Associa-

ate, passage was delayed until August, due to debate over the Anderson-Kennedy amendment substituting benefits for all aged under Social Security. The amendment was defeated by the conservative coalition, 44–51, but H.R. 12580 passed 91–2, with the bipartisan nays from Republican Barry Goldwater and Democrat Strom Thurmond. *Congressional Record*, 23 August 1960, 17220, 17235.

tion reacted much more strongly, and considered hospital insurance for the aged the wedge that might open the door to national health insurance. Nevertheless, the medical lobby had to subdue its rhetoric when faced with a politically appealing target group and growing public consensus on the issue.

This consensus was being reinforced by the American labor movement. Labor leadership was a guiding force in the formulation of the limited proposals for hospital insurance targeted to the aged in the Forand Bill. Organized labor's campaign for this legislation contributed to its emergence as an effective political counterweight to the medical lobby. The retreat from national health insurance to what was considered a more feasible reform strategy was deeply influenced by the political boundaries that labor faced within the Democratic party coalition. Within the constraints of a two-party system, in which labor had hitched its star to the Democratic party, the design of health reform would have to overcome congressional resistance and recapture public support.

The Canadian and American labor movements went through similar structural changes and mergers of their principal organizations during the 1950s. But while health insurance continued to be central to their legislative agendas, organized labor in the two countries embarked on separate roads to health reform. Canadian labor did not waver from its demands for universal, comprehensive health insurance, and its support for hospital insurance was based on the conviction that this would be the first step to such an outcome. The Canadian labor movement also distinguished itself by moving closer to a social-democratic third party.

Although the Liberal party in Canada, like the Democratic party in the United States, remained divided on health reform, it faced considerably more pressure from the politically mobilized Left on the health insurance issue. The social-democratic CCF clearly had a role in prompting legislative action, both through its advocacy role in the federal Parliament and in the demonstration effect of the Saskatchewan hospital insurance program. The CCF continued to exercise both these roles as Canada moved toward a comprehensive system of health insurance system in the next decade.

CHAPTER SIX

The 1960s: The Political Battle for Health Insurance

BY THE EARLY 1960s, health insurance reform was rapidly gaining public support and political momentum in Canada and the United States, but the political debates surrounding the issue took two distinct directions. At the close of the decade, each country had put in place its own system of government-sponsored health insurance covering hospital and medical benefits. In Canada, this was a period of consolidation of existing federal-provincial arrangements based on universal health insurance principles. The debate centered not on providing health insurance to certain groups, but on the extension of benefits beyond hospital insurance to cover the costs of medical services. In the United States, the 1960s represented a watershed period of political compromise, resulting in a multitiered system of health insurance. This system embodied both social insurance principles and private insurance subsidization for a portion of the population, namely the aged, under Medicare Part A (compulsory hospital insurance) and Part B (supplementary medical insurance), plus means-tested coverage for the medically indigent under Medicaid.

MEDICAL INSURANCE AND SOCIAL DEMOCRACY IN CANADA

The CCF Initiative in Saskatchewan

By 1961, all ten Canadian provinces had introduced hospital insurance programs under the cost-sharing provisions of the Hospital and Diagnostic Services Act. The Saskatchewan precedent had provided both the impetus for federal involvement and the model for other provinces. As Taylor suggests, "In the educational process through which Canadian governments learned how to administer universal hospital insurance, Saskatchewan paid most of the tuition fees."[1]

After a decade of financing its own hospital insurance program, the Saskatchewan government found that federal money provided under the arrangement offered some fiscal room to maneuver and to experiment

[1] Taylor 1987, 104.

with the next stage in health reform: medical care insurance. On the political front, medical insurance would give the CCF an effective issue to revive its support in the 1960 provincial election. Premier Tommy Douglas had a personal commitment to ensuring the fulfillment of his government's health insurance program. Since he would soon be recruited to lead the CCF's federal wing as leader of the New Democratic party, the establishment of medical insurance seemed a fitting apogee to his provincial career. It would also reaffirm continuity with the CCF's social-democratic principles as the party readied itself for a formal rapprochement with Canadian labor.[2]

The CCF government unveiled its medical insurance plan in December 1959. It provided for universal medical insurance under public administration, financed by contributory premiums, and "acceptable" to both patients and doctors.[3] The CCF was prepared to implement a fee-for-service (as opposed to salaried) system that seemed a more feasible way of getting the medical profession's support. Despite these assurances, Saskatchewan doctors felt they were being railroaded into the program. The relationship between the CCF and the medical profession, represented by the Saskatchewan College of Physicians and Surgeons (SCPS), had become increasingly strained over the years. Saskatchewan doctors traditionally played an integral role in rural life, and the devastating effects of the Depression had made them more conscious of the need for health insurance. Attitudes were changing, however, for several reasons: a thriving economy; the increasing power of urban-based specialists; and the influx of "refugees" from Britain's National Health Service who had come to fill much-needed positions in the doctor-scarce province.[4] The SCPS had only grudgingly accepted a medical insurance experiment under fee-for-service in the Swift Current region, and it resisted efforts to extend this to other regions in the 1950s.

As the provincial election approached in 1960, the medical lobby in Saskatchewan was faced with the same specter of Armageddon that had haunted American doctors in the 1940s. Indeed, the stakes were even higher, because if the CCF were to be reelected with a majority government, it would be extremely difficult to block legislative passage of medical insurance. Although the SCPS did not formally endorse any party, it outspent all of them in waging "a political campaign against the government." Having "studied the tactics of the American Medical Association in opposing legislative action in the United States," the medical lobby

[2] Tollefson 1968, 239.

[3] Taylor 1987, 278.

[4] McLeod 1971, 88–89. Since 1936, the SCPS had also represented the Saskatchewan branch of the Canadian Medical Association, thus performing the dual role of regulation and of representation. Taylor 1987, 241.

launched a public relations campaign to mobilize doctors and their patients against the "evil" compulsion of the CCF government's medical insurance plan.[5]

The June 1960 election turned into a referendum on the government's plan for medical insurance, and the CCF interpreted its victory as a mandate for immediate action on the measure. At its annual general meeting later that month, an anxious Canadian Medical Association reiterated its opposition to the CCF plan. A revised statement on medical care insurance made clear that the CMA would accept government involvement in medical insurance only if there was recognition of the profession's autonomy in the plan's administration and control of the method of payment.[6]

A clash of wills was evident as the SCPS attempted to delay passage and implementation of the program (as the B.C. medical lobby had successfully done in the 1930s), while the Saskatchewan government was determined to act on the measure. In September 1961, soon after the CCF became the New Democratic party under Tommy Douglas's leadership at the federal level, Premier Woodrow Lloyd introduced a medical care bill into the Saskatchewan legislature. Despite opposition from the medical lobby and the business community (who proposed government subsidies for the purchase of private insurance instead), and protests from organized labor (over the use of premiums and fee-for-service payment), the bill became law on November 17, 1961.[7]

Having failed to thwart the CCF in its reelection and in the passage of medical insurance, the medical lobby now attempted to block the new law's implementation. As the starting date of the program was postponed to July 1962, the SCPS marshaled opposition to the plan and solidified its hard-line stance. In early May, the SCPS called a special meeting and prepared for strike action. The "Keep Our Doctors Committees" that had originated as grass roots movements, soon became antisocialist organizations mobilized by doctors and their allies, including business groups and the Liberal party.[8] Their frenzied rallies and ideological appeals contributed to the abysmal federal election results of the New Democratic party in Saskatchewan in June (even its leader, Tommy Douglas, was unable to win a seat). In spite of this, the Saskatchewan government

[5] Badgley and Wolfe 1967, 30–31. The SCPS levied a "nonpolitical" $100 assessment on doctors to finance the campaign, while the Canadian Medical Association donated $35,000 to the SCPS's efforts.

[6] "The Canadian Medical Association Statement on Medical Services Insurance, 1960," in Blishen 1969, 187–188.

[7] Tollefson 1968, 245–48; "Submission to the Advisory Council, SFL, 1961," in NAC; MG 28; I–103; CLC Papers; Vol. 274; File "Medical Care, SFL."

[8] Krueger 1971, 405–34. On the impasse leading up to the strike, see Badgley and Wolfe 1967, 42–60.

refused to back down: the medical insurance plan went into effect on July 1, 1962, and the doctors' strike began.[9]

Apart from the Saskatchewan press (allied with Liberal party interests), media coverage in Canada and even the United States was highly critical of the strike, more on ethical and legal grounds than on the issue of medical insurance; the *Washington Post*, for example, termed it "a betrayal of their profession" and "bad medicine."[10] The AMA, fighting its own battle against more limited government intervention in the United States, also threw its support behind Saskatchewan doctors. The Canadian Medical Association, certain that the Saskatchewan experience would influence other provinces contemplating medical insurance plans, also stood behind the SCPS.[11] Yet, in the end, the medical lobby retreated first. Aware of increasing public resentment, the SCPS agreed to negotiate, and the strike ended three weeks after it began.[12] The medical insurance plan would continue to be universal and compulsory, but doctors could choose not to join, and they were allowed to "extra-bill" their patients directly at higher rates.[13]

The Saskatchewan program represented the first medical insurance plan in North America, just as the doctors' strike represented the first withdrawal of services by the medical profession. While the medical lobby was able to influence some of the important features of the plan, including fee-for-service payment and extra-billing concessions, it was unable to prevent its passage and implementation. The strike "did much to erode the profession's mystique" and to associate doctors' opposition to health reform with their narrow self-interest.[14] Although the government was defeated in the 1964 provincial election, medical insurance was not withdrawn.[15] Rather, the success of this provincial innovation would have

[9] Emergency services in hospitals were retained, and the Saskatchewan government "imported" about one hundred doctors, mainly from England, to provide temporary medical services; teams of American specialists from major U.S. cities were also on "stand-by arrangement." Badgley and Wolfe 1967, 67–68.

[10] Quoted in Taylor 1987, 311. Very few major newspapers outside Saskatchewan supported the doctors; one notable exception was the *Montreal Gazette*. NAC; MG 28 IV-1; CCF Papers; Vol. 500; File "Medicine—News and Publications."

[11] Naylor 1986b, 205.

[12] The strike was mediated by the "colourful, hyperactive" Lord Stephen Taylor, a former Labour M.P., who had helped set up the British National Health Service. Badgley and Wolfe 1967, 71–72; Naylor 1986b, 209–11.

[13] Extra-billing allowed physicians to bill patients directly at rates above negotiated fee schedules; patients were reimbursed by the provincial government for the negotiated fee but had to absorb the "extra" fees.

[14] Coburn, Torrance, and Kaufert 1983, 407–32, 419.

[15] The Liberal party now pledged to *extend* the program; this, in addition to the polarization unleashed during the crisis, and a farmer backlash against the labor element in the NDP, contributed to the 1964 defeat. Ward 1967, 187–88.

a considerable impact on the development of health insurance across Canada.

The Hall Commission and the Debate over Health Reform

The battle over medical insurance in Saskatchewan had immediate echoes at the federal level. While the CCF government was formulating its health program, the Canadian Medical Association was fashioning a strategy to deal with the medical insurance issue. Part of the strategy was aimed at diminishing the momentum for health reform, and it was with this in mind that the CMA asked the federal government to appoint a Royal Commission to study the "health needs and resources of Canada." The Conservative government was receptive to this request, as it was not anxious to immediately reopen legislative debate on health insurance either.[16] Royal Commissions serve the dual function of allowing a public arena for societal groups and of providing research and recommendations to government from an expert group, but their reports are not necessarily acted upon; indeed, a cynical view of such commissions is that they "take the heat off the government in connection with some problematic situation in the hope that by the time the commission's report is published, the problem will have evaporated."[17] The Royal Commission on Health Services was the fifth appointed by Prime Minister Diefenbaker after two years in office, leading to criticism that he used them as an "escape mechanism" for postponing legislative action and "then shelving their recommendations."[18]

The Royal Commission on Health Services, however, ended up fanning the flames of the health insurance debate in Canada rather than subduing them. The Commission was appointed in June 1961 to make a "comprehensive and independent study . . . of the needs of the Canadian people for health services and the resources available to meet such needs."[19] Because they coincided with the conflict over medical insurance in Saskatchewan, however, the hearings and final report were dominated by the issue of the government's role in financing the costs of medical care.

Diefenbaker appointed Emmett Hall, the Chief Justice of Saskatchewan (and former law school classmate), as chair of the Royal Commission, with representatives from the medical, nursing, and dental professions. The Hall Commission, as it came to be known, received hundreds

---

[16] Canada, House of Commons, *Debates*, 21 December 1960, 1023–25.
[17] Dyck 1996, 463.
[18] Newman 1963, 82.
[19] NAC; RG 33; Vol. 1128; File 504-4-12, Pt.1; P.C. 1961–883, 20 June 1961.

of submissions and held public hearings across Canada from the fall of 1961 through the spring of 1962.

As had been the case at the 1943 Special Committee hearings, a clear division between societal groups on the issue of health reform emerged during the Hall Commission hearings. At one end of the spectrum were labor and farm groups. The Canadian Labour Congress advocated a "two-stage" medical insurance plan that would first cover general and specialist medical services and eventually all dental and drug costs. But, as it did in the Saskatchewan debate, labor underscored the need for public control of the plan, and expressed serious reservations about fee-for-service payment. The CLC also directly attacked the claims of the medical lobby and the insurance industry on the advantages of a private, multicarrier voluntary health insurance system.[20] The Canadian Federation of Agriculture was less concerned with issues of payment and control, and more with redistribution of income and universal access to health care.[21] In contrast to the divisions in the United States, the Canadian farm movement appeared united on health reform, and it actively supported the CCF initiatives in Saskatchewan.

Facing these groups were medical, insurance, and business interests. As in the United States, organized medicine had recognized the need to build alliances with the private sector, and it had been strengthening ties with these interests since the 1950s. Putting aside differences over private and physician-controlled plans, the CMA and the Canadian Health Insurance Association joined in opposition against further government intervention in the health sector. In briefs to the Hall Commission, both the CMA and the CHIA supported the voluntary medical insurance plans being considered in Alberta and Ontario and offered an alternative, means-tested plan in which government subsidies would allow the medically indigent to purchase medical insurance. Even though the medical lobby seemed to be endorsing a position similar to its American counterpart, CMA representatives at the hearings labeled these comparisons with the AMA "entirely unacceptable."[22]

Yet, in tandem with developments in the United States, the position of medical and insurance lobbies was now publicly reinforced by powerful business interests. The Canadian Manufacturers Association later supported the voluntary approach and cautioned that "no government-oper-

---

[20] CLC, Submission to the Royal Commission on Health Services, 25 May 1962; Supplementary Brief, 16 October 1962; "CLC Brief to Health Commission" June 1962, 15; and "Congress Critical of CMA, Insurance Assoc.," *Canadian Labour*, November 1962, 28.

[21] Canadian Federation of Agriculture, Submission to the Royal Commission on Health Services, 19 March 19 1962.

[22] "CMA, Commission Clash," *The Globe and Mail*, 16 May 1962. Hall found the CMA "unnecessarily touchy" in its defensive attitude.

ated health scheme, applicable to Canadians generally, should be undertaken."[23] The Chamber of Commerce warned of the adverse economic effects of increased government expenditures, and instead recommended locally administered care for the indigent; other Canadians were urged to assume their own responsibilities by placing a "higher priority on budgeting for health care."[24]

Despite the powerful voices, the Hall Commission's final report, released in June 1964, recommended that "the Federal Government enter into agreement with the provinces to provide grants on a fiscal need formula to assist the provinces to introduce and operate comprehensive, universal, provincial programs of personal health services."[25]

The Hall Report attempted to build from a set of fundamental principles about the role of the individual and the state in health care, embodied in the "Health Charter for Canadians," based on government-sponsored, comprehensive, universal health services.[26] The second volume of the report, published in 1965, not only pointed out the inadequacies of the voluntary approach, but also went on to reject extra-billing, the basis of the Saskatchewan compromise. Justice Hall explicitly designed this to be "the definitive rebuttal of the CMA and other [allied] groups"; in so doing, Hall lost the support of the medical representatives on the commission.[27]

The Hall Report and its Health Charter became rallying points for organized labor as it called for immediate action on the recommendations. Both labor and farmer organizations felt the Hall Commission had "vindicated" their position on health insurance, as the recommendations resembled more closely their demands than those of organized medicine.[28] Indeed, for the medical lobby, the report was a bitter pill to swallow, particularly since the CMA had requested the inquiry in the first place. The medical lobby was stunned by the report, feeling "the rug has been pulled from under [our] feet."[29] The first official reply stated that the

[23] Canadian Manufacturers Association, Submission to the Royal Commission on Health Services for Canada, 19 April 1962.

[24] Canadian Chamber of Commerce, Submission to the Royal Commission on Health Services for Canada, 19 March 1962.

[25] Royal Commission on Health Services for Canada, *Final Report*, vol. 1, p. 19. These services included medical, drug, prosthetic, and home care for all, and dental and optical services for specific groups.

[26] Royal Commission on Health Services, 1964, 11–12. For the evolution of the charter idea, see NAC; RG 33; Vol. 25; File 1-6-1, Pt.2.

[27] NAC; RG 33; Vol. 26; File 1-6-1A; Naylor 1986b, 232.

[28] NAC; MG 32 C-59; Knowles Papers; Vol. 46; File 6 (57–64); CLC press release, 19 June 1964, and CFA Statement in Support of the Royal Commission Report, 18 August 1964.

[29] NAC; RG 33; Vol. 26; File 1-6-1, Pt.5; Van Wart to Hall, 24 June 1964.

CMA "cannot agree with all of the recommendations as they relate to the provision of personal medical services under single provincial plans."[30] At the CMA convention just days later, criticism was more forceful against what was seen as an arbitrary imposition of federal policy resembling Saskatchewan's "socialized medicine." A special meeting was announced for January 1965, the first such convention since the 1943 social security proposals. The CMA's allies in the insurance and pharmaceutical sectors expressed concern over the danger of compulsory public insurance for the future of their industries, while the Chamber of Commerce attacked the regressive effects of massive government expenditures on health insurance.[31]

Medical Insurance and Canadian Party Politics

By the time the Hall Report was released in 1964, the Liberal party was back in power, but with a minority government that had to count on the support of third parties in the House of Commons. The Liberal government faced a precarious situation in the House of Commons and, as the Saskatchewan conflict and the Hall Report fueled the debate, found it more difficult to hedge on health reform. The Liberals were under pressure to complete the health insurance program they had promised in 1945 and had begun implementing with the National Health Grants Program in 1948 and the federal-provincial hospital insurance plan in 1957.

The Liberal party went through a significant transformation after its devastating loss to the Conservatives in 1958.[32] Although the CCF had also fared dismally in 1958, the Conservative sweep had called into question the role of the "center party" in Canada and raised the specter that had so haunted Mackenzie King: a British-style Left-Right polarization in Canadian politics, of the kind that could squeeze out the center party. The role of the center party in what was now a fragmented Canadian party system was ambiguous, as the Liberals had to steer their message between opposing social-democratic and populist ones. In parallel to the strategy that Mackenzie King had successfully exploited, it became neces-

---

[30] NAC; RG 29; Vol. 1128; File 504-4-12, Pt.3; Frank Turnbull, president of CMA (telegram), to Prime Minister Lester Pearson, 26 June 1964.

[31] Mercer Actuarial *Bulletin*, August 1964; Chamber of Commerce *Newsletter*, July–August 1964; both in NAC; MG 32 C-59; Knowles Papers; Vol. 46; File 6 (57–64). Also, NAC; MG 26N; Pearson Papers; Vol. 175; File 354; H. D. Cook (president, CPMA) to Lester Pearson, 3 July 1964.

[32] The Liberals won 34 percent of the popular vote and were reduced to forty-nine seats, or 18 percent of the House of Commons, while the Conservatives captured 53 percent of the vote and 78 percent of the seats. Beck 1967, 22–23.

sary to refashion the Liberal party as the party of social reform. The difference now was that the strategy required more than shifting the message to attract the working-class vote. Instead, it would entail concrete policy action and party change from the leadership to the grassroots.

By 1960, the old guard of the Liberal party was in decline. A policy conference in September—similar to the 1933 conference that had discussed the relevance of the New Deal—and a National Rally a few months later focused on the need to expand the party base by building a new policy platform that could capture the center, and the left of center, in the political spectrum.[33] In contrast to King's reticence in the 1930s, however, these reforms were supported by the party's new leader. Lester Pearson, who had had an illustrious career as Secretary of State for External Affairs and had won the Nobel Peace Prize while serving as President of the General Assembly at the United Nations, was receptive to the demands of the progressive wing of the party for social reform. As a pragmatic politician, he realized the need to build a new agenda to revive the party's fortunes and respond to the social-democratic threat: "My desire was to forget about the old party, to stop looking to the past. . . . We no longer believed in the old-fashioned doctrine of laissez-faire liberalism. We could no longer be successful unless we were a truly liberal party, progressive enough to attract people who might otherwise turn to the New Democratic Party."[34]

The new emphasis on "welfare liberalism" centered around health reform.[35] The party's new platform promised a health plan, to cover medical costs, within five years. While the plan was to be universal, it would also meet the "stated conditions of the Canadian Medical Association."[36] After the plan was unveiled in 1961, Pearson urged that "we proceed to develop it in greater detail and then arrange to give it as much publicity as possible."[37] Like the Democratic party in the United States, the Liberal leadership was aware of the political effectiveness of such an issue in electoral campaigns. The Liberal party hired Lou Harris, the Kennedy administration pollster who had reinforced support for the medicare issue, as an adviser in the 1962 campaign.[38] Although it did not completely embrace

[33] Wearing 1981, 16–20.

[34] Pearson 1975, 54.

[35] Campbell and Christian (1996, 77–79) make a distinction between "business" and "welfare" liberalism in the Liberal party's ideological mix.

[36] NAC; MG 26N; Pearson Papers; Vol. 114; File Health and Welfare-Liberal Health Plan; "The Health Plan of the Liberal Party," 10 January 1961.

[37] NAC; MG 26N; Pearson Papers; Vol. 114; File Health and Welfare–Liberal Health Plan; Pearson to Tom Kent, 7 February 1961.

[38] Stursberg 1978, 69–70. The Liberal party attempted to model Pearson after Kennedy in the election campaign, but with obviously limited success. Wearing 1981, 33–35.

social-democratic principles on medical insurance, the new Liberal platform was aimed at co-opting the CCF-NDP's health reform agenda, and
it was used as such in both the 1962 and 1963 election campaigns.

The 1963 elections finally brought the Liberal party back into power,
but with a minority government, as the Social Credit held the balance of
power in the House of Commons. It was the first time the Liberals were
in a minority situation since the early 1920s, when King had briefly gov-
erned with the support of the Progressives. This time, however, the support of the third party could not be taken for granted. Pearson did attempt to get the NDP to agree to a "formula" to support the Liberal
government, but the NDP refused any "working arrangement" with the
Liberal party.[39] It would be much more difficult to postpone action on
health insurance, or to propose measures that the NDP would threaten
to defeat.

The New Democratic Party, Organized Labor, and Health Insurance

As the Liberal party moved to the left to co-opt potential CCF support,
the CCF was moving toward a more moderate position in the hopes of
distancing the party from the Cold War connotations of "socialism" and
attracting a wider electoral base among the working class. In 1956, the
CCF replaced its Regina Manifesto, which called for the "eradication of
capitalism," with the Winnipeg Declaration, which emphasized the goals
of "equality and freedom."[40]

The disastrous results of the 1958 election, coupled with declining
membership and finances, served as a catalyst for immediate action and
broke down some of the resistance to change in the party.[41] Broadening
the electoral base, shoring up finances, and attracting a wider audience to
the social-democratic message logically meant forging closer ties with organized labor. Although few labor delegates were at its founding in
1932, the CCF had actively defended worker interests and attempted to
"court" labor support from the very beginning. By the 1940s, the CCF
had established close ties with industrial unions in the Canadian Congress of Labour, and this was reflected in important gains for the party in
provincial election in British Columbia and, to a lesser extent, in Ontario.

The road toward labor affiliation was nevertheless a long one, hampered both by fears within the party of labor domination and by the
traditional resistance by craft unions toward political engagement, partic-

[39] Smith 1973, 190–191.
[40] Penner 1992, 88–89.
[41] Lewis 1981, 485.

ularly with a "socialist" party. The Trades and Labor Congress had long maintained an American-influenced position on nonpartisan political action. But the merger of the AFL-CIO reinforced American labor's political association with the Democratic party and also served to loosen American influence on Canadian labor, in particular the choice of political-action strategies.[42] At the time of the merger between the Trades and Labor Congress and the Canadian Congress of Labour in 1956, there were signs that the new labor leadership was already favorable to some type of formal support for the CCF. At the convention of the new Canadian Labour Congress (CLC) in April 1958 (two months before the federal election), the delegates endorsed the formation of "an effective, alternative political force . . . a broadly-based peoples' political movement which embraces the CCF, the Labour movement, farm organizations, professional people and other liberally-minded persons, interested in basic social reform and reconstruction through our Parliamentary system of government."[43]

Organized labor had an important role in transforming the CCF into the New Democratic party (NDP), although as a "marriage of notables" this did not create a truly "labor" party.[44] Given the structure of the Canadian labor movement and the nature of the CCF, the CLC would not "itself become an integral part" of the new party, but would instead encourage voluntary affiliation, allowing unions to "maintain a position of political neutrality."[45] This position appeased wary unionists, while at the same time it presented the New Democratic party as a broader organization to CCF supporters and the Canadian electorate. In the 1962 and 1963 federal elections the NDP made modest but important gains in urban Ontario and in British Columbia.[46]

Although the NDP's new platform was less radical in tone than the CCF's, it reaffirmed the party's commitment to social reform.[47] This was immediately reinforced by the facts that the party was founded in midst of the bitter conflict in Saskatchewan and that its new federal leader, Tommy Douglas, had been responsible for setting the medical insurance

---

[42] Abella 1973, 214–16.

[43] CLC, *Proceedings*, 1958, Substitute Resolution on Basic Political Party, 45.

[44] Brodie and Jenson 1988, 242–43.

[45] CLC, *Proceedings*, 1960, Substitute Resolution on Affiliation with New Political Party, 44.

[46] The NDP won nineteen seats in 1962 (six from Ontario, ten from British Columbia) and seventeen in 1963 (six from Ontario, nine from British Columbia), and its share of the popular vote climbed to 14 percent. Beck, 1967.

[47] "The New Democratic Party Program" (1961 founding convention), *Canadian Labour*, September 1961, 7; see also "The New Democratic Platform of 1962" in Carrigan 1968, 270–83. On the "de-radicalizing" influence of organized labor in the new party, see Penner 1992, 101–3; Brodie and Jenson 1988, 272–73.

plan in motion. The CLC actively supported both the Saskatchewan Federation of Labour and the CCF government in the fight against the medical lobby. Even though several labor leaders had expressed misgivings that fee-for-service payment would benefit the "inefficient, uneconomical and backward medical organization,"[48] the CLC endorsed the model, opposing the type of voluntary medical plans contemplated by provincial governments in Ontario, Alberta, and British Columbia.[49]

Meanwhile, in the House of Commons, the NDP pressured the Liberal government to use the Saskatchewan model as a basis for forging a "national" health insurance system. As in the debate over hospital insurance in the 1950s, there were two principal attacks: first, public demand for action on medical insurance and the lack of a federal response; and second, the success of the CCF initiative in Saskatchewan, which became "like Banquo's ghost, a constant spectre" before the Liberal government.[50]

Trying to avoid NDP badgering on the issue, Pearson indicated he would wait for the Hall Commission to report first. Once the report was released in 1964, the margin for maneuvering became more limited for the Prime Minister. Within the Liberal party, power struggles sharpened as the report became "a rallying cry of support" for progressive Liberals, in opposition to the old guard.[51] In addition, the Hall recommendations reinforced the social-democratic principles advocated by the NDP, and the third party spared no effort in pressuring the government on them. By 1965, Stanley Knowles and the NDP were "pressing for such action literally every week" in the House of Commons,[52] and, with organized labor, the party launched the "Health Charter Campaign" to mobilize public opinion around an attractive target date: 1967, Canada's upcoming centennial year.[53]

---

[48] NAC; MG 28 I-103; CLC Papers; Vol. 274; Ted Goldberg (United Steel Workers) to Andrew Andras (CLC legislation department). The CLC had even discussed the matter with I. S. Falk, who felt this practice would be "a tremendous mistake."

[49] CLC, *Proceedings*, 1962, Substitute Resolution No. 2, Health Insurance ("carried by an enthusiastic standing vote"), 92–93; CLC, *Proceedings*, 1964, Medicare Resolutions, 47–49.

[50] Taylor 1987, 353. NDP members repeatedly goaded Pearson on the release of the Hall report; see Canada, House of Commons, *Debates*, 1963, 1964 (*passim*); NAC; MG 26N; Pearson Papers; Vol. 175; File 354–Health Services; T. C. Douglas to Lester Pearson, January 1964.

[51] Taylor 1987, 353.

[52] NAC; MG 32 C-59; Knowles Papers; Vol. 46; File 7 (57–64).

[53] On this campaign, see *Canadian Labour*, February 1965; NAC; MG 32 C-59; Knowles Papers; Vol. 46; File 7 (57–64); NAC; MG 26N; Pearson Papers; Vol. 175; File 354–Health Services, Pt. 2.

Legislative Action on Medical Insurance

By early 1965, strategists began to discuss whether a health and social reform platform could help propel the Liberals to a majority government in the next election. In April, the Liberal government signaled its first formal commitment to medical insurance legislation in the Throne Speech, the promise of "ensuring that all Canadians can obtain needed health care, irrespective of their ability to pay."[54] The speech also included a new welfare plan and sweeping promises for the "the elimination of poverty among our people"—prompting one Conservative M.P. to label it, "the left-over breakfast from President Johnson's Great Society campaign."[55] Undeterred, Prime Minister Pearson was sure the Liberals had scored a political coup in seizing the health reform issue from the NDP: "We have stolen some of their clothes while they were bathing in holy water!"[56]

The federal government indicated it would immediately start discussions with the provinces, but the provincial governments had not yet had their last say in the matter. The relatively "cooperative" relationship between the federal government and the provinces that had facilitated the implementation of hospital insurance and other programs was waning, as the provinces flexed their political muscle and developed their own state capacities in social and economic domains.[57] This was particularly the case in Quebec, where the Liberal government of Jean Lesage was ushering in a period of unprecedented social reform embedded in the pivotal role of the modern provincial state—a period that came to be known as the "Quiet Revolution." While committed to public medical insurance, the Quebec government insisted the provincial program should be free of federal interference.[58]

Other provinces were also wary of federal government interference in medical insurance, but for reasons that had to do with opposition to the principles enunciated in the Hall Report. In contrast to, and as a counter-reaction against, the CCF approach in Saskatchewan, conservative governments in Ontario, British Columbia, and Alberta were designing medical insurance plans based on voluntary health insurance principles. The first of these was introduced in 1963 by Alberta's charismatic Social Credit leader, Ernest Manning, who launched a campaign against "social-

---

[54] Canada, House of Commons, *Debates*, 5 April 1965, 1–3.
[55] Jack Horner, Canada, House of Commons, *Debates*, 7 April 1965, 86.
[56] Pearson 1975, 200.
[57] Mallory 1965, 9–11.
[58] McRoberts 1993, 131–32; Taylor 1987, 380–81.

istic" health insurance that represented "the flagrant violation . . . of freedom of choice in a free society."[59] The "Manningcare" plan reflected two basic principles, shared by medical and insurance interests: voluntary health insurance for the majority of residents and means-tested government subsidies to enable lower-income residents to purchase private insurance. Similar "voluntary" plans were introduced in British Columbia and Ontario, although these were under the control of a provincial agency (administered by government and medical representatives), responsible for enrolling residents, collecting premiums, and paying claims.[60]

The lack of uniformity in provincial proposals unnerved the federal NDP and the Canadian labor movement, who feared that the implementation of voluntary medical insurance by conservative provincial governments would jeopardize universality and access to health care for Canadians. The Liberal government, however, was also unsettled by the prospect of a crazy quilt of medical insurance plans in the provinces, particularly as the Prime Minister considered social programs part of a strategy to strengthen the presence of the federal government and encourage "nation" building across Canada.

A compromise of sorts was presented at the July 1965 Federal-Provincial Conference, where Prime Minister Pearson introduced a shared-cost program for medical insurance. On the one hand, it responded to provincial wariness by limiting federal involvement to financial participation and raised the possibility of "opting-out," which Quebec preferred, to allow provinces to receive financial compensation if they chose not to adhere to the program. On the other hand, the federal government insisted on a set of necessary criteria that the provinces would have to meet for federal funding: public administration of medical plans; comprehensive benefits, including generalist and specialist services; the portability of these benefits across provinces; and universality, so that all Canadians would be covered "on uniform terms and conditions."[61]

These principles relied heavily on the existing arrangements of the hospital insurance plan and the Saskatchewan medical insurance program, and reflected the emphasis on universality promoted by the recommendations of the Hall Report, the platform of the NDP, and its allies in the labor movement.[62] Of course, these principles were squarely at odds with the stated interests of medical, insurance, and business organizations. Al-

---

[59] NAC; MG 32 C-59; Knowles Papers; Vol. 46; File 7 (57–64).

[60] Taylor 1987, 338–41.

[61] Opening Statement by Prime Minister Lester B. Pearson, Federal-Provincial Conference, Ottawa, 19 July 1965, 16–17.

[62] The main drafter of the policy was Al Johnson, a former Saskatchewan senior civil servant, who had come to Ottawa after the CCF-NDP's defeat in 1964. Granatstein 1986, 195–96.

though private insurers could cover services not provided under public plans, the emphasis on public administration excluded the cohabitation of private and public insurance in the provinces. The emphasis on "uniform terms and conditions," meanwhile, translated into universal access to health care, regardless of residence, age, or level of income, and ruled out the development of "two-tiered" medical provision.

With the Hall Report recommendations and the announcement of these federal principles for medical insurance, it appeared that the CMA's strategy to contain the Saskatchewan experiment was faltering. The lobby turned to damage control, directing its opposition at the principles of compulsion, universality, and government administration. The CMA supported the principle of medical insurance, as well as the idea of government involvement, but it rejected "compulsory" public insurance, affirming that: "We believe that through co-operation between governments, insurance agencies, the public, and the medical profession, voluntary insurance can in fact be made accessible to every resident of Canada."[63] Although the CMA made clear the reluctance of doctors to participate in compulsory medical insurance, its strategy did not include strike action as in Saskatchewan; indeed, "the ultimate result of this strike had a major deterrent effect on the Canadian Medical Association . . . to even mention that possibility as a negotiating tool."[64] Instead, the CMA focused its energies on lobbying the Cabinet to delay or modify the medical insurance program, as medical associations in the provinces would also do. The medical lobby in Canada did not target individual legislators to the same extent that one could have in the United States, as the CMA's general perception was that "party discipline effectively prevents the use of MPs to alter government policy."[65]

The profession did win some important concessions, however, including the use of physician-sponsored nonprofit insurers in initially collecting premiums in certain provinces (notably Ontario and British Columbia). In addition, extra-billing would be tolerated in most of the provinces (mainly in Ontario and Alberta) except Quebec, where it was prohibited.[66]

Concern about the federal initiative was not confined to the medical

[63] "The Canadian Medical Association Statement of Policy on Medical Services Insurance, 1965," in Blishen 1969, 189–91; "News and Views on the Economics of Medicine," CMA *Newsletter* no. 129 (21 May 1966).

[64] Leclair 1975, 21.

[65] Weir 1973, 164–65.

[66] In use until the 1984 Canada Health Act banned the practice, extra-billing was not very widespread, but this concession had a significant impact on political developments in other provinces, including doctors' strikes in Quebec (in 1970) and Ontario (in 1986). Tuohy 1988, 267–96.

profession. There was also opposition from Conservative and Social Credit members of Parliament, who preferred a voluntary approach. More significant was the resistance of certain members of the Liberal caucus and the Cabinet, with regard to the financial burden medical insurance would impose on government, reflecting the tensions between the old guard and more reformist wings of the party. These tensions were exacerbated by the results of the November 1965 federal election. The reformers urged Pearson to call the election to form a majority government by capitalizing on the health reform promises and siphoning support away from the NDP. The strategy backfired, as the NDP made significant gains in Ontario and won 18 percent of the popular vote, higher than any third party at the federal level since the Progressives in 1921. Liberal support remained unchanged, and the party again formed a minority government, dependent on NDP support in the House of Commons.[67]

The NDP lost no time in interpreting the combined support of the Liberal and NDP parties as a mandate for federal action on medical insurance. As soon as Parliament reconvened in early 1966, the NDP pressured the government to introduce legislation and to confirm the plan's July 1967 starting date. In May, Health and Welfare Minister Alan MacEachen formally confirmed the plan's starting date, and in July he finally introduced medical care legislation (Bill C-277). Several Conservative M.P.'s balked at this "haste," but the NDP immediately pledged its full support of the legislation.[68] Amid rumors of rifts within the Liberal party, the NDP's main focus was to have legislation passed and implemented as quickly as possible before opposition forces both in and out of Parliament could gather any more momentum.

These rumors were justified. When the House reconvened after the summer recess, Finance Minister Mitchell Sharp announced the plan's starting date would be deferred to July 1968, due to fiscal priorities.[69] This postponement, and the storm of protest that followed, reflected bitter internal battles on the issue within the Liberal party. The controversy had come to embody the division between fiscal conservatives, like Finance Minister Sharp, and the more progressive wing led by his predecessor, Walter Gordon.[70] Although the Cabinet finally accepted Sharp's

---

[67] Popular vote results remained unchanged from 1963 for the two major parties, while the NDP's increased from 13 to 18 percent. The two majors gained two seats each, the NDP four; by 1965, the NDP had 18 percent of the vote (higher than any CCF result) and twenty-one seats. Beck, 1967.

[68] Canada, House of Commons, *Debates*, 12 July 1966, 7544, 7591.

[69] Canada, House of Commons, *Debates*, 8 September 1966, 8217.

[70] On the Liberal party split, see Pearson 1975, 226–27; see also Smith 1973, 335–36. Gordon resigned from the Cabinet after urging Pearson to call the 1965 election. Wearing 1981, 64–68.

decision, the frustration of several ministers (some of whom threatened to resign over the issue) and the party caucus (many of whom had campaigned during the election on the issue) was palpable. Unlike the American system, reformers inside the center party were constrained by party discipline; but when the pressure of this discipline became too great, they could also resort to the threat of jumping ship completely. Pearson, fearing that the split "might lead to a drift of some [left Liberals] to the NDP,"[71] promised there would be no further delays, neither in the passage of the legislation nor in its new starting date of July 1968. The Liberal caucus, with the help of the NDP, voted down several attempted amendments to the legislation introduced by Conservative and Social Credit M.P.'s. By now, it was evident that the NDP would not support any watered-down version of the bill. The medical insurance proposals had become "politically potent; no one could afford to be seen as opposed."[72] This was evident at the bill's final passage, by a vote of 177 to 2.[73]

The prolonged and bitter debate in the House over the legislation, the divisions within the Liberal party, the delayed implementation, and the small but significant concessions offered to the medical profession indicate that the development of medical care insurance was a far from effortless procedure. The fact that all Canadian parties ended up endorsing the measure reflected more the political stakes that its proponents had built up around the issue than an ideological convergence on national health insurance in the Canadian political community.

THE MEDICARE COMPROMISE IN THE UNITED STATES

The Kennedy Medicare Initiative

Like the Liberal government in Canada, the Democratic administration in the United States realized the political saliency of health reform in the 1960s. Health insurance was an important issue in the 1960 presidential campaign, but the Democratic victory did not ensure passage of legislation since a political consensus on the issue was not yet evident, particularly in the Congress. Nevertheless, mounting public support for health insurance for the aged, and dissatisfaction with the limits of the Kerr-Mills program, ensured health insurance a prominent place on the domestic agenda. President John F. Kennedy stressed health insurance in

[71] Pearson 1975, 228.
[72] Granatstein 1986, 196.
[73] Canada, House of Commons, *Debates*, 8 December 1966, 10881–82. Howard Johnston of the Conservative party and Social Credit leader Robert Thompson were the nays.

his first State of the Union address and shortly afterwards presented a special message to Congress on health insurance for the aged, one that would be repeated again in 1962 and 1963.[74]

Strategists in the Kennedy administration were receptive to health reform because of public support for extending Social Security benefits for the aged. A Gallup poll published in June 1961 indicated that 67 percent of Americans favored medicare for the aged, even with increases in Social Security taxes, and Kennedy's private polls corroborated this widespread popularity.[75] Like Roosevelt in the debate over the Social Security Act, Kennedy realized that his popularity would be affected by the response to politically attractive social reform. In attempting to impose such policy on a recalcitrant Congress, Kennedy was faced, like Truman, with a party divided on health reform and an openly hostile conservative coalition of Republicans and southern Democrats, particularly in the House of Representatives.

In spite of the more limited nature of the 1960s proposals, the public and legislative battles over "medicare"[76] would not be easy. The focal point was the King-Anderson bill, introduced in February 1961 by Democrats Cecil King of California (H.R. 4222) and Clinton Anderson of New Mexico (S. 909), which outlined the administration's version of the Forand proposals, specifically limiting hospital benefits to the aged and omitting physician services.[77] The bill was heavily influenced by Wilbur Cohen, the new Assistant Secretary in the Department of Health, Education, and Welfare. A veteran of Democratic administrations' health policy battles since the 1930s, Cohen understood the potential roadblocks to health reform and realized the necessity of both emphasizing its political legitimacy and avoiding direct confrontation with doctors.[78] While Cohen

[74] "Health and Hospital Care—Message from the President," *Congressional Record*, 9 February 1961, 2000–2003.

[75] Gallup 1971, Vol. 3, 1721; for an analysis of the role of polling during this period, see Jacobs 1993, 137–40.

[76] The term "medicare" refers to the King-Anderson bill and its successors; it was first used to denote the 1956 Dependents' Medical Care Act program for the armed forces. Altmeyer 1966, 283.

[77] The Forand bill covered all OASDI beneficiaries, plus inpatient surgical procedures. The King-Anderson bill was limited to OASDI beneficiaries over 65, providing ninety days of hospital care, one hundred and eighty days of nursing home care, and outpatient diagnostic services ("Summary Comparison of the King-Anderson and Forand Proposals," 19 July 1961; Health Insurance 1962; Box 31; Cohen Papers; SHSW).

[78] Cohen had been part of Senator Kennedy's informal "Academic Advisory Committee" since 1958 (Sorensen 1965, 117–18). He also headed Kennedy's Task Force on Health and Social Security, which presented a report to the President-elect: "Health and Social Security for the American People," in January 1961 (File 5; Box 4; Altmeyer Papers; SHSW).

was considered pragmatic—too much so, perhaps, for many of his critics[79] —this was precisely the skill the Kennedy and Johnson administrations sought in their efforts to forge the necessary compromises for the passage of medicare legislation.

The King-Anderson Bill Hearings and the Debate over Medicare

The first round of hearings on the medicare bill took place in the House Ways and Means Committee during the summer of 1961.[80] Legislative action did not look very promising, for two reasons. First, many congressional Democrats had reservations about the bill, including the same members of the committee and its chairman (Wilbur Mills) that had previously rejected the Forand bill and supported Kerr-Mills in 1960. The Kerr-Mills alternative had become an instrument for opponents of medicare who advocated limiting government action to a means-tested program.[81] In addition, the 1960 election had reduced the Democratic majority in the House by some twenty seats, many of which had been held by prolabor members who would have been more supportive of medicare.[82]

For the AMA, however, the new proposals were a real threat. Even though the AMA had already won what was in a sense the major battle, since physician services were omitted from the bill, the medical lobby still felt threatened by a social insurance measure that involved government funding of the health care system. The AMA perceived King-Anderson, like Forand, as the looming "foot in the door toward all-out socialized medicine."[83] The events unfolding in Canada also gave the AMA reason to pause. By 1961, hospital insurance had been implemented in all ten Canadian provinces, and, true to the medical lobbies' fears on both sides of the border, this had proved to be the first step toward medical insurance. "Anyone who thought that socialized health care could not happen there was wrong," wrote one Canadian insurance official, suggesting that American physicians "guard themselves" against this eventuality.[84]

Given the strong support of the administration and the more limited

[79] Derthick 1979, 54.

[80] U.S. Congress, House, Committee on Ways and Means, *Health Services for the Aged under the Social Security System: Hearings on H.R. 4222*, 87th Cong., 1st sess., July-August 1961.

[81] On the means-test versus social insurance approach, see Marmor 1973, 40.

[82] "Elections Weaken Labor in Congress," *Congressional Quarterly Almanac*, 1960, 769–70.

[83] Editorial, "Foot in the Door," *AMA News*, 6 February 1961, 4.

[84] Kilgour 1963, 726–31.

nature of the proposals, the AMA feared medicare had better chances of passing Congress than had the Truman reforms. An AMA survey of the Eighty-seventh Congress revealed that a majority of legislators were against King-Anderson, but only by slim margins, and that "mounting pressure could shift the balance." The AMA's strongest support in Congress was found in "the South and the Southwest," reinforcing the idea of an AMA-conservative coalition consensus on the health insurance issue.[85]

A special meeting of AMA delegates was convened to plan a counter-offensive, raising dues to launch a new campaign aimed at influencing the public and their representatives in Washington. Although the AMA had long been involved in political campaigns, the formation of the AMA's Political Action Committee (AMPAC) in July 1961 represented a formal commitment to participate in elections specifically on the medicare issue. It also signaled the AMA's determination to do battle with medicare's major supporters in the Congress and in the labor movement, by setting up a political machine to challenge the AFL-CIO's Committee on Political Education (COPE). The AMA's president, Edward Annis, openly acknowledged that AMPAC was formed because "[w]e were being clobbered around the country by COPE" and that the organization was "sort of patterned after COPE" in both its organization and financial support.[86] While the AMPAC's impact in congressional elections achieved only mixed results in the 1960s, the AMA was more successful in reinforcing opposition to medicare by shoring up support from influential Republican and Democratic members of the conservative coalition in Congress, particularly those from the South. The AMA also had a great deal of influence with representatives of tobacco-producing states, who applauded the AMA's refusal to endorse the Surgeon-General's linkage of cancer and smoking in 1964, and vigorously supported the AMA's opposition to medicare.[87]

Despite the more limited nature of Medicare as compared to the Truman proposals of the 1940s, at the congressional hearings on the bill the AMA still emphasized the "loss of freedom" associated with government control. Aware of the pitfalls of attacking provisions for the aged, the AMA instead warned that the administration proposals were "wrong in principle" and would destroy the "moral fiber" of family responsibility. A better solution, claimed the AMA, was to "give additional dollars with which [the aged] could buy their own insurance, pay their hospital, or

---

[85] "AMA Staff Assesses Mood of Congress," *Medical World News*, 23 June 1961, 33–35.

[86] U.S. Congress, House, Committee on Ways and Means, *Medical Care for the Aged: Hearings on HR. 3920*, 88th Cong., 1st sess., 21 November 1963, 785.

[87] Harris 1966, 159–61.

drug, or doctor bills."[88] The medical lobby's position converged with its Canadian counterpart in preferring that government involvement be limited to enabling the elderly to purchase their own medical insurance.

Although the AMA restrained its antisocialist attacks at congressional hearings, its public education campaign made extensive use of the slogan, "Socialized Medicine and YOU."[89] The AMA was careful not to target the goal of reform (helping the aged) but rather the means ("socializing" the delivery of medical care). The virulent tone of the 1940s was now moderated, but the supporters of medicare were still associated with dangerous leftism and un-Americanism.[90] Repeating Cold War rhetoric from 1949, the AMA warned, "History shows that government control over health care is either the first step or one of the early steps toward government domination over all aspects of a people's life."[91]

Like the medical lobby in Canada, the AMA counted on the support of business, pharmaceutical, and insurance interests. The American Pharmaceutical Association and the Health Insurance Association of America testified against King-Anderson, as they had against Forand, reiterating the principles of individual responsibility and freedom. The Chamber of Commerce of the United States (CCUS) and the National Association of Manufacturers (NAM), like their Canadian counterparts, balked at the cost of the medicare program and the fiscal implications of government involvement in health care. In its testimony the NAM argued that American business provided adequate health benefits, and repeated the AMA's stance that "many families still have the moral fiber . . . to provide security, medical and otherwise, for their beloved parents."[92] The American Farm Bureau Federation, closely allied with business interests and political representatives form the South, also continued its vehement resistance to government involvement in health insurance.

The AMA nevertheless had difficulty maintaining a watertight coalition with other health professionals. Dissension among physicians, evident since the 1930s, resurfaced once again. The Physicians Forum challenged the AMA, as it had in the 1940s, claiming that most American doctors were not opposed to health reform. These groups of doctors were now

[88] U.S. Congress, House, Testimony of Leonard Larson, AMA president, on H.R. 4222, 2 August 1961, 1309.

[89] The AMA also launched "Operation Coffee Cup," run by doctors' wives and featuring antisocialism recordings by Ronald Reagan. Harris 1966, 139.

[90] Wilbur Cohen was the focus of the attention of the American Association of Physicians and Surgeons, which warned of his "extreme leftist-un-American leanings" (AAPS Membership Committee for Missouri, 24 March 1962; File Personal Attacks; Box 56; Cohen Papers; SHSW).

[91] Annis (AMA president) 1963, 104.

[92] U.S. Congress, House, Testimony of John E. Carroll, National Association of Manufacturers, on H.R. 4222, 4 August 1961, 1790.

attracting much more public legitimacy as they organized to support the medicare bill.[93] The American Nurses' Association, representing the care-givers for the elderly in hospitals and nursing homes, enthusiastically endorsed the King-Anderson bill, as it had the Forand bill, cementing the group's defection from the AMA coalition. The American Hospital Association (AHA), meanwhile, aware of the financial problems that the indigent and the aged posed for hospitals, vacillated on the issue. Although reluctant to endorse any compulsory measures for health insurance, the AHA stated instead that "if we come to the point that we feel that the voluntary programs will not meet the needs, then in the interest of health care of the people of the country, we would support social security."[94] In January 1962, the AHA held a special meeting on the medicare issue, and indicated that it supported government funding for health insurance for the aged as long as this was administered by voluntary nonprofit carriers (e.g., Blue Cross), but added that "the tax source of the funds is of secondary importance to us," leaving the door open for Social Security tax financing.[95]

Although the medical lobby's opposition to health insurance was not mitigated by the more limited medicare proposals, its effectiveness did suffer from the dissension of other health professionals. The AMA was also faced with a widening public and political consensus for medicare, bolstered by the mobilization of organized labor. A consistent obstacle to health reform in the past had been the absence of an effective counter-weight to the AMA from the labor movement.[96] Although labor had been at the forefront of health reform debates before, the unified AFL-CIO was now the central force in organizing the public campaign for medicare.

Labor's political muscle was rejuvenated by the merger of the AFL-CIO, increased levels of unionization, and the return to power of a Democratic administration. Although Kennedy had not been labor's choice in the Democratic primaries, the AFL-CIO was willing to support the administration on its health reform agenda. Organized labor had not forgotten the lessons of 1949, and it realized that even with the limited medicare proposals, a Democratic administration and Congress did not

[93] An example of this was the Bay Area Committee for Medical Aid for the Aged through Social Security, formed in 1961 to publicize the support of doctors for medicare. BACMA to Wilbur Cohen, 19 June 1961; Cohen Papers; Box 32; Support (by doctors) Health Insurance 1961–62; SHSW. The national Physicians' Committee for Health Care of the Aged through Social Security, was eventually also organized.

[94] U.S. Congress, House, Testimony of Frank Groner, AHA President, on H.R. 4222, 24 July 1961, 259.

[95] U.S. Congress, House, 20 November 1963, 35.

[96] See discussion in Altmeyer, COHC, 145.

ensure passage of health reform. Labor's campaign for medicare against the AMA was made more effective, especially in the public eye, since the beneficiaries of the proposed legislation were not active union members. As such, labor was not perceived to be acting out of narrow self-interest in the same way as the medical profession.

Just as organized medicine tried to link health insurance for the aged to national health insurance, and the social insurance approach to unnecessarily helping those that could help themselves, organized labor would carefully avoid making any linkages between medicare and national health insurance, while at the same time applauding Social Security and its crucial role in assuring the "deserving" aged their proper entitlements. This message was brought out at the King-Anderson bill hearings. When asked whether the medicare plan would be the first step toward a system of universal coverage such as that proposed in the 1940s, UAW president Walter Reuther replied:

> When the Wagner-Dingell bill was submitted to Congress . . . we supported it because, at that time, we did not have comprehensive voluntary programs. . . . Since then we have made great progress. Therefore, we believe that we now have a system under which, if the minimums are met by a Government program, we will encourage the expansion of voluntary programs . . . in the end, it is going to be the adequacy of the voluntary programs that will limit governmental action.[97]

This position shows the extent to which American labor leaders had diverged from their Canadian counterparts on health reform. Of central importance was that the American labor movement associated itself with the Democratic administration's position on health insurance. This stands in contrast to the Canadian labor movement, which adopted a health insurance platform that reflected the principles of a social-democratic third party. Although the AFL-CIO kept abreast of developments in Canada, support for health reform there put American labor leaders on a precarious tightrope with respect to their legislative agenda. In the context of the highly politicized debate over health reform in the United States, labor was obviously wary of supporting proposals for universal health insurance introduced by a social-democratic government. Although American labor leaders denounced the Saskatchewan doctors' strike, they were careful not to get involved in the conflict. Requests by Premier Douglas to American labor experts involved in health bargaining to testify or help the Saskatchewan Federation of Labour prepare submis-

---

[97] U.S. Congress, House, Testimony of Walter P. Reuther, UAW President, on H.R. 4222, 3 August 1961, 1656.

sions in support of health insurance were turned down and deemed "unwise":

> The one interest of organized labor in the health insurance field at this time in the United States is getting through legislation for health care of the elderly. They are being extremely quiet about mentioning next steps such as extending health insurance to others in the population. . . . [If we were] to promote a pattern of medical care publicly that goes far beyond the kind of compulsory health insurance that one hardly dares mention in the United States, with resulting publicity rapidly reaching medical circles here, some of the results might be unfortunate.[98]

Although national health insurance had been mentioned in the AFL-CIO's 1955 platform, after the 1957 Forand bill was introduced labor shifted its attention to health insurance for the aged. The previous emphasis on universal health insurance for all Americans had, for the moment, disappeared. In the AFL-CIO's convention proceedings during this period, the emphasis was almost exclusively on public coverage of the aged through Social Security, and on reform of the existing private insurance system for the rest of the population to ensure complete coverage of services and of high-risk groups through prepaid plans.[99]

The AFL-CIO's campaign for medicare in the United States was a two-pronged approach: an offensive attack to mobilize support for King-Anderson; and defensive measures against the "ominous threat" of "the political efforts of business, medicine and the right wing."[100] This involved enlisting the support of union affiliates, building ties with other interest groups, and working closely with reformers in the Democratic party and the DHEW. The AFL-CIO's Social Security department became a clearinghouse for the public education campaign for medicare, tracking legislative activities in Congress and coordinating the efforts of other proreform groups. Public health and welfare groups (many of which had supported national health insurance since the 1940s), includ-

[98] F. D. Mott, Executive Director, Community Health Association, Detroit [of which Walter Reuther was president], to Alex Robertson, Professor of Social and Preventive Medicine, University of Saskatchewan [active in the CCF medical insurance effort], 12 September 1960; in NAC; MG 28; CLC Papers; Vol. 274. In December, Reuther refused CLC president Claude Jodoin's personal appeal to allow Mott to testify at the Saskatchewan hearings; I. S. Falk (of the USW) also turned down the CLC's appeal.

[99] "Health Insurance and Medical Care," Report of the AFL-CIO Executive Council, 1961, 139–42; and 1963, 146–48.

[100] Political Education Resolution No. 195, AFL-CIO, *Proceedings*, 1963, 187. In addition to AMPAC (American Medical Association Political Action Committee), the National Association of Manufacturers had set up BIPAC (Business-Industry Political Action Committee). See "Is Big Business-AMA Political Alliance Emerging?" COPE Political Memo, 30 July 1962.

ing the American Public Health Association and the American Public Welfare Association (formerly led by Wilbur Cohen), now lent their full support to the medicare proposals. In addition, religious-based social welfare organizations, representing a wide array of denominations, also endorsed the King-Anderson bill. Catholic organizations, which had opposed Truman's compulsory plan in 1949, now embraced health insurance for the aged. The National Farmers Union, the progressive Midwestern wing of the American farm movement, was also active in its support for medicare and its opposition to the American Farm Bureau Federation (AFBF) on the issue.[101]

An important part of the campaign for medicare was directed at staging a counterattack against the AMA. Organized labor's most effective allies in this strategy were the elderly themselves.[102] In addition to forging alliances with existing groups, organized labor was also instrumental in the formation of the Senior Citizens for Kennedy movement during the 1960 election campaign. Labor leaders, particularly within the UAW, convinced the Democratic National Committee to set up the group to attract elderly voters around the medicare issue, as a way of "expanding the political constituency of the Democratic party," namely lower-income, "relatively Republican" older Americans.[103] The organizational and financial resources of labor's Committee on Political Education (COPE) provided essential support in this effort, as did retirees of major unions (railroad, steel, auto, and garment workers). Although it is not clear whether these efforts were decisive in Kennedy's 1960 victory, the high profile of the Senior Citizens for Kennedy movement did shore up support for issues such as medicare within the Democratic party.[104]

The National Council of Senior Citizens (NCSC), set up in July 1961, was an outgrowth of this group.[105] Although the NCSC would become an important interest group for senior citizens, its initial force was as a single-issue lobby for medicare, and as a visible counterweight against the AMA's campaign: as one NCSC leader noted, "The AMA had all the

---

[101] U.S. Congress, House, 27 July 1961 and 30 July 1961.

[102] Seniors' groups that testified in support of King-Anderson included the Council of Golden Ring Clubs of Senior Citizens and the National League of Senior Citizens. The American Association of Retired Persons (AARP), formed in 1958, also testified in support of King-Anderson. Pratt 1976, 89–90.

[103] Pratt 1976, 59–62.

[104] Pratt 1976, 64–65. The most significant impact of the vote of the elderly for Kennedy was in Florida (especially Miami Beach) and in parts of New York City and Los Angeles County.

[105] Nelson Cruikshank initially feared the group would turn into the "Townsend people" and play havoc with medicare and other social reform (Harris 1966, 136); later, he became head of the NCSC after its first leader, Aimé Forand. On the NCSC's formation, see Pratt 1976, 88–89.

money, and we had all the old people."[106] Indeed, the group directly attacked the medical lobby through an "Operation Negative" campaign, warning that the AMA's "illogical opposition to government programs" showed that "the AMA believes what's good for doctors is not always good for their patients."[107] Meanwhile, promedicare Democrats focused on the political clout of the aged in trying to get the legislation through Congress: "It was one thing to write off socialism; but the risks of writing off the aged would give the wise politician second thoughts."[108]

Partisan Politics and the Legislative Saga of Medicare

If Republicans and southern Democrats were not about to write off the aged, they were not yet ready to accept medicare either. At the same time that interest groups were beginning to wage the public battle over medicare in 1961, opponents of the measure in Congress were stalling the King-Anderson bill. Despite the administration's backing, it faced a divided congressional leadership, and overt hostility within the Ways and Means Committee and among southern Democrats.

President Kennedy's efforts on behalf of medicare legislation tactics involved a counteroffensive, coordinated with the AFL-CIO and the NCSC, to lower the heat of the AMA's attacks. This included strong attacks on the AMA at a series of highly publicized events, culminating in Kennedy's televised appearance before an NCSC rally at Madison Square Garden in New York. The AMA responded in kind, renting the Garden for a paid television broadcast the next night.[109] Kennedy also inflamed AMA leaders by suggesting their position on medicare stemmed from their original opposition to social security in the 1930s and by charging the AMA of deliberately misleading Americans.[110] Nevertheless, Kennedy's oratory was not enough to sway public opinion, which remained divided on medicare.[111]

---

[106] NCSC Executive Director William R. Hutton, quoted in Pratt 1976, 88.

[107] "Operation Negative" pamphlet, Box 32; Cohen Papers; SHSW.

[108] Marmor 1973, 28.

[109] Sundquist 1968, 310–11.

[110] Press release by HEW Secretary Ribicoff, 22 May 1962; Cohen Papers; Box 32; SHSW; Presidential Press Conference, 21 May 1962, in U.S. President, *Public Papers of the Presidents*, 1962, 432.

[111] In a series of polls in 1962 on preferences for a Social Security–based plan for older Americans or a voluntary health insurance plan, Americans preferred the latter 55 to 34 (March), 48 to 44 (May), and 44 to 40 (July); Gallup 1972, Vol. 3, 1759, 1774, 1781; Schiltz 1970, 140. The use of two alternatives was thought misleading by Cohen and his staff, and the SSA, concerned about the impact of such polls on Congress, tried to get Gallup to avoid such wording; such questions were not asked again until 1965 (Confiden-

Kennedy was also unsuccessful in pressuring Congress to vote on the issue. House Speaker Sam Rayburn supported medicare, but "lacked formal means to enforce party discipline" on the President's proposals.[112] In addition, many members of Congress were sensitive to their own district polls, which did not show clear majorities in favor of medicare.[113] To the relief of members facing midterm election and uneasy about the issue, the House did not vote on the King-Anderson bill in 1962. Despite heavy lobbying by the administration, the bill remained stuck in the Ways and Means Committee, where it faced the same "negative majority" as the Forand bill before it, including Chairman Wilbur Mills and six southern Democrats.

With these obstacles in the House, the bill's sponsor in the Senate, Clinton Anderson, attempted to develop a compromise with Republican Jacob Javits of New Mexico that would be palatable to Republicans and conservative Democrats. The compromise, supported by the administration and the AFL-CIO, extended coverage to elderly non-OASDI recipients, and incorporated the use of Blue Cross or other nonprofit carriers to administer the hospital insurance plan.[114] Five Republican senators finally voted in favor of the Anderson-Javits amendment, but the rest allied with southern and border Democrats to defeat it.[115]

Although the 1962 elections did not substantially alter the partisan balance on health reform in Congress, the results indicated that medicare had a growing measure of popular support. Even though the conservative coalition held, the Democratic party was able to stave off midterm losses (for the first time since 1934), and gained three seats in the Senate.[116] Most significant was that medicare's friends were rewarded while its enemies were not. In the House, the issue cost the Democratic primary for at least one of its opponents in Ways and Means (James Frazier of Tennessee), and also ensured the reentry into Congress of ardent health reformer Claude Pepper.[117] In the Senate races, several promedicare candidates defeated Republican opponents on the strength of the issue, and,

---

tial: Ball to J. Douglas Brown, 3 August 1962; File Support [Health Insurance] 1961–62; Box 32; Cohen Papers; SHSW).

[112] Marmor 1973, 46.

[113] Tabulated by members in their districts, these polls showed 54 percent opposed and 40 percent in favor of the social security approach for health insurance for the aged (*Congressional Record*, 10 July 1962, 13070–71). While these polls were drawn from nonrandom samples, they reflect the pressures facing members of Congress.

[114] Sundquist 1968, 312–13.

[115] The motion to table the amendment to the Social Security bill (H.R. 10606) was very narrowly passed, 52 (21D–31R) to 48 (43D–5R). *Congressional Quarterly Almanac*, 1962, 670.

[116] *Guide to U.S. Elections*, 1987, 1116; *Congressional Quarterly Almanac*, 1962, 1029.

[117] Sundquist 1968, 315.

despite the entry of AMPAC and heavy spending by the AMA, no overtly promedicare candidates were defeated.[118]

Convinced that the midterm elections reflected a mandate for health reform, the administration focused it efforts on passing medicare through the Eighty-eighth Congress. In early 1963, Kennedy reiterated his commitment to medicare in two separate addresses to Congress, and a new King-Anderson bill was introduced (H.R. 3920; S. 880), based on the Anderson-Javits compromise.[119] Meanwhile, however, other urgent domestic matters took the forefront, notably the omnibus tax bill and the pressing controversy over civil rights. Hearings on King-Anderson were delayed until November, to allow time to clear the tax bill through Ways and Means and avoid further confrontation with southern Democrats.

Although the composition of the Ways and Means Committee had changed slightly, Wilbur Mills was still leading powerful legislative opposition to medicare. Mills's resistance to medicare was based on several factors. He was part of the conservative coalition in Congress, representing an Arkansas district not known for its liberal leanings. Mills sensed the ambivalence surrounding the issue, and he was not convinced that the bill would secure enough votes, no matter how forceful his committee's recommendations. Finally, Mills was worried that the comprehensive "medicare" label was misleading the public about the quite limited scope of hospital benefits being offered, and as a fiscal conservative, he was uneasy about the unpredictable costs involved.[120]

As part of the commitment to the Kennedy program, the Johnson administration continued a high-profile campaign for medicare, beginning with a special message to Congress early in 1964. Johnson also sent an antipoverty message to Congress, but made no mention of health insurance for the poor, or what would later become Medicaid.[121] Yet again, however, a medicare bill failed to get out of House Ways and Means, and attention turned to the Senate, where Albert Gore of Tennessee proposed an amendment to another Social Security bill (H.R. 11865), already passed by the House.[122] Supporters again proved willing to compromise with Republican alternatives, in this case Senator Javits's plan for a private

---

[118] Sundquist 1968, 314–15; Harris 1966, 149.

[119] "Health Protection Recommendations" (H. Doc. No. 60), *Congressional Record*, 7 February 1963, 1940–43; "Aid for Elderly Citizens" (H. Doc. No. 72), *Congressional Record*, 21 February 1963, 2693–99.

[120] Marmor 1973, 56–57; Derthick 1979, 327.

[121] H. Doc. No. 224, *Congressional Record*, 10 February 1964, 2805–7; H. Doc. No. 243, *Congressional Record*, 16 March 1964, 5287–88.

[122] During the Senate Finance Committee's August hearings on H.R. 11865, Gore and other senators backed testimony by HEW Secretary Celebrezze and the AFL-CIO's Cruikshank urging the inclusion of hospital insurance for the aged. *Congressional Quarterly Almanac*, 1964, 235–36.

supplemental insurance program. In September 1964, the gamble paid off, and the Senate narrowly passed the Gore amendment (49–44).[123] It was a historic moment, the first roll call in favor of medicare in either house, but Mills and other House opponents refused to concede on the medicare issue in conference committee, and H.R. 11865 remained deadlocked.

Cohen and DHEW officials, convinced that Congress would legislate on medicare in 1964, were disheartened by these repeat failures.[124] Johnson, for his part, was determined to use the health issue in the presidential campaign against Senator Barry Goldwater, an ardent foe of medicare and a close ally of the AMA. For Johnson, the health issue represented a way of unifying legislative policymakers.[125] Medicare was highlighted in the "Great Society" platform that stressed continuity not only with Kennedy's New Frontier, but also with the New Deal and the Fair Deal.[126] It had resonance among voters in both the presidential and congressional elections. In congressional races, the promedicare side gained four seats in the Senate and forty-four in the House; in addition, almost all the doctors (eleven of fourteen) who ran for Congress were defeated.[127]

In a political climate charged with the promise of reform, and with a newly energized Congress, the measure looked as if it had the chance to finally pass. Public opinion polls following the election in December 1964 recorded 65 percent approval of medicare.[128] Lawmakers were faced with the political saliency of the issue, especially in terms of public enthusiasm for reform as manifested in both the presidential and congressional races. Still faced with the institutional constraints of the American political system, however, health reform proponents resisted the urge to use this political mandate to fashion broader health reform like that being developed in Canada. Despite the sweeping promise of the Great Society, and the limited nature of the medicare plan, health reform still carried the heavy baggage of past battles for health insurance reform and the legacies of those defeats.

[123] Five Republicans voted for medicare; the difference was the defection of three Democrats from the conservative coalition to join the party line. *Congressional Quarterly Almanac*, 1964, 715. Two southern senators, Russell Long and George Smathers (a longtime AMA ally), also ended up supporting the administration. Harris 1966, 170–71.

[124] In May, Cohen had offered to pay the President "one dollar for every vote above 15 against the bill. He [LBJ] said it was a bargain and shook my hand" (Confidential memo from Cohen to the Secretary [Celebrezze], 25 May 1964; File Executive Sessions—1964; Box 33; Cohen Papers; SHSW).

[125] Jacobs 1993, 194–95.

[126] Campaign speech on 3 October 1964 at Chicago Stadium, in U.S. President, *Public Papers of the Presidents*, 1963–64, 620–22.

[127] Harris 1966, 174; Sundquist 1968, 317.

[128] Gallup 1972, Vol. 3, 1915. The White House's private polls confirmed this. See Jacobs 1993, 191–96.

Work on the new medicare bills (symbolically numbered H.R. 1 and S. 1), began immediately after the election.[129] When the Eighty-ninth Congress reconvened in January 1965, medicare was the first order of business.[130] With the new configuration in Congress, including majority support for medicare in the Ways and Means Committee, Mills showed willingness to act on the measure.[131] But caution was in order given the resurgence of alternative plans by opponents of medicare. Derthick describes the two tactics of these opponents to health insurance reform as delay and preemption.[132] Delay had been the tactic of choice ever since the Forand bill had surfaced in the 1960 election campaign. By 1965, delay was no longer a politically feasible option. As in Canada, rising public expectations, coupled with a political balance swaying in favor of reform, was forcing legislative action on the issue. In Canada, delay tactics had a certain impact, but preemption was practically impossible, both for reasons of parliamentary procedure and because the NDP, holding the balance of power in the House, would not support fundamental changes to the health insurance proposals. In the United States, however, the failure of delay tactics gave way to a final preemptive strike by the AMA as the medicare bills were introduced in Congress.

As in the 1940s, the AMA concentrated on offering an alternative to the administration's proposals: then, it had been the endorsement of voluntary health insurance; now, it would involve efforts to institutionalize the voluntary approach through "Eldercare," introduced by a bipartisan team of AMA allies on the Ways and Means Committee, Sydney Herlong (D-Fla.) and Thomas Curtis (R-Mo.). Eldercare provided for comprehensive health insurance through the expansion of the Kerr-Mills program to include medical insurance for the aged, subsidized by federal-state grants according to income, and provided by private insurers.[133]

Congressional Republicans supported these principles, but they endorsed another alternative. The "Bettercare" bill, as Republicans called it, was meant to provide voluntary hospital and medical insurance through the federal government. It was introduced by John Byrnes, the ranking Republican on the Ways and Means Committee.[134] The Byrnes bill was

[129] Wilbur Cohen, "Specifications for New Medicare Bill," 25 November 1964; File Hospital Insurance; Box 33; Cohen Papers; SHSW.

[130] State of the Union Address, 4 January 1965; see also "The Nation's Health," Message to Congress, *Congressional Record*, 7 January 1965, 365–66.

[131] Marmor 1973, 60; Sundquist 1968, 317.

[132] Derthick 1979, 327.

[133] *Congressional Quarterly Almanac*, 1965, 248–49; "Comparison of Three Proposals for Health Care of the Aged," Binder 4; Box 35; Cohen Papers; SHSW.

[134] The Byrnes bill was modeled on the federal government's employee health plan, run by Aetna Life Insurance. Marmor 1973, 63–64.

"tactically . . . preemptive" in the sense that it was designed to stave off compulsory, Social Security–based health insurance for the aged in favor of voluntary health insurance that preserved the private delivery system.[135] It was also based on the Republicans' perception of medicare's long-term political portent and their realization that, if legislation was inevitable, they wanted some substantive input and political recognition for the measure.[136] Wilbur Mills also saw the Byrnes bill as a way of assuaging conservative resistance to medicare, of responding to Republican and AMA criticisms of medicare's limited scope, and of foiling inevitable future demands for expansion of the administration's hospitalization plan.[137]

Mills's strategy to combine the administration proposal and the Byrnes bill into what became known as Medicare Part A and Part B was indeed a stroke of political brilliance.[138] Part A would include the benefits under H.R. 1 for compulsory hospital insurance coverage, financed by the Social Security payroll tax; the new Part B would incorporate the Byrnes proposals for supplementary voluntary insurance for physician, surgical, and diagnostic services financed by monthly premiums paid by participants. Supporters of Medicare in the administration were amenable to the compromise, especially as this would mitigate opposition to health reform and speed it through Congress. President Johnson lost no time in publicly endorsing the new compromise measure (H.R. 6675) after it had passed the House, and he pressured recalcitrant Democrats to do the same.[139] After extensive hearings in the Finance Committee, the new bill passed the Senate in early July. After the conference committee reached accommodation on details of the benefits, the Medicare compromise bill passed both the House and the Senate with substantial majorities. On July 30, 1965, President Johnson signed the Medicare bill into law.

The final voting masks, as in the Canadian case, the difficulties in reaching legislative agreement on the Medicare issue. Although the final votes reflected Democratic party-line voting in the House (Democrats 237–48 versus GOP 70–68), many Democrats had favored the Byrnes alternative to H.R. 6675. In the Senate, a larger majority of Democrats voted for Medicare (57–7 for Democrats, compared to 13–17 for Republicans), but two influential southern Democrats (Harry Byrd and Russell Long) put up the most resistance to block the legislation in the

---

[135] Derthick 1979, 332.

[136] Marmor 1973, 63.

[137] Derthick 1979, 332.

[138] On the Mills compromise, see Marmor 1973, 64–68; Derthick 1979, 331–33. On the changes to the Medicare bill through the legislative process, see *Congressional Quarterly Almanac*, 1965, 252–68.

[139] "Remarks to the Press," 26 March 1965, U.S. President, *Public Papers of the Presidents*, 1965, 327–30.

final stages.[140] Republicans split almost evenly on the Medicare vote, showing that the compromise had succeeded in its goal of attracting bipartisan support.

Organized labor accepted the compromise measure, although it did express concern over the high deductible being assessed by the supplementary plan. Labor leaders were happy to gloat over the foiled attempts of Medicare opponents to block reform, especially the AMA, whose attacks on Medicare's insufficiency "backfired as few such efforts have ever done. In this strange way, the people are indebted to those who opposed" health insurance reform.[141]

The AMA, for its part, was "shocked and opposed" despite the support for the compromise measure among erstwhile AMA allies in Congress.[142] During the final weeks of congressional activity on the issue, the AMA mounted another massive publicity campaign, reportedly spending almost $1 million in the first quarter of 1965 alone, a record "exceeded only by the AMA's spending in 1949–50."[143] At the Senate hearings in May, the AMA again warned this would be "the first step toward establishment of socialized medicine in the United States" despite the fact that the plan now embraced a voluntary health insurance model (Medicare Part B) for physician services. The insurance industry also protested against the new supplementary plan, which they considered a threat to the future of private insurance. The only victory the AMA and its private insurance allies could claim was the extension of Kerr-Mills for the medically indigent, the third layer of Mills's compromise known as "Medicaid."

The AMA had managed to limit government involvement in health insurance, and the supplementary plan for medical insurance would in fact work in favor of the medical profession, consolidating, for the time being, the principles of professional autonomy and freedom of choice. In effect, both the Canadian and American health insurance systems would be based on similar fee-for-service delivery, but while in Canada this would involve fee negotiations with provincial medical associations, the Medicare system effectively allowed U.S. physicians to continue doing business a usual with elderly patients, the only new guideline being that they billed according to "reasonable charges." Part of this hands-off atti-

---

[140] Harry Byrd (D-Va.), chair of Senate Finance, broke party ranks to vote against the bill; Russell Long (D-La.), the Majority Whip, caused a commotion with proposed amendments for "catastrophic coverage" (see Harris 1966, 196–204; vote tallies in *Congressional Quarterly Almanac*, 1965, 982, 1062).

[141] AFL-CIO Convention, *Proceedings*, 1965, pt. 2, 123–24.

[142] Memo to Douglas Cater from Wilbur Cohen, 10 March 1965; File AMA and Hospital Insurance; Vol. 33; Cohen Papers; SHSW.

[143] *Congressional Quarterly Almanac*, 1965, 247.

tude by government may have resulted from fears that doctors would not cooperate in the implementation of the Medicare Act. The AMA leadership did not believe that strike action was feasible, but individual doctors had the option of participating in the program or not. At the June 1965 AMA annual meeting, AMA president James Appell instead exhorted doctors to "comply with any health care legislation enacted by Congress, while at the same time work toward amending the law."[144]

The 1965 Medicare and Medicaid provisions were a "three-layer" compromise, designed to appeal to different political constituencies. In Medicare, the Democratic administration and reform proponents, including labor, succeeded in obtaining compulsory hospital insurance for the aged. Republicans gained their proposals for supplementary medical insurance, and the AMA and insurers managed to get expanded government coverage of the medically indigent. The health insurance program put into place in the United States thus served to reflect and institutionalize conflicting perspectives on social reform: the Social Security entitlement approach (based on a specific demographic group); the voluntary insurance approach (based on individual choice and payment); and the means-tested welfare approach (based on income-related need).

CONCLUSION

By the end of the 1960s, the health insurance systems of Canada and the United States were in place, setting the parameters of government involvement in care. In the United States, health insurance reflected the legacy of previous social reform: an emphasis on means-tested and partial coverage of the population, with a mixture of private and public responsibility. This targeted approach reflected the recognition of the aged as a deserving political constituency and of the poor as a group at risk in terms of both their physical and financial health. In Canada, a universal health insurance system developed that reflected intergovernmental arrangements, shared-cost financing coupled with certain "standards," but one in which doctors were able to retain professional autonomy and fee-for-service delivery.

The legislative outcomes of the decade reveal the impact of institutions and of partisan politics. As in the past, compromise politics on the health issue set the tone of health care debates in the United States. Even limited reform, however, involved protracted legislative struggle. The enduring split in the Democratic party on health reform allowed opponents of

[144] *AMA News*, 28 June 1965. Doctors were wary of the legality of organized boycotts under the Sherman Antitrust Act. AMA Board of Trustees to Delegates, 10 August 1965; File AMA and Hospital Insurance; Vol. 33; Cohen Papers; SHSW.

the measure to wield powerful influence through their control of institutional levers such as the committee system. This was strengthened by the influence of the medical lobby, particularly in the regional configurations of legislative opposition. Although the AMA was initially successful in blocking reform, the lobby was undermined by the growing political legitimacy surrounding Medicare and the effective counterweight exerted by the labor movement.

In Canada, different institutional configurations led to a very different legislative outcome: a federal-provincial system of universal medical insurance. The presence of a social-democratic third party and the constraints and opportunities of Canadian federalism and parliamentary government were particularly decisive. In the Canadian federal system, provincial responsibility over most areas of social policy encouraged subnational innovations in the health area. The medical care initiative in Saskatchewan both continued the path of past reform, based on compulsory and universal principles, and set the stage for further government involvement in the health sector.

At the federal level, the CCF-NDP played a crucial role in pressuring the Liberal government for legislative action. This effectiveness was reinforced by the rules of the game of the parliamentary system, in particular the influence it could exert as a third party in the House of Commons in a minority Liberal government situation. In addition, reformers in the Liberal party could use the potential threat of the Left (in capturing working-class votes or as an exit option) to exercise influence in the health reform debate. Finally, opponents of the measure, both in and out of government, could not wield effective institutional "veto points" in the same way that this could be done in the United States through the committee system and amendments to the legislative proposals.

The way in which government-funded health insurance was finally realized in Canada and the United States in the 1960s has had lasting effects on future reform attempts. In the United States, universal health insurance initiatives continued to be stymied by the medical lobby and its allies in the Congress. The institutionalization of the Medicare and Medicaid systems, meanwhile, set precedents for the role of the federal government in health care and shaped future reform debates. In Canada, some elements of the medical lobby opposed the implementation of provincial medical care plans, but once in place, the system took on a momentum of its own, and conflicts between government and providers were contained within institutionalized bargaining frameworks. The development and popular success of health insurance led to a widespread consensus in Canada on the role of government in health care. This type of consensus was not reached in the United States.

CHAPTER SEVEN

Why Did They Part?
Explaining Health Policy Trajectories in the United States and Canada

THIS BOOK began with a simple question: Why did Canada and the United States develop two different systems of government-funded health insurance? The answer, as the historical evidence suggests, involves crucial divergence at the crossroads of health reform. In the United States, there was considerable interest in health insurance in the early decades of the century, but the first federal activity in this area was as part of the research surrounding the Social Security Act. Health insurance proposals were not a part of this legislation, however; nor did they succeed in passing in 1939 or 1943. In the second half of the 1940s, President Truman took the initiative in presenting a national health insurance plan, but this was stalled by both Republican and Democratic Congresses. During the 1950s, health reform proposals were narrowed down to focus on hospital insurance for the elderly under Social Security. President Kennedy's attempts to implement this program were also thwarted by Congress, and it was only after the 1964 election that the publicly financed health insurance programs under Medicare and Medicaid were passed in the United States.

The Canadian health reform trajectory begins at a similar starting point but ends up with very different outcomes. In Canada, there was no federal involvement in the health insurance area until the 1940s. Prior to this, health reform was studied by several provinces but legislation was passed only in one, British Columbia, in the midst of the Depression; this legislation was never implemented. In 1943, special hearings were held on health insurance proposals, and two years later a national health insurance plan was presented as part of the Liberal government's postwar reconstruction package. This package, however, was blocked due to fiscal conflict with the provinces, and a system of federal health grants was eventually passed instead. Meanwhile, the Co-operative Commonwealth Federation (CCF) government in Saskatchewan initiated its own hospital program in 1947. Ten years later, the federal government introduced a coordinated plan to fund hospital insurance in the provinces. Again, Saskatchewan took the initiative and passed medical insurance, although its implementation was delayed by a doctors' strike in 1962. By 1966, the minority Liberal government had introduced a federal-provincial program to fund medical insurance in the provinces.

REVIEWING THE HISTORICAL EVIDENCE

What explains this parting at the crossroads? This comparative historical analysis has emphasized how divergent policy outputs in the two countries reflected the different institutional attributes of their political systems. Both the Canadian and American experiences in health insurance involved fundamental struggles between proponents and opponents of reform. In both cases, medical groups wished to retain professional and economic control over the organization and delivery of health care. They were confronted by proponents of health insurance in government, political parties, and the labor movement, who were interested in building a system of universal access and comprehensive coverage of health care through government intervention. Translated through the political process, these conflicts resulted in very different health insurance policy outcomes. The crucial difference between the two cases lies not only in the different political institutions but, most importantly, in the way in which they conditioned the party system. Specifically, what mattered was the presence of a social-democratic party in the Canadian case, and its influence in the debates about public health insurance. The following section assesses some of the most significant explanatory factors in light of the historical evidence.

The Medical Lobby's Struggle for Control

Organized medicine is often presented as a structural barrier to health reform. However, the comparative analysis shows that what determines the medical lobby's effectiveness is related to the constraints and opportunities of the political system. The effectiveness of this resistance depends on the institutional and political context. Organized medicine in Canada and the United States shared similar concerns about maintaining the autonomy of professional and economic interests. They were also wary of government intervention and national health insurance. In fact, the only such direct intervention that was explicitly endorsed in either country was coverage of the low-income or medically indigent. By 1949, both the Canadian Medical Association and the American Medical Association were on record favoring voluntary health insurance.

There were, however, differences in the strategies and in the relative influence of organized medicine across the two cases. In the United States, the AMA had a hostile relationship with health reformers in the Democratic party from the outset. They were especially suspicious of the influence of social policy "experts" who were very visible during the Roosevelt years. Reformers within the Committee on Economic Security, and later the Social Security Board, were equally wary of the AMA. Neither side felt it could gain concessions from the other on the health insurance issue, which may have stiffened the resolve of the AMA to fight any type of government intervention.

The AMA's concerted campaign against national health insurance reached its apogee against the Truman administration in the second half of the 1940s. This suggests two interpretations. First, the AMA felt this legislative initiative sponsored by the President was a serious threat, because it had the potential to garner both public sympathy and congressional support. Second, the AMA turned its attention toward capturing the public agenda and building up strategic alliances and congressional support for a specific alternative, the voluntary approach to health insurance. This signals that the AMA was conscious of public demand for health reform and was determined to use its campaign to channel the public debate away from national health insurance to voluntary alternatives. It was also able to polarize the health issue along ideological lines, by using Cold War symbols to reinforce its opposition to "socialized medicine."

The medical lobby was successful in burying national health insurance because it was fighting an initiative from a party decidedly split on the issue (and the Democrats would become even more divided on health reform as a result of AMA pressure tactics). Thus, the separation of powers presented an institutional opportunity for organized medicine. But also important were the workings of Congress itself, particularly the institutional features related to the partisan system, such as the key role of committee leadership, the strategic importance of regional voting blocs, and the absence of party discipline. The AMA exercised its influence by cultivating supporters in the conservative coalition, and attacking "liberal" opponents in the Democratic party. This divide-and-conquer strategy was clearly suited to the institutional rules of the American legislative game.

While the AMA succeeded in splintering the health reform debate, it was not entirely successful in its attempts to completely prevent government intervention in the health sector. When health reformers shifted their focus to the politically appealing group of "deserving" elderly Americans, and mounted an extensive publicity campaign coordinated by organized labor, they succeeded in beating the AMA at its own game of symbolic rhetoric in capturing the public agenda. The AMA was able to transform the health agenda in the United States, but it was unable to completely stifle reform.

Compared to the AMA, the Canadian Medical Association was decidedly less successful in dictating the health reform agenda in Canada. Again, this was due both to institutional factors and to the impact of party politics. The CMA's position was initially more ambiguous than the AMA's. It supported the insurance "principle" as early as 1934, but it never explicitly endorsed universal, public health insurance. The CMA did consider government intervention as serving the economic interests of the profession, through subsidies to secure private insurance for low-income workers and for covering the costs of indigent care; the AMA also supported the same principles to some extent (and these were realized somewhat through the Medicaid program).

Organized medicine in Canada had a different relationship with the federal Liberal government, as compared to the AMA and Democratic administrations in the United States. Canadian medicine was initially quite involved with the formulation of health insurance proposals, and it enjoyed cordial relations with government elites. An important difference is the political strategy the Canadian medical lobby used. Part of its closeness to government elites stemmed from the fact that such connections were the main path for pressure groups in the parliamentary system. Since legislators are bound by party discipline once the executive proposes legislation, groups are more likely to lobby the Cabinet and government departments to influence policy in its formative stages.

Both reformers and providers felt there was room to maneuver on the health insurance issue. However, when political actors were forced to modify their position on health insurance for political reasons (such as pressure from the Left), the medical lobby distanced itself from health reform. When government initiatives were seen to directly threaten the medical profession's interests, they fought back. The clearest example of this was the CCF'S plan for universal medical insurance in Saskatchewan, which was fought with resistance to "socialized medicine" and, ultimately, strike action by the province's doctors. In sharp contrast with the AMA's experience in the anti-Truman campaigns of the 1940s, this strategy backfired on Saskatchewan doctors. It proved much more difficult to attack a legitimately elected social-democratic government on the issue in Canada. The political agenda on national health insurance had already been set in Canada, and it conformed to the universal and comprehensive principles influenced by the social-democratic party presence in federal and provincial politics and its allies in the labor movement. The medical lobby thus faced a direct counterweight on the health insurance issue, and one whose political weight was brought to bear more effectively in the Canadian political system than in the American.

The medical lobby did, however, influence some of the defining features of health insurance programs in Canada. For example, the staging of health insurance beginning with hospital insurance was partly due to concerns about the reaction of organized medicine to health reform. The retention of health delivery systems based on fee-for-service remuneration was also a choice made in anticipation of doctors' reactions. Finally, specific compromises, such as allowing extra-billing, were seen as necessary concessions toward the medical profession.

Organized Labor as Counterweight: Similar Pressures, Different Levers

Just as institutions affected the political action of organized medicine, they also had an important impact on organized labor. Labor was a crucial actor in the health reform debate because of its role as a counterweight to organized medicine, both in the political sphere and in its ability to mobilize other societal actors for health reform. The Canadian and American labor movements initially had similar positions and were supportive of a public, universal health insurance system. The important difference between the two in the health insurance debate lay in their respective ability to translate their demands through the political system. In Canada, organized labor did not waver from its support of universal health insurance, while in the United States it was forced to accept a political compromise on the issue.

After 1935, organized labor in the United State was as supportive of national health insurance as its Canadian counterpart. Indeed, it was even more politically active on the issue than Canadian labor in the 1940s. Even after the decision was made to support a limited program of health insurance for the aged, the American labor movement represented the primary counterweight to organized medicine in the public battle over the issue. The difference between the two cases was that American labor was compelled to make and accept a fundamental compromise on national health insurance. This compromise transformed health reform from a universal and comprehensive policy to one that was partial and limited. This choice was conditioned by two factors: first, the nature of labor's political alliances in the party system; and second, the constraints these alliances imposed on labor's platform for health reform.

By the end of the Second World War, organized labor in the United States could no longer afford to maintain a nonpartisan stance. Given the structural constraints facing an independent labor-based third party in the American political system, and the openings that the New Deal coalition created, organized labor found itself under the Democratic umbrella. This umbrella, however, was large and diverse, and labor and its health reform allies found themselves at odds with the opposition of the conservative coalition and their medical lobby allies. In this context, organized labor was forced to retreat from national health insurance to a more politically practicable alternative to overcome congressional resistance and AMA opposition and recapture the public agenda on health reform.

In embracing health insurance for the aged, American labor effectively abandoned any immediate action toward national health insurance. Labor leaders accepted the voluntary alternative for their own constituents, namely workers, and aligned themselves with the politically feasible position of supporting the "deserving" elderly. Part of this strategy may have stemmed from the fact that labor was enjoying its highest levels of unionization in the 1950s and early 1960s, and perceived union-negotiated health plans as an acceptable alternative at the time. In Canada, meanwhile, where unionization levels were similar during this period, these alternatives were not satisfying. American labor felt that it could successfully reopen the national health insurance debate at a later date, and that coverage of the aged could be a first step in the staging of health benefits for all Americans.

A social-democratic third party was crucial for the labor movement, because its presence offered labor the possibility of expressing an independent political voice on the health insurance issue. This was the case even though, paradoxically, the third party in question had agrarian regional roots and first came to power at the subnational level in a province characterized by agrarian radicalism rather than labor militancy. But the CCF-NDP's presence forced the major parties, at both the provincial and federal levels, to recognize the potential of the labor vote, and it gave Canadian labor significant leverage on the political agenda for health reform. Public health insurance remained on the political agenda, and the voluntary alternative was never endorsed by Canadian labor. The concessions that labor accepted were provincial rather than federal administration of health insurance and fee-for-service payment, both precedents set by the CCF-NDP in Saskatchewan.

This analysis did not focus on health in terms of the class struggle between capital and labor. However, the evidence does show that business organizations in both countries were generally opposed to health insurance reform proposals. This may have stemmed from fears of high taxes or employer contributions to finance such plans, and more generally from shared concerns about free enterprise. American business groups were highly visible AMA allies, along with pharmaceutical and insurance interests. The same kinds of groups opposed medical insurance in Canada, especially private insurers, who felt directly threatened by government-sponsored health insurance reform. While the implementation of publicly administered health plans in Canada effectively weakened the further development of such private insurers, in the United States private insurers have become among the most severe opponents of health reform.

Bureaucrats and Reform Initiatives: No Escape from Politics

In both countries, bureaucrats involved with the health agenda were clearly constrained in their policy formulation by political and institutional factors. Overall, senior Canadian officials were less politicized than their reformist American counterparts and also less likely to independently initiate reform proposals. This does not mean, however, that the Canadian civil service was more sheltered from political pressures. Officials were consistently aware that their minister's directives were dictated by Cabinet decisions based upon collegial consensus and direct responsibility to the House of Commons. The minister and senior civil servants were also more permeable to influential groups such as the medical lobby, whose access to individual legislators was hampered by the dictates of party discipline. But this influence on bureaucrats was tempered by other exigencies. For example, Heagerty's proposals in 1943 tried to appeal to the interests of the CMA, and the staging of hospital benefits was in part a way of avoiding direct conflict with the medical profession. Nevertheless, once the political agenda for universal, public health insurance was set, the medical lobby in Canada found its influence and veto power considerably reduced.

In the United States, lobbyists targeted the Congress, since individual members of Congress can play influential roles in the committee system and on the floor of the Senate and the House. Senior bureaucrats, meanwhile, exercised a more independent influence in the formation of health proposals than did their Canadian counterparts. Although they, too, were working under administrative directives, these bureaucrates were instrumental in designing proposals for health reformers in Congress, as for example the Wagner bill of 1939, or the Wagner-Murray-Dingell bill of 1943. In a sense, reform-minded bureaucrats kept the health agenda alive in the Democratic party, and they developed reform proposals, in tandem with Congress or allies outside government (such as labor), that would be acceptable as feasible alternatives (e.g., the Forand bill). But the shape and success of these proposals were related to political factors. A national health insurance program, and hospital insurance for the aged, two very different policies, were both spearheaded by several of the same reform-minded New Deal "veterans" who were conscious of what was politically feasible in the context of the legislative system and the American health insurance debate.

Federalism and Health Insurance:
Decentralization and Policy Innovation

In Canada, federalism tended at some junctures to slow the progress of health reform, but it also provided crucial opportunities for innovation. Jurisdictional conflicts posed some problems for initial action, as the case of British Columbia demonstrates. Concerns about responsibility for the administration and cost of health insurance obviously made both provincial and federal governments cautious about health reform. As was the case in 1945, health and social insurance initiatives could also be lost within larger issues of fiscal and constitutional wrangling between federal and provincial governments. And, in addition, powerful conservative provincial governments in Quebec and Ontario were suspicious of federal interference in their spheres of jurisdiction. On the other hand, the federal propensity to shift the burden of health and social reform initiatives on to the provinces was also very much in evidence. In fact, it was provincial pressure that was critical in finally getting the federal government into the health arena, and this pressure was often politically motivated by public demands and electoral threats from labor and the Left. In addition, provincial innovations, most notably Saskatchewan's hospital and medical insurance programs, became constructive models for federal involvement in health. These programs, undertaken by a social-democratic government because action was not forthcoming from the federal government, served as "experiments" that turned the principles of universal health insurance into concrete legislation, demonstrated they could succeed, and also served as test cases that defused conflict with opponents of the reformers, particularly doctors.

The comparative analysis shows it is difficult to evaluate the impact of federalism without examining its relationship to other institutional arrangements. As a comparison between the Canadian and American cases shows, it depends on the type of federal structure and the opportunities open to forces for social reform. In the United States, there were few state-level initiatives in health insurance, and even fewer instances of social-democratic subnational governments. The reasons have to do with the nature of American political institutions, and the evolution of federalism in the United States. The 1930s were a watershed decade not only for the accommodation of the Left into the Democratic party coalition, but also because of the centralizing effects of the federal government's response to the Great Depression. In the area of social policy, this was especially important. The decline of regional agrarian movements and left-wing parties decreased the chances for breakthrough groups such as the CCF in Saskatchewan. Also, by shifting the focus of social policy initiative to the central government, American states were not under the same pressure to initiate innovations in the controversial health area (although there were some attempts, as the California example in the 1940s shows). While in Canada provincial initiatives were encouraged and could serve as models for other provinces and federal action, in the United States this kind of diffusion process or bottom-up reform was more problematic. The institutional features in the United States that hinder the formation of coherent policy at the federal level—especially the separation of powers, lack of party discipline, and multiple veto points for the expression of opposition—are also present in each of the fifty states.

The tendency in American federalism for regions to express their interests in the national political arena also works against reforms such as universal health insurance. Regional factors, such as the influence of the southern bloc in Congress, effectively stalled legislation and limited the realm of possible outcomes. And, although race was not explicitly enunciated in the health insurance debate, it is evident that the Medicaid compromise has tended to reinforce these cleavages in American society.

Parties and Institutions

The institutional constraints associated with the American political system, such as the separation of powers, offer significant "veto points" for potential health reform. These types of constraints are much fewer in the Canadian parliamentary system where, once the executive decides on a policy, legislative action generally follows. However, institutions in and of themselves do not determine outcomes; political configurations, particularly party politics, are also relevant to the story. For example, Democratic Presidents like Truman or Kennedy could not push forward health reform even though the Democratic party controlled Congress. A reluctant Prime Minister, such as St. Laurent, for his part, was compelled to implement reform.

In Canada, the conflict around the control of the health agenda was profoundly affected by the existence of a third party of the Left. At every stage in the health insurance debate in Canada, reform initiatives by both federal and provincial leaders were influenced by this social-democratic force. Duff Pattulo's health policy in British Columbia in the 1930s was influenced by the electoral impact of the CCF, which pulled the provincial Liberal party (temporarily) to the left in that province's polarized political spectrum. King's postwar federal reform proposals were also directly linked to the potential electoral threat posed by the CCF. The pressures for federal action brought to bear by Premier Frost of Ontario, and by St. Laurent's hesitant hospital insurance initiative, were also conditioned by the CCF and its growing ties to the labor movement. More-over, Pearson's push for medical insurance can be seen in important part as a consequence of the precedent set by the CCF in Saskatchewan and of the institutional power the CCF-NDP could wield as the third party of the Left upon on a succession of minority Liberal governments. Al-though health insurance was part of the Liberal party platform, actively supported by several reformers within the party, the political decisions of the Liberal governments were in part reactions to the pressures engen-dered by the CCF and NDP.

This third party's viability and longevity were themselves the functions of institutional structures, such as the rules of the game of the Canadian parliamentary system. These rules facilitated the party's formation and gave the reformist Left an important, independent national forum for its platform. With the requirements of party discipline in the Canadian par-liamentary system, and the antipathy of the major parties toward both social reform and western protest in Canada, the Co-operative Common-wealth Federation emerged as the third party of the Left in Canada in the 1930s. Its regional nature gave it both a foothold in the federal parlia-ment (since this concentrated support was well suited to the single-mem-ber plurality system) and the chance to exert considerable political muscle at the provincial level, where third parties with concentrated support could form their own governments.

Even though it was regionally based, the CCF-NDP exerted an impor-tant influence in the national health insurance debate because of its pivo-tal position as the third party of the Left in a political system dominated by a center party. Constrained by party discipline, the Liberal party could not completely absorb the CCF-NDP, but neither could it remain obliv-ious to its message. The third party was able to articulate and sustain the demand for universal and comprehensive government-financed health in-surance by providing an effective public counterweight to the opposition of the medical lobby in setting the public debate on the health insurance issue. The CCF-NDP's presence on the left of the political spectrum made it a potential threat as a vehicle for working-class protest. Because of this, and through its effective manipulation of the parliamentary sys-tem, the CCF-NDP was able to exert considerable pressure on the major parties for health reform. Vis-à-vis the Liberal party, the CCF-NDP repre-sented a potential electoral threat, but also an internal threat. Its presence offered reformers within the center party ammunition to convince their colleagues of the need for action. At the provincial level, the CCF experi-ments in Saskatchewan provided the opportunity to implement hospital and medical insurance along social-democratic principles of universality and comprehensiveness. These experiments served to further influence the national health agenda through the reform precedent they set, the demand for reform they engendered in other provinces, and the successful skirmishes that were fought with health care providers.

In the United States, conflict around the control of the health agenda was considerably more entangled and complex. This is because the most influential messages about health insurance came from a powerful professional lobby that could penetrate a political system with multiple veto points. The counterweights to this message could not exert an independent political voice as in Canada. That is, demands for national health insurance in the United States were most frequently channeled through political institutions under the form of legislative proposals defended by the Democratic party. The Democrats remained deeply divided on questions of health and social policy, and these divisions forced health reformers to strike compromises in order to get legislative progress on the issue and effective party-line voting. The clienteles that favored national health insurance, most importantly labor and the reformist Left, were effectively captured by the Democratic party. As a consequence, these compromises had to appeal to other elements within the party, including influential southern conservatives who controlled powerful institutional levers in the congressional leadership.

Another institutional constraint was the fact that Congress was easily penetrable to the political tactics of organized medicine and the effect of these on individual members. Indeed, this strong medical lobby succeeded both in convincing allies in the two parties to support its position and in targeting proreform legislators in the Democratic party. Because of the forceful nature of the medical lobby's public discourse, health insurance proponents in the United States had to formulate a politically acceptable compromise. This compromise built on existing and successful precedents under the Social Security Act, covering health care benefits for the aged, a specific group around whom a wide base of public support could be built and maintained.

The Limits of Political Culture

The comparative historical analysis reveals that the explanatory power of political culture is related to how culture is "embedded" in institutional phenomena and changes over time. Health policy outcomes were affected by the way in which demand for health insurance was translated through the political system and by how the party system was able to express the different points of view on the issue of health reform. In the American case, the national health insurance platform was effectively stifled within the Democratic party, while in Canada it was a continuous presence in the debate over reform, most visibly through the CCF-NDP.

The passage of health insurance in both countries involved a political struggle that was conditioned by the way societal and political actors were forced to play by the rules of the political game. In Canada, the presence of a party of the Left profoundly shaped the health insurance debate by focusing on the role of government in health care financing, and by influencing the federal and provincial governments to fulfill this role. Universal health insurance did not initially enjoy blanket consensus from political or societal actors. It was the dynamics of the Canadian party system that helped keep it on the public agenda and the structure of Canadian federal and provincial governments that facilitated its passage and enactment.

The two aspects of political culture that are dissimilar in Canada and the United States are cleavages based on language and and on race. However, it is not clear that linguistic cleavages played a role in the development of public health insurance in Canada. There was resistance on the part of Quebec's Union Nationale government to health reform in the 1940s and 1950s, but this was related more to reasons of ideology and of provincial autonomy, similar to resistance from conservative governments in Ontario and Alberta. In the American case, some weight could be given to racial cleavages, although these were not an explicit factor in the health insurance debate. These cleavages were translated in the political system through the strength of southern conservatives within the Democratic party, who were instrumental in stymieing many health reform initiatives. Absent in the American case was a social-democratic counterweight to such resistance.

Canada and the United States have different systems of government-sponsored health insurance because these systems were shaped by different institutional and political dynamics. The establishment of public health insurance in Canada and the United States has also had lasting effects on possibilities for future reform. The institutionalization of universal health insurance in Canada involved a long process of change and experimentation, accomplished in a sense through a series of leaps in the dark. This process was marked first by provincial innovations and then by their diffusion through the involvement of the federal government, wielding the carrot of financing and the stick of sanctions. The favorable public consensus that now exists about the role of government in the Canadian health care system was built up over time and as a result of the relative success of the public system in ensuring the basic health needs of Canadians. While confrontation between government and medical interests persists, these disputes have not yet called into question the fundamental precepts of government-financed health care. This consensus has remained viable not simply because the system is perceived as successful, but also because the fundamental principles underlying universal health insurance have been defined by the extent to which this consensus has become "embedded" in the Canadian political culture.

Such a consensus has yet to be realized in the United States. The limited programs of the 1960s, based on Social Security precedents, reflect the tendency toward compromise inherent in American political institutions and the party system. These compromises have in turn become embedded in the American health care system, and in dominant perceptions of the government's role in health and social reform. The institutionalization of Medicare and Medicaid, while widening the role of government involvement in the health sector, has also set limits on the feasibility of further reform. Health reform continues to be embroiled in political battles involving powerful interest groups, a divided Democratic party, and the confines of bipartisan compromise. But the recurrent resurfacing of national health insurance on the political agenda indicates that the enduring demand for reform still persists and will continue until a satisfactory compromise on health policy is reached in the United States.

If institutions can help explain the divergence in historical developments, they also reveal the constraints and limits to health reform in the new political context ushered in by the implementation of publicly funded health insurance in Canada and the United States. The next chapter reveals how the debates over health care have changed in the two countries since the momentous reforms of the 1960s, and how institutional arrangements and past policy choices have conditioned the direction and fate of subsequent reform strategies.

CHAPTER EIGHT

Point of No Return?
Policy Legacies and the Politics of
Health Reform

THIRTY YEARS after the passage of health insurance legislation in the United States and Canada, health reform remains a controversial issue on both sides of the border. The concerns look the same—cost, access, quality health care—but the controversies and the political contexts are much different. In the United States, recent health reform debates have been framed in terms of whether and how to extend government intervention in the health care sector. In Canada, meanwhile, attention has been focused on whether and how the long-term viability of the single-payer system is threatened by continued cuts in public expenditures.

The way in which health insurance developed in the two countries has had an effect on these recent debates, as institutional arrangements and past policy choices condition subsequent reform strategies. The institutionalization of health policies has contributed to a changing of the rules of the game of health politics, creating new political dynamics between actors and institutions and in turn shaping policy "feedback" and the outcomes of future reform.[1] Thus, although the basic parameters of the debate over health care cost and access remain similar in Canada and the United States, the policies implemented in the 1960s have created very different settings for the politics of health care reform in the 1990s and beyond.

RECENT HEALTH REFORM EFFORTS IN THE UNITED STATES: THE ENDURING DEBATE OVER GOVERNMENT INTERVENTION

With the passage of Medicare and Medicaid in 1965, the U.S. government took on the responsibility of guaranteeing access to health care for those groups most likely to be shut out of the voluntary and employer-based market for health insurance, relegating government's role to that of insuring groups with the highest actuarial risk. The public sector,

---

[1] On policy feedback and institutionalist analysis, see Pierson 1993.

therefore, was constrained to participate in the private market for health care, but with little control over costs. Although both insurance and medical interests were initially hostile to government action, they soon recognized the favorable financial implications of these programs. Senior citizens' groups, relatively minor players in health reform until the 1960s, soon emerged as the powerful "gray lobby," devoted to protecting their entitlements.[2]

The new arrangement suited both providers and recipients of care so long as governments were willing to reimburse them for any "reasonable costs" billed by hospitals and doctors. With the steep increase in the price of health care and the explosion of public expenditures in the United States, however, the focus of health reform soon shifted from improving access to controlling costs. Throughout the 1970s, Democrats in Congress attempted to link access and cost concerns with renewed demands for national health insurance; Senator Edward Kennedy and others even touted the Canadian model as a "natural experiment" for the United States that combined universal access, low costs, and high quality.[3] The enduring divisions within the Democratic party on the issue, the vigor of Republican opposition, and the persistent resistance of provider groups precluded such reform.[4]

Instead of attempting to regulate the costs of health through public administration of universal health insurance (as in Canada), U.S. governments relied on the microregulation of health care provision. The Republican Nixon administration's strategy was to offset renewed pressures for health reform by encouraging private-sector initiatives. The Health Maintenance Organization Act of 1973, for example, was designed to encourage the development of prepaid group plans that could restrain providers and centralize health care delivery.[5] The federal government also attempted to control public expenditures by instituting a "peer review" process among physicians, while states imposed reviews of hospital service utilization under Medicaid. The arrival in power of the Reagan administration accelerated pressure on health care as part of a larger agenda to reduce federal spending in entitlement programs. Federal payments for Medicaid programs were substantially reduced, forcing states to modify their benefits and eligibility criteria. Medicare was a more difficult target, since it enjoyed widespread bipartisan support, bolstered by the political influence of the aged as a clientele group. Instead of dismantling the program, retrenchment efforts focused on regulating the market

---

[2] Pratt 1976, chap. 7.
[3] Lee 1974, 713–16; see also Marmor 1975.
[4] Marmor 1983.
[5] On the development of HMOs, see Brown 1983.

for Medicare services by imposing direct limits on payments to doctors and hospitals. In 1982, the reimbursement of "reasonable costs" was replaced with a prospective schedule of fees based on "Diagnostic Related Groups," and Medicare beneficiaries were encouraged to use "Preferred Provider Organizations."[6]

Cost concerns were not limited to government programs. The establishment and maintenance of negotiated health benefits became a central battle for labor, as business looked for ways to reduce the burgeoning costs associated with providing health insurance for workers. Private insurers, meanwhile, attempted to secure their bottom line by raising premiums, competing for and selecting individuals according to their health risks, and regulating providers in their provision of health care to patients. In addition, the growing number of uninsured strained the capacity of hospital facilities and led to cost-shifting toward patients and their insurers to cover losses.[7] Ironically, American doctors, who had long fought against compulsory national health insurance on the grounds of physician autonomy, now found themselves increasingly regulated by governments, private insurers, and pressure from health maintenance organizations (HMOs)—more regulated, some were even led to think, than their Canadian colleagues working within a public health insurance system.

As health expenditures continued to soar in the United States in the late 1980s, cost concerns became inextricably linked with questions of access to care. The economic downturn of 1990–91 exacerbated the growing uneasiness about health care and costs. Public opinion polls revealed that Americans were increasingly concerned about their access to health insurance and the future viability of the health care system.[8] By 1991, influential business leaders, unions, and provider groups were sounding the alarm on the need for government action to reform the health care system; later that year, Harris Wofford's upset victory over former Attorney General Richard Thornburgh in a special Pennsylvania Senate race revealed the political stakes of the issue. Early in 1992, President Bush proposed a tax credit and health insurance voucher program, but the public's growing dissatisfaction with administration inaction on health reform intensified during the presidential campaign. The recasting of health reform as a "middle-class" issue that affected the health care of working Americans propelled health reform to the forefront of domestic policy debate and contributed to President Bill Clinton's first victory.[9]

---

[6] On a review of these regulatory initiatives, see Morone 1990, chap. 7; and Ruggie 1996, 150–60.

[7] Aaron 1991, 27–37, 73–77.

[8] Jacobs, Shapiro, and Schulman 1993, 394–427.

[9] Peterson 1993, 435–38. On the pivotal events of the early 1990s, see Skocpol 1996, chap. 1; and Hacker 1997, chap. 1.

By the time the Clinton administration began to tackle health reform, several potential alternatives were already being discussed in policy circles.[10] On the one hand, there were proposals emphasizing universal health insurance coverage and access to health care. Interest in the Canadian model resurfaced because of its ability to balance cost control and access to care, leading to suggestions for a "single-payer" government-financed health insurance system, supported by influential health care experts, consumer lobby groups, union organizations, and a sizable number of progressive Democrats.[11] Others in the Democratic party considered a logical approach to health reform to be the extension of universal coverage through Medicare, given the widespread support the program enjoyed in American public opinion. The Democratic leadership in Congress, meanwhile, conscious that the majority of Americans were insured through work-related health benefits, had been promoting the idea of a "play or pay" requirement that would oblige employers to cover their employees or contribute to finance government subsidies for the uninsured. On the other hand, Republican proposals focused on the affordability of health care for individual consumers, and emphasized more incremental reforms in the health care market, such as malpractice reform, and tax credits, vouchers, and medical savings accounts to defray the costs of private insurance.[12]

The solutions proposed reflected the institutional configuration of the American polity and the legacies of existing policies. The Clinton plan that emerged in 1993 was a self-conscious "amalgam of alternatives" that represented a departure from both the basic social insurance precedent of the existing Medicare program and the emphasis on private fee-for-practice health care delivery.[13] The President's Health Security Plan was designed at once to ensure health care coverage for all Americans and to act as a mechanism for cost control through "managed competition" in health insurance markets. This involved government regulation of private insurers through the creation of regionally based "health alliances" that would act as consumer cooperatives to control costs through competition and the spread of managed care. Clinton's reform proposal thus recognized the principle of government intervention in health care, while retaining the legitimacy of private markets in health insurance. As such, it represented an attempt to embrace universality, portability, and accessibility (the premises of the Canadian model), but it sought to achieve these goals through the provision of insurance by third-party payers, rather than through a publicly administered system.

---

[10] For a review of these alternatives, see Blendon, Edwards, and Hyams 1992, 2509–20.

[11] Tolchin 1989, IV–4; Toner 1993, A22.

[12] For a discussion of the congressional bills that represented these different alternatives, see Rubin 1994, 23–28; Rubin and Donovan 1994, 2201–12.

[13] For a discussion of the plan, see Starr 1994.

Nevertheless, the Clinton compromise, aimed at forging a middle path through the public regulation of private health insurance, failed to rally enough support. While social reform advocates were increasingly marginalized in public debates, the insurance and medical lobbies, in alliance with grass-roots advocacy groups, waged highly effective public campaigns against the Clinton proposals and, more broadly, against government involvement in health care. Despite the fact that there had been a widespread recognition of the need for some kind of health reform by business leaders and the health care community, the administration plan also faced powerful opposition from small business. Significantly, the medical lobby, which had waged the previous battles against government intervention in health care, was now overshadowed by the vociferous opposition of the insurance lobby, which had a vested interest in preserving the profitable private health care market.[14]

The President's erstwhile allies, meanwhile, were deeply divided, a situation that did not bode well for health reform. While the AFL-CIO supported the plan, many unions, such as the American Federation of State, County and Municipal Employees, made clear their opposition to "managed competition." Organized labor, however, was itself overshadowed in this round of the health reform debate by the seniors' groups it had helped mobilize during the push for medicare legislation in the 1960s. The American Association of Retired Persons (AARP), whose main concern was the preservation of Medicare and Medicaid, was hesitant about campaigning for the bill and only officially endorsed it in the waning days of the legislative debate. Among consumer groups there was also division, as the Consumers' Union eventually rallied to the President, while Citizen Action remained committed to single-payer health insurance. Within Congress, the Clinton administration faced opposition not only from Republican opponents but also from both the left and right wings within the Democratic caucus.[15] As health care reform collapsed under the weight of widespread public confusion over the complex details of the President's health plan, the spectacle of warring factions on Capitol Hill, and the doomsday prophecies of its opponents, its demise became linked with the Republican "anti-government" crusade against the basic premise of social services provision by the government, including substantial cuts to existing programs.[16]

Institutional constraints led the Clinton administration to embrace managed care competition as an alternative to more sweeping govern-

---

[14] For an overview of interest-group positions, see *Well-Healed: Inside Lobbying for Health Care Reform* (Washington: Center for Public Integrity, 1994).

[15] See Skocpol 1996, chap. 3; Center for Public Integrity 1994, 35–74.

[16] Skocpol 1996, chap. 5: For detailed and vivid accounts of the defeat of the Clinton health plan, see Johnson and Broder 1996; Hacker 1997.

ment involvement, but these constraints also contributed to the demise of the Clinton health reform proposal. The most important constraint had to do with party politics and the internal divisions within the Democratic party on the issue of health reform. Initially, the only unified bloc in Congress included the supporters of the Canadian single-payer model and their allies among consumer and labor groups. The reformist wing of the Democratic party, however, was itself divided on how to approach health reform and unable to capture momentum to build a coalition around alternative strategies. Its support was taken for granted by the Democratic administration, which refused to entertain proposals that were seen as too "radical" and, more importantly, too vulnerable to attack from the Republican opposition and that opposition's allies in the insurance and medical lobbies.[17] But the legacy of Clinton's defeat, like that of Harry Truman's, was to force reform proponents again to retreat to a defensive position and refocus their energies on more incremental strategies.

Meanwhile, however, in the absence of federal action to legislate health reform, the states have been forced to address the issues of access to health care and cost containment. Compared to the Canadian experience, subnational innovation has been more limited in the United States. Although the American states do not have the same jurisdictional responsibility for health policy as the Canadian provinces, state-level administrative strength in this area has expanded considerably, as states developed the capacity to administer jointly funded Medicaid programs. The economic and political constraints faced by the American states, however, have largely precluded their becoming "laboratories" for health care reform.[18] Even if states did have bold plans to extend health care coverage, their limited fiscal capacity makes it extremely difficult for them to implement such reform. This is exacerbated in each state by the same opposition forces that scuttled federal efforts at health reform. The states also face federal constraints such as the Employee Retirement Income Security Act (ERISA), which prevents state legislatures from imposing mandates on employers to provide health insurance for workers. This explains in part why Hawaii's acclaimed "universal" health insurance through employer-based coverage has not been widely adopted by other states.

Under the Clinton plan, the states would have been responsible for administering health insurance reform, with the ability to experiment in doing so, even with a single-payer mechanism. In some state legislatures, particularly in Vermont, Minnesota, and Florida, there was support for

---

[17] On the role of the Left in American health reform, see Navarro 1994.
[18] On the limits of the "laboratory" analogy, see Sparer and Brown 1996, 1181–202.

the single-payer model but no legislation was passed.[19] Although most states have launched health care initiatives in the past decade, their reform efforts have been only incremental for the major part. Indeed, state-level reforms focused primarily on ways to reduce the costs associated with Medicaid and, to some extent, increase access to health care for the uninsured.[20] These incremental and limited health reform efforts point to the limits of state-led reform in the absence of a clear federal policy direction.

The process of "shifting the burden"[21] of health care to the subnational level and the rhetoric of retrenchment of public expenditures are also evident in recent health reform initiatives in Canada. In the Canadian case, however, a different political discourse surrounds the debate, one that is conditioned by the distinct institutional configuration of the Canadian polity and the political stakes associated with a fully institutionalized system of publicly financed universal health insurance.

RECENT HEALTH REFORM IN CANADA: THE SEARCH FOR BALANCE BETWEEN COSTS AND ACCESS

As in the United States, the principal health reform debate in Canada until the 1960s centered on the extent to which government should be responsible for improving access to health care. With the offer of federal cost-sharing guarantees, the provinces rapidly implemented health insurance programs by the early 1970s. The development of a publicly financed system, with negotiated medical fee schedules and hospital budgets, allowed for some measure of cost control. It also avoided many of the problems encountered in the United States, where the public sector participated in private markets with little control over the price of health. However, the fee-for-service system did inflate the demand for health services and overall health expenditures in Canada, and the "open-ended" cost-sharing arrangements of 1957 and 1966 that obliged the federal government to cover almost half of provincial expenditures exacerbated the problem.

By the mid-1970s, the federal government began placing more emphasis on controlling health expenditures. In 1977, the Established Programs Financing Act (EPF) replaced cost sharing with block grants that were tied to GNP growth and, in addition, transferred federal tax points

---

[19] Reformers favoring the single-payer model in the states were advised to "not call it a Canadian system, even if you want one" (Nelson 1994, 11).

[20] On the states and health care reform, see Iglehart 1994, 75–79; and the review in Holahan and Nichols 1996, 50–53.

[21] This expression is, of course, borrowed from Martin, *Shifting the Burden*, 1991.

to the provinces to raise additional revenues.[22] In so doing, the federal government effectively shifted the responsibility to exercise restraint over health care costs to the provinces.

Many of the practices instituted by the provinces to control public expenditure on health care, including allowing for the increased use of extra-billing by doctors and the imposition of user fees, were considered contrary to the spirit of the principles the provinces were pledged to adhere to by federal legislation. The Canada Health Act of 1984, which amalgamated hospital and medical insurance into one statute, attempted to reinforce provincial adhesion to these standards by imposing financial penalties on a province if it violated the principle of equal access to health services. This sparked considerable controversy about federal interference in provincial jurisdiction, in addition to resistance by doctors to what was felt to be a violation of their autonomy and of the terms of their agreement with governments under public health insurance.[23]

As in the United States, concerns about government spending on social programs were reinforced by the arrival in power in September 1984 of the Progressive Conservative party, which was committed to reducing the federal deficit. Like the Republicans in the United States, however, the Conservative government in Canada found its social agenda constrained by public support for existing programs.[24] In the same way that Social Security set the contours of American political discourse, so too had universal health insurance become "embedded" in Canadians' perceptions of their political culture. The institutionalization of a public health insurance system created its own support constituency across a wide spectrum of recipients, but also providers, of health care.

Because of the program's widespread popularity, the federal government was loathe to be saddled with dismantling universal health insurance. Nevertheless, the Conservatives did attempt to rein in social expenditures, generally by applying the same "blame avoidance" tactics as the Reagan administration had in the United States.[25] These attempts to "offload" the deficit onto the provinces involved curtailing federal spending in the health sector, reducing the growth of block grants in 1986 and freezing them in 1991, which effectively further shifted the burden of cost control to the provinces.[26]

The Liberal government that regained power in 1993 pledged to pre-

---

[22] Cost-sharing arrangements and the EPF reforms are discussed in Soderstrom 1978, chap. 4.

[23] On the Canada Health Act and its repercussions, see Taylor 1990, 165–83.

[24] The Mulroney government's social reform agenda is analyzed by Johnson 1988; Rice and Prince 1993.

[25] On "blame avoidance" and public policy strategies, see Weaver 1986, 371–98.

[26] On "deficit offloading," see Boothe and Johnson 1992.

serve funding levels and the federal conditions of the Canada Health Act, but nevertheless followed a somewhat contradictory strategy on health reform.[27] On the one hand, the Liberal government emphasized the importance of the welfare state, and of health insurance in particular, as the epitome of Canadian solidarity and identity. In part to capitalize on this popularity and to appease public concern over the future of the health care system, the Chrétien government convened the National Forum on Health in 1994. The majority of the provinces, however, resisting the federal government's unilateral initiatives in this area of provincial jurisdiction, refused to participate.[28] In addition, the party's centralized vision of the Canadian federation led it into conflict with several provinces as it attempted to pursue a more aggressive strategy in enforcing the terms of the Canada Health Act.

The flipside of this pledge to maintain the welfare state was the Liberal government's commitment to constrain public expenditures. In the virtual absence of the Left in the House of Commons, the Liberal party's drive for deficit reduction met with relatively little resistance. Indeed, the opposition consisted for the most part of two regional third parties with distinct political agendas. The Bloc Québécois included several members from social-democratic backgrounds, but its primary objective was Quebec sovereignty, and thus it argued for more provincial autonomy. At the right end of the Canadian political spectrum, the Reform party was a western-based protest movement with a platform centered on devolution to the provinces to let them introduce market mechanisms into their health care systems.[29] Using the rhetoric of "flexible federalism" to respond to these political challenges, the Liberal government amalgamated health care and other social program funding arrangements into a "super" block grant to the provinces, the Canada Health and Social Transfer. This consolidation, however, was accompanied by substantial cuts in the cash portion of federal transfers, leading to an outcry from the provinces over unilateral imposition of this revenue squeeze, as well as concerns that this withdrawal of funding could disarm the federal government's ability to impose a "national" health care system across the country.[30]

Today, the fiscal pressure on provincial governments has forced them

[27] Keith Banting, quoted in Edward Greenspon: "Ottawa quietly repealing health act, expert alleges," *The Globe and Mail*, 3 May 1995, A4.

[28] Indeed, only three provinces (New Brunswick, Nova Scotia, and Manitoba) sent representatives. On these and other recent conflicts, see Maioni 1996.

[29] "Political Views on Health Care Reform," *Leadership in Health Services* 2, no. 5 (September–October 1993): 25–30.

[30] Phillips 1995, 84; see also Armstrong and Armstrong 1996, 158–160.

to reduce health expenditures, while at the same time try to find a viable balance between access and costs.[31] Although there has been considerable variation among the provinces on how to achieve this, almost all provincial health care systems have been subject to restructuring to some extent in recent years, with primary emphasis on reducing expenditures and reorganizing the delivery of health care.[32] In the provinces this has involved further shifting of responsibility to regional boards charged with controlling the supply of health care. The provincial governments have also tried to shift the burden of cost control by controlling the demand for services and the rationalizing of delivery of care. Pressure from cost control has also reopened the debate, in some provinces, about the viability of the single-payer model, and the potential for privatization of certain parts of the health care sector.[33]

The implementation of health insurance in the provinces involved considerable compromise and sometimes bitter confrontation with medical interests, but the consensus was that doctors would accept negotiated fee schedules in return for professional autonomy. Medical services have continued to be offered on a fee-for-service basis, but cost and access concerns have led many provincial governments to attempt to regulate the supply of health care by imposing limits on physician billing and by intervening in the redistribution of doctors across specialties and regions. While the Canadian Medical Association remains committed to the principle of health insurance, debates over the funding of health care have emboldened certain provincial organizations to flex political muscle. The resurfacing of this issue has provided a window of opportunity to open discussion about the relative merits of the private market and the coexistence of public and private health care. Meanwhile hospital administrators, faced with reduced global budgets that are more stringently enforced, have had to find ways to juggle increasingly limited resources. This has included the reduction of hospital beds, the limitation of new equipment and construction, and the reallocation of services through waiting lists and outpatient or home-based care. In many provinces, including NDP governments in Saskatchewan and British Columbia, hospital closures have been mandated by provincial authorities in an attempt to reduce expenditures. In Quebec, where the health care system was founded on explicitly social-democratic principles of collective responsibility and equal access to care, a succession of governments have at-

---

[31] During the 1980s, numerous provincial commissions and task forces undertook studies of health care. For a review, see Angus 1992, 50–54.

[32] Deber, Mhatre, and Baker 1994, 91–121.

[33] Ruggie 1996, 197–205; Armstrong and Armstrong, 1996, 205–9.

tempted to shift demand away from institutionalized care to alternative forms of health care delivery.[34]

Some provincial governments, particularly Conservative regimes in Ontario and Alberta, have shown an interest in market mechanisms to control the demand for health care. In addition, there has been renewed interest in increasing individual responsibility to pay for health care through co-payments, deductibles, and the imposition of specific "health taxes." The opening of the health care system to the private sector has also been increasing. Several provinces have reduced the range of services covered by public insurance, such as optometry, pharmaceuticals, or dental care. Others have allowed the expansion of private clinics in which medical procedures are covered by public insurance but patients are charged facility fees. In the drive to control health care budgets, however, governments are faced with public resistance to change. Like their neighbors to the south, Canadians are preoccupied with controlling public expenditures and are concerned with the long-term viability of government health programs. At the same time, they remain resistant to change that would infringe upon access to what they consider to be the "right" to health care.

CONCLUSION

Although Canada and the United States took divergent paths in the development of their health care systems, until the 1960s the two polities were engaged in similar public debates about the extent of the role of the state in ensuring access to health care. These debates, however, were conditioned by the presence of different political institutions and partisan systems. In Canada, decentralized federal arrangements encouraged subnational innovations that tested the feasibility of public health insurance. The parliamentary system allowed the federal government to take the lead in diffusing state intervention in the health care sector across Canada.

In the American case, the constraints of the separation of powers and the imperatives of partisan coalition building hampered consensus on health reform. In a highly fragmented political arena, competition between the executive and the legislature precluded the development of coherent health reform. The absence of party discipline and the permeable nature of congressional politics allowed opponents of universal health insurance a greater voice in the political process. State-level innovation was hampered by the absence of federal direction and, in the ab-

---

[34] On the specifics of the Quebec model, see Bergeron and Gagnon 1994.

Canada. House of Commons. 1930–1966. *Debates.*

———. Select Standing Committee on Industrial and International Relations. 1929. *Report, Proceedings and Evidence . . . upon the question of Insurance against Unemployment, Sickness and Invalidity.* Ottawa: King's Printer.

———. Special Committee on Social Security. 1943. *Minutes of Proceedings and Evidence*, Nos. 1–28. Ottawa: King's Printer.

———. Royal Commission on Dominion-Provincial Relations. 1940. *Final Report.* Book 2: Recommendations. Ottawa: King's Printer.

———. Royal Commission on Health Services. 1964. *Final Report.* Vol. 1. Ottawa: Queen's Printer.

United States. Committee on Economic Security. 1935. *Report to the President.* Washington, D.C.: U.S. Government Printing Office.

———. 1935. *Risks to Economic Security Arising Out of Illness.* Washington, D.C.: U.S. Government Printing Office.

United States. Congress. 1935–1965. *Congressional Directory.* 78th–89th Congress. Washington, D.C.: U.S. Government Printing Office.

———. 1935–1965. *Congressional Record.* 78th–89th Congress. Washington, D.C.: U.S. Government Printing Office.

United States. House. 1949. Committee on Interstate and Foreign Commerce. *Hearings on H.R. 4312 and H.R. 4313.* 81st Cong., 1st sess. Washington, D.C.: U.S. Government Printing Office.

———. Committee on Ways and Means. 1959. *Hospital, Nursing Home, and Surgical Benefits for OASI Beneficiaries: Hearings on H.R. 4700.* 86th Cong., 1st sess. Washington, D.C.: U.S. Government Printing Office.

———. 1961. *Health Services for the Aged under the Social Security System: Hearings on H.R. 4222.* 87th Cong., 1st sess. Washington, D.C.: U.S. Government Printing Office.

———. 1963, 1964. *Medical Care for the Aged: Hearings on H.R. 3920.* 88th Cong., 1st and 2d sess. Washington, D.C.: U.S. Government Printing Office.

———. Subcommittee of the Committee on Labor. 1935. *Unemployment, Old Age and Social Insurance: Hearings before a Subcommittee of the Committee on Labor on H.R. 2827 (H.R. 2859, H.R. 185, H.R. 10).* 74th Cong., 1st sess. Washington, D.C.: U.S. Government Printing Office.

United States. Senate. Committee on Education and Labor. 1939. *To Establish a National Health Program: Hearings before a Subcommittee of the Committee on Education and Labor on S. 1620.* 74th Cong., 1st sess. Washington, D.C.: U.S. Government Printing Office.

———. Committee on Finance. 1946. *National Health Program: Hearings before the Committee on Finance on S. 1606.* 79th Cong., 2d sess. Washington, D.C.: U.S. Government Printing Office.

———. Committee on Labor and Public Welfare. 1947, 1948. *National Health Program: Hearings before a Subcommittee of the Committee on Labor and Public Welfare on S. 545 and S. 1320.* 80th Cong., 1st and 2d sess. Washington, D.C.: U.S. Government Printing Office.

———. 1949. *National Health Program: Hearings before a Subcommittee of the Committee on Labor and Public Welfare on S. 1106, S. 1456, S. 1581, and S. 1679.* 81st Cong., 1st sess. Washington, D.C.: U.S. Government Printing Office.

sence of federal standards, by the tendency of states to compete against one another in the "race to the bottom" in social policy matters.

In the decades since the implementation of health insurance, the delivery of health care in Canada and the United States has remained relatively similar, but the two countries have continued to differ significantly on the extent of government intervention in the system. Canada has institutionalized universal, publicly financed health insurance, while the United States has engaged on a path that has targeted specific groups for public coverage. Nevertheless, the basic priorities of health reform have remained remarkably similar: how to render health care more accessible and how to make the system more cost efficient. The difference has been that, in Canada, policy solutions to these problems have continued to rely upon government intervention, while in the United States the battle has placed proponents of moderate public involvement in opposition to advocates of free markets in health care.

In Canada, the extent to which provincial health care systems can allow a private market to exist for insurance and services is limited by two things: the federal conditions of equal access and public administration; and, significantly, public opinion. Federal governments have been adroit at claiming credit for the popularity of health insurance and defending the principles of the Canada Health Act, but they have recently been engaged in avoiding blame for the problems confronting the system in the wake of reduced social expenditures. The Liberal party, which had embraced the Left's health policy agenda in the 1960s, is moving right of center to face new political challenges in the 1990s.

As the federal government continues to cut transfer payments to the provinces, the legitimacy of the federal government's actions in imposing the norms of the system may be eroding. The sustaining feature of public health insurance in Canada has been the consensus and satisfaction of the "stakeholders" in the system, the recipients and providers of health care. Reductions in public spending on health care have already led to protest and resistance. In the long run, however, the more enduring consequence of these cuts may be the further erosion of the consensus in favor of funding of the system by taxpayers. As the rhetoric of the Right gains currency in many provinces, it is clear that Canada is not immune to polarized ideological debates about the role of the state in the social arena.

While the early 1990s saw pundits asking whether the United States would adopt a "Canadian-style" single-payer model, a new question may be to what extent is Canada converging toward an "American-style" market-based system. There is an inherent irony in the situation that, as some Americans glance northwards for a model of health care reform, some Canadians may be tempted to look south in search of alternative solutions. Whether Canada and the United States will somehow meet at a midpoint is unlikely, but this will depend on the nature of the political institutions that condition the health care debate in the two countries, and on their different policy histories in health insurance development.

The United States and Canada face important choices about the future direction of the welfare state. Although the two countries took divergent paths in the past, Canadians are concerned with essentially the same issues as are their American neighbors, namely how to fashion an affordable, comprehensive health care system that ensures access to fine-quality health care. In Canada, support for universal health insurance took many years to develop, as evidenced by the political struggles and practical experiments in its history, and it is likely to endure so long as the system is perceived as successful in responding to the needs of Canadians. In the American context, this process has taken much longer and has involved even more bitter political struggles. The emergence of a consensus over the right to health care and the role of government in guaranteeing that right is possible, but it will depend on the ability of the health reformers to harness support from political actors and the general public behind a program that promises fundamental change and effectively delivers on that promise.

Bibliography

Manuscript Collections

National Archives of Canada, Ottawa, Ontario (NAC)
  Record Group 29, *Records of the Department of National Health*
  Record Group 33, *Records of the Royal Commission on Health Ser*
  Manuscript Group 26 J, *William Lyon Mackenzie King Papers*
  Manuscript Group 26 N, *Lester Bowles Pearson Papers*
  Manuscript Group 27 III B 5, *Ian A. Mackenzie Papers*
  Manuscript Group 28 I 103, *Canadian Labour Congress*
  Manuscript Group 28 IV 1, *Co-operative Commonwealth Fed
    Democratic Party*
  Manuscript Group 32 B 12, *Paul Martin Papers*
  Manuscript Group 32 C 59, *Stanley H. Knowles Papers*
National Archives and Records Administration, Washington, D.C. (
  Record Group 47, *Central Files of the Social Security Board (CEN*
  Record Group 47, *Committee on Economic Security (CES)*
  Record Group 47, *Records of the Office of Research and Statistics (*
  Record Group 174, *Records of the Department of Labor (DOL)*
  Record Group 235, *Records of the Federal Security Agency (FSA)*
State Historical Society of Wisconsin, Madison, Wisconsin (SHSW)
  Arthur J. Altmeyer Papers
  Wilbur J. Cohen Papers
  Edwin E. Witte Papers
  American Federation of Labor Records (AFL)
Columbia Oral History Collection, Columbia University, New York, N
  Reminiscences of Arthur J. Altmeyer

Government Documents

British Columbia. 1932. *Final Report of the Royal Commission on
  Insurance and Maternity Benefits.* Victoria: King's Printer.
———. 1935. *A Plan for Health Insurance for British Columbia.*
  partment of the Provincial Secretary.
Canada. Dominion-Provincial Conference on Reconstruction. 1945
  the Government of Canada. Ottawa: King's Printer.
———. Federal-Provincial Conference. 1955 *Proceedings of the Fe
  cial Conference, 1955.* Ottawa: Queen's Printer.
———. 1965. *Proceedings of the Federal-Provincial Conference, 1
  Queen's Printer.
———. Health Canada. 1996. *National Health Expenditures in Ca
  1994.* Ottawa: Minister of Supply and Services Canada.

United States. General Accounting Office. 1991. *Canadian Health Insurance: Lessons for the United States.* Washington, D.C.: U.S. Government Printing Office.

————. Interdepartmental Committee to Coordinate Health and Welfare Activities. 1938. *Proceedings of the National Health Conference.* Washington, D.C.: U.S. Government Printing Office.

————. President. *Public Papers of the Presidents of the United States: Harry S. Truman, 1945–1953.* Washington, D.C.: U.S. Government Printing Office.

————. *John F. Kennedy, 1960–1963.* Washington, D.C.: U.S. Government Printing Office.

————. *Lyndon B. Johnson, 1963–1969.* Washington, D.C.: U.S. Government Printing Office.

Primary Sources

American Federation of Labor. 1934–1955. *Report of Proceedings of the [. . .] Annual Convention of the American Federation of Labor.* Washington, D.C.: AFL.

American Federation of Labor–Congress of Industrial Organizations. 1957–1965. *Report of the Proceedings of the AFL-CIO [. . .] Constitutional Convention.* Washington, D.C.: AFL-CIO.

Canadian Congress of Labour. 1941–1955. *Proceedings of the [. . .] Annual Convention.* Ottawa: The Congress.

Canadian Labour Congress. 1956–1966. *Report of the Proceedings of the [. . .] Constitutional Convention.* Ottawa: The Congress.

Congressional Digest. 1946. *The Proposal for a Compulsory Federal "Health Insurance" Program.* Vol. 25, Nos. 8–9. Washington, D.C.: Congressional Digest Corporation.

Congressional Quarterly. 1946–1965. *Congressional Quarterly Almanac.* Washington, D.C.: Congressional Quarterly.

Congress of Industrial Organizations. 1938–1955. *Proceedings of the [. . .] Constitutional Convention of the Congress of Industrial Organizations.* Washington, D.C.: The Congress.

Gallup, George H. 1972. *The Gallup Poll: Public Opinion, 1935–1971.* Volumes 1, 2, 3. New York: Random House.

Organisation for Economic Co-operation and Development. 1985. *Measuring Health Care, 1960–1983.* Social Policy Studies No. 2. Paris: OECD.

————. 1987. *Financing and Delivering Health Care: A Comparative Analysis of OECD Countries.* Social Policy Studies No. 4. Paris: OECD.

————. 1990. *Health Care Systems in Transition: The Search for Efficiency.* Social Policy Studies No. 7. Paris: OECD.

————. 1995. *New Directions in Health Care Policy.* Health Policy Studies No. 7. Paris: OECD.

Trades and Labor Congress of Canada. 1931–1955. *Report of the Proceedings of the [. . .] Annual Convention.* Ottawa: Progressive Printers.

Secondary Sources

Aaron, Henry J. 1991. *Serious and Unstable Condition: Financing America's Health Care.* Washington: Brookings Institution.

Abella, Irving. 1973. *Nationalism, Communism and Canadian Labour.* Toronto: University of Toronto Press.

Alford, Robert R. 1975. *Health Care Politics: Ideological and Interest Group Barriers to Reform.* Chicago: University of Chicago Press.

Altmeyer, Arthur J. 1966. *The Formative Years of Social Security.* Madison: University of Wisconsin Press.

Amenta, Edwin. 1991. "Making the Most of a Case Study: Theories of the Welfare State and the American Experience." *International Journal of Comparative Sociology.* 32 (January/April): 172–94.

Anderson, Odin W. 1968. *The Uneasy Equilibrium: Private and Public Financing of Health Services in the United States, 1875–1965.* New Haven: College and University Press.

Andrews, Margaret W. 1983. "The Course of Medical Opinion on State Health Insurance in British Columbia, 1919–1939." *Histoire sociale/Social History* 25 (May): 129–41.

Angus, Douglas E. 1992. "A Great Canadian Prescription: Take Two Commissioned Studies and Call Me in the Morning." In R. Deber and G. Thompson, eds., *Restructuring Canada's Health Services System: How Do We Get There from Here?* pp. 49–62. Toronto: University of Toronto Press.

Annis, Edward R. 1963. "Government Health Care: First the Aged, Then Everyone." *Current History* 45 (August): 104–9.

Anton, Thomas J. 1989. *American Federalism and Public Policy: How the System Works.* Philadelphia: Temple University Press.

Armstrong, Pat, and Hugh Armstrong. 1996. *Wasting Away: The Undermining of Canadian Health Care.* Toronto: Oxford University Press Canada.

Babcock, Robert H. 1974. *Gompers in Canada: A Study in American Continentalism Before the First World War.* Toronto: University of Toronto Press.

Badgley, Robin F., and Samuel Wolfe. 1967. *Doctors' Strike: Medical Care and Conflict in Saskatchewan.* Toronto: Macmillan of Canada.

Banting, Keith G. 1987. *The Welfare State and Canadian Federalism.* 2d ed. Montreal: McGill-Queen's University Press.

Beck, J. Murray. 1967. "The Democratic Process at Work in Canadian General Elections." In J. Courtney, ed., *Voting in Canada*, pp. 2–31. Scarborough, Ont.: Prentice-Hall of Canada.

Bell, David J. 1992. *The Roots of Disunity: A Study of Canadian Political Culture.* Toronto: Oxford University Press Canada.

Bennett, Arnold. 1987. *The History of the Labour Movement in Quebec.* Montreal: Black Rose Books.

Bensel, Richard F. 1984. *Sectionalism and American Political Development: 1880–1980.* Madison: University of Wisconsin Press.

Bergeron, Pierre, and France Gagnon. 1994. "La prise en charge étatique de la santé au Québec." In V. Lemieux, P. Bergeron, C. Bégin, and G. Bélanger, eds., *Le Système de santé au Québec: Organisations, acteurs et enjeux*, pp. 9–32. Sainte-Foy: Presses de l'Université Laval.

Berry, Jeffrey M. 1984. *The Interest Group Society*. Boston: Little, Brown.

Blendon, Robert J. 1989. "Three Systems: A Comparative Survey." *Health Management Quarterly* 9(1): 2–10.

Blendon, Robert J., Jennifer N. Edwards, and Andrew L. Hyams. 1992. "Making the Critical Choices." *Journal of the American Medical Association* 267 (May 13): 2509–20.

Blendon, Robert J., Robert Leitman, Ian Morrison, and Karen Donelan. 1990. "Satisfaction with Health Systems in Ten Nations." *Health Affairs* 9 (summer): 185–92.

Blendon, Robert J., et al. 1995. "Who Has the Best Health Care System? A Second Look." *Health Affairs* 14 (winter): 220–30.

Blishen, Bernard R. 1969. *Doctors and Doctrines: The Ideology of Medical Care in Canada*. Toronto: University of Toronto Press.

Boothe, Paul, and Barbara Johnson. 1992. "Stealing the Emperor's Clothes: Deficit Offloading and National Standards in Health Care." *Papers in Political Economy*. London, Ont.: University of Western Ontario.

Bothwell, Roberts. 1978. "The Health of the Common People." In J. English and J. O. Stubbs, eds., *Mackenzie King: Widening the Debate*. Toronto: Macmillan.

Bothwell, Robert S., and John R. English. 1981. "Pragmatic Physicians: Canadian Medicine and Health Care Insurance, 1910–1945." In S.E.D. Shortt, ed., *Medicine in Canadian Society: Historical Perspectives*, pp. 479–93. Montreal: McGill-Queen's University Press.

Brodie, Janine, and Jane Jenson. 1988. *Crisis, Challenge and Change: Party and Class in Canada Revisited*. Ottawa: Carleton University Press.

Brown, Lawrence D. 1983. *Politics and Health Care Organization: HMOs as Federal Policy*. Washington: Brookings Institution.

Bryden, Kenneth. 1974. *Old Age Pensions and Policy Making in Canada*. Montreal: McGill-Queen's University Press.

Burnham, Walter Dean. 1970. *Critical Elections and the Mainspring of American Politics*. New York: W. W. Norton.

Burrow, James G. 1963. *AMA, Voice of American Medicine*. Baltimore: Johns Hopkins University Press.

Cairns, Alan C. 1968. "The Electoral System and the Party System in Canada, 1921–1965." *Canadian Journal of Political Science* 1 (March): 55–80.

———. 1977. "The Governments and Societies of Canadian Federalism." *Canadian Journal of Political Science* 10 (December): 695–725.

———. 1986. "The Embedded State: State-Society Relations in Canada." In K. Banting, ed., *State and Society: Canada in Comparative Perspective*, pp. 53–86. Toronto: University of Toronto Press.

Cameron, David R. 1978. "The Expansion of the Public Economy: A Comparative Analysis." *American Political Science Review* 72 (December): 1243–61.

Campbell, Colin, and William Christian. 1996. *Parties, Leaders, and Ideologies in Canada*. Toronto: McGraw-Hill Ryerson.

Caplan, Gerald. 1973. *The Dilemma of Canadian Socialism: The C.C.F. in On-tario.* Toronto: McClelland and Stewart.

Carrigan, D. Owen. 1968. *Canadian Party Platforms 1867–1968.* Toronto: Copp Clark.

Carty, R. K., ed. 1992. *Canadian Political Party Systems.* Peterborough, Ont.: Broadview Press.

Carty, R. K., and David Stewart.1996. "Parties and Party Systems." In C. Dunn, ed., *Provinces: Canadian Provincial Politics*, pp. 63–94. Peterborough, Ont.: Broadview Press.

Castles, Francis G. 1982. "The Impact of Parties on Public Expenditure," pp. 21–96. In F. Castles, ed., *The Impact of Parties.* Beverly Hills, Calif.: Sage.

Castles, Francis G., and Vance Merrill. 1989. "Towards a General Model of Pub-lic Policy Outcomes." *Journal of Theoretical Politics* 1 (April): 177–212.

Cates, Jerry. 1983. *Insuring Inequality: Administrative Leadership in Social Secu-rity, 1935–54.* Ann Arbor: University of Michigan Press.

Center for Public Integrity. 1994. *Well-Healed: Inside Lobbying for Health Care Reform.* Washington: Center for Public Integrity.

Clarke, Harold D., Jane Jenson, Lawrence Le Duc, and Jon H. Pammett. 1996. *Absent Mandate: Canadian Electoral Politics in an Era of Restructuring.* Van-couver: Gage.

Coburn, David, George M. Torrance, and Joseph M. Kaufert. 1983. "Medical Dominance in Canada in Historical Perspective: The Rise and Fall of Medi-cine?" *International Journal of Health Services* 13:407–32.

Contandriopoulos, André-Pierre, et al. 1993. *Regulatory Mechanisms in the Health Care Systems of Canada and Other Industrialized Countries: Description and Assessment.* Working paper no. 93-01, Cost-effectiveness of the Canadian Health Care System, Queen's-University of Ottawa Economic Projects.

Coughlin, Richard M. 1980. *Ideology, Public Opinion and Welfare Policy: Atti-tudes toward Taxes and Spending in Industrialized Societies.* Berkeley: Institute of International Studies, University of California.

Crotty, William. 1985. *The Party Game.* New York: W. H. Freeman.

Cutright, Phillips. 1965. "Political Structure, Economic Development and Na-tional Social Security Programs." *American Journal of Sociology* 70 (March): 537–50.

Danzon, Patricia. 1992. "Hidden Overhead Costs: Is Canada's System Really Less Expensive?" *Health Affairs* 11 (spring): 21–43.

Davis, Mike. 1986. *Prisoners of the American Dream: Politics and Economy in the History of the US Working Class.* London: Verso.

Deber, Raisa B., Sharmila L. Mhatre, and G. Ross Baker. 1994. "A Review of Provincial Initiatives," pp. 91–124. In A. Blomqvist and D. Brown, eds., *Limits to Care: Reforming Canada's Health System in an Age of Restraint.* Toronto: C. D. Howe.

Derthick, Martha. 1979. *Policymaking for Social Security.* Washington: Brookings Institution.

Dick, William. 1972. *Labor and Socialism in America: The Gompers Era.* Port Washington, N.Y.: Kennikat Press.

Doern, G. Bruce, and Richard W. Phidd. 1992. *Canadian Public Policy: Ideas, Structure, Process.* 2d ed. Scarborough, Ont.: Nelson Canada.

Duverger, Maurice. 1954. *Political Parties: Their Organization and Activities in the Modern State.* Translated by Barbara and Robert North. London: Methuen.

Dyck, Rand. 1996. *Canadian Politics: Critical Approaches.* 2d ed. Scarborough, Ont.: Nelson Canada.

Ehrenreich, Barbara. 1970. *The American Health Empire: Power, Profits, and Medicine.* New York: Random House.

Elkins, David J., and Richard Simeon. 1979. "A Cause in Search of an Effect, or What Does Political Culture Explain?" *Comparative Politics* 11 (January): 127–45.

Epstein, Leon D. 1964. "A Comparative Study of Canadian Parties." *American Political Science Review* 58 (March): 46–59.

Erskine, Hazel. 1975. "The Polls—Health Insurance." *Public Opinion Quarterly* 39 (spring): 128–43.

Esping-Andersen, Gøsta. 1985. *Politics against Markets: The Social Democratic Road to Power.* Princeton: Princeton University Press.

———. 1990. *The Three Worlds of Welfare Capitalism.* Princeton: Princeton University Press.

Evans, Robert G. 1982. "Health Care in Canada: Patterns of Funding and Regulation." In G. McLachlan and A. Maynard, eds., *The Public/Private Mix for Health: The Relevance and Effects of Change*, pp. 369–424. London: Nuffield Provincial Hospitals Trust.

———. 1990. "Tension, Compression, and Shear: Directions, Stresses, and Outcomes of Health Care Cost Control." *Journal of Health Politics, Policy and Law* 15 (winter): 101–28.

Evans, Robert G., et al. 1989. "Controlling Health Expenditures—The Canadian Reality." *New England Journal of Medicine* 320 (March 2): 571–77.

Falk, I. S. 1936. *Security against Sickness: A Study of Health Insurance.* Garden City, N.Y.: Doubleday, Doran and Company.

Finkel, Alvin. 1989. *The Social Credit Phenomenon in Alberta.* Toronto: University of Toronto Press.

Fishbein, Morris. 1947. *A History of the American Medical Association, 1847 to 1947.* Philadelphia: W. B. Saunders.

Fisher, Robin. 1991. *Duff Pattullo of British Columbia.* Toronto: University of Toronto Press.

Flanagan, Thomas. 1995. *Waiting for the Wave: The Reform Party and Preston Manning.* Toronto: Stoddart.

Fox, Daniel M. 1986. *Health Policies, Health Politics: The British and American Experience 1911–1965.* Princeton: Princeton University Press.

Free, Lloyd, and Hadley Cantril. 1967. *The Political Beliefs of Americans.* New Brunswick, N.J.: Rutgers University Press.

Fuchs, Victor R., and James S. Hahn. 1990. "How Does Canada Do It? A Comparison of Expenditures for Physicians' Services in the United States and Canada." *New England Journal of Medicine* 323 (September 27): 884–90.

Fulton, M. Jane. 1993. *Canada's Health Care System: Bordering on the Possible.* New York: Faulkner & Gray.

Fulton, M. Jane, and W. T. Stanbury. 1985. "Comparative Lobbying Strategies in Influencing Health Care Policy." *Canadian Public Administration* 28 (summer): 269–300.

Gais, Thomas L. 1996. *Improper Influence: Campaign Finance Law, Political Interest Groups and the Problem of Equality.* Ann Arbor: University of Michigan Press.

Gais, Thomas L., Mark A. Peterson, and Jack L. Webb. 1984. "Interest Groups, Iron Triangles, and Representative Institutions in American National Government." *British Journal of Political Science* 14 (April): 161–85.

Galenson, Walter. 1986. "The Historical Role of American Trade Unionism." In S. M. Lipset, ed., *Unions in Transition: Entering the Second Century*, pp. 39–73. San Francisco: Institute for Contemporary Studies.

Gibbins, Roger. 1993. "A Tale of Two Senates." In D. Thomas, ed., *Canada and the United States: Differences that Count*, pp. 162–176. Peterborough, Ont.: Broadview Press.

Gillespie, J. David. 1993. *Politics at the Periphery: Third Parties in Two-Party America.* Columbia: University of South Carolina Press.

Goldmann, Franz. 1948. "Labor's Attitude Toward Health Insurance." *Industrial and Labor Relations Review* 2 (October): 90–98.

Granatstein, J. L. 1967. *The Politics of Survival: The Conservative Party of Canada, 1939–1945.* Toronto: University of Toronto Press.

———. 1986. *Canada, 1957–1967.* Toronto: McClelland and Stewart.

Gray, Gwendolyn. 1991. *Federalism and Health Policy: The Development of Health Systems in Canada and Australia.* Toronto: University of Toronto Press.

Grayson, Linda, ed., 1971. *The Wretched of Canada: Letters to R. B. Bennett 1930–1935.* Toronto: University of Toronto Press.

Greenstone, J. David. 1969. *Labor in American Politics.* Chicago: University of Chicago Press.

Guest, Dennis. 1980. *The Emergence of Social Security in Canada.* Vancouver: University of British Columbia Press.

Hacker, Jacob S. 1997. *The Road to Nowhere: The Genesis of President Clinton's Plan for Health Security.* Princeton: Princeton University Press.

Hamby, Alonzo. 1972. "The Vital Center, the Fair Deal and the Quest for a Liberal Political Economy." *American Historical Review* 77 (June): 653–78.

Hanson, Russell L. 1993. "Defining a Role for States in a Federal Health Care System." *American Behavioral Scientist* 36 (July–August): 760–81.

Harris, Richard. 1966. *A Sacred Trust.* New York: New American Library.

Hartmann, Susan M. 1971. *Truman and the 80th Congress.* Columbia: University of Missouri Press.

Hartz, Louis. 1955. *The Liberal Tradition in America: An Interpretation of American Political Thought Since the Revolution.* New York: Harcourt, Brace.

Hatcher, Gordon. 1981. *Universal Free Health Care in Canada, 1947–1977.* Bethesda, Md.: U.S. Department of Health and Human Services, National Institute of Health.

Hatcher, Gordon H., Peter R. Hatcher, and Eleanor C. Hatcher. 1984. "Health

Services in Canada." In M. Raffel, ed., *Comparative Health Systems: Descriptive Analyses of Fourteen National Health Systems*, pp. 86–132. University Park: Pennsylvania State University Press.

Heclo, Hugh. 1974. *Modern Social Policies in Britain and Sweden*. New Haven: Yale University Press.

Hellander, Ida, J. Moloo, D. Himmelstein, S. Woolhandler, and S. Wolfe. 1995. "The Growing Epidemic of Uninsurance: New Data on the Health Insurance Coverage of Americans." *International Journal of Health Services* 25, no. 3: 377–92.

Hicks, Alexander, M., and Duane H. Swank. 1992. "Politics, Institutions, and Welfare Spending in Industrialized Democracies, 1960–82." *American Political Science Review* 86 (September): 658–74.

Hirschman, Albert O. 1970. *Exit, Voice and Loyalty: Responses to Decline in Firms, Organizations, and States*. Cambridge: Harvard University Press.

Hirshfield, Daniel. 1970. *The Lost Reform: The Campaign for Compulsory Health Insurance in the United States from 1932 to 1943*. Cambridge: Harvard University Press.

Holahan, John, and Len Nichols. 1996. "State Health Policy in the 1990s." In R. Rich and W. White, eds, *Health Policy, Federalism, and the American States*, pp. 39–70. Washington: Urban Institute.

Hollingsworth, J. Rogers. 1986. *A Political Economy of Medicine: Great Britain and the United States*. Baltimore: Johns Hopkins University Press.

Horowitz, Gad. 1966. "Conservatism, Liberalism and Socialism in Canada: An Interpretation." *Canadian Journal of Economics and Political Science* 32 (May): 143–71.

Iglehart, John K. 1986. "Health Policy Report: Canada's Health Care System, Part 2." *New England Journal of Medicine* 315 (September 18): 778–85.

———. 1994. "Health Care Reform—The States." *New England Journal of Medicine* 330 (January 6): 75–79.

Immergut, Ellen M. 1992. *Health Politics: Interests and Institutions in Western Europe*. New York: Cambridge University Press.

Irving, Allan. 1987. "The Development of a Provincial Welfare State: British Columbia, 1900–1939." In A. Moscovitch and J. Albert, eds., *The Benevolent State: The Growth of Welfare in Canada*, pp. 155–74. Toronto: Garamond Press.

Jacobs, Lawrence R. 1992. "Institutions and Culture: Health Policy and Public Opinion in the U.S. and Britain." *World Politics* 44 (January): 179–209.

———. 1993. *The Health of Nations: Public Opinion and the Making of American and British Health Policy*. Ithaca: Cornell University Press.

Jacobs, Lawrence R., and Robert Y. Shapiro. 1993–94. "The Duality of Public Opinion: Personal Interests and National Interest in Health Care Reform." *Domestic Affairs* 2 (winter): 245–59.

———. 1994. "Questioning the Conventional Wisdom on Public Opinion toward Health Reform." *PS: Political Science & Politics* 27 (June): 208–14.

Jacobs, Lawrence R., Robert Y. Shapiro, and Eli C. Schulman. 1993. "Trends: Medical Care in the United States—an Update." *Public Opinion Quarterly* 57 (fall): 394–427.

Johnson, Andrew F. 1988. "Canadian Social Services Beyond 1984: A Neo-Liberal Agenda." In A. Gollner and D. Salée, eds., *Canada Under Mulroney: An End of Term Report*, pp. 265–83. Montréal: Véhicule Press.

Johnson, Haynes, and David S. Broder. 1996. *The System: The American Way of Politics at the Breaking Point*. Boston: Little, Brown.

Kaim-Caudle, P. R. 1973. *Comparative Social Policy and Social Security: A Ten-Country Study*. London: Martin Robertson.

Kelley, Stanley. 1956. *Professional Public Relations and Political Power*. Baltimore: Johns Hopkins University Press.

Kennedy, Frank R. 1954. "The American Medical Association: Power, Purpose, and Politics in Organized Medicine." *Yale Law Journal* 63 (May): 938–1022.

Key, V. O. 1964. *Politics, Parties, and Pressure Groups*. 5th ed. New York: Thomas Crowell Company.

Kilgour, D. E. 1963. "Canadian Health Insurance: Observations from Ringside." *New York State Journal of Medicine* 63 (March 1): 726–31.

King, Anthony. 1973. "Ideas, Institutions and the Politics of Government: A Comparative Analysis." Pts. 1 and 2; pt. 3. *British Journal of Political Science* 33 (July): 291–313; 33 (October): 409–23.

Kitchen, Brigitte. 1987. "The Introduction of Family Allowances in Canada." In A. Moscovitch and J. Albert, eds., *The Benevolent State: The Growth of Welfare in Canada*, pp. 222–41. Toronto: Garamond.

Klass, Gary M. 1985. "Explaining America and the Welfare State: An Alternative Theory." *British Journal of Political Science* 15 (October): 427–50.

Korpi, Walter. 1983. *The Democratic Class Struggle*. London: Routledge and Kegan Paul.

———. 1989. "Power, Politics and State Autonomy in the Development of Social Citizenship: Social Rights During Sickness in Eighteen OECD Countries Since 1930." *American Sociological Review* 54 (June): 309–28.

Krueger, Cynthia. 1971. "Prairie Protest: The Medicare Conflict in Saskatchewan." In S. M. Lipset, *Agrarian Socialism: The Cooperative Commonwealth Federation in Saskatchewan*. Rev. ed., pp. 405–34. Berkeley: University of California Press.

Kudrle, Robert T., and Theodore R. Marmor. 1981. "The Development of Welfare States in North America." In P. Flora and A. Heidenheimer, eds., *The Development of Welfare States in Europe and America*, pp. 81–121. New Brunswick, N.J.: Transaction Books.

Kunitz, Stephen J. 1992. "Socialism and Social Insurance in the U.S. and Canada." In C. Naylor, ed., *Canadian Health Care and the State: A Century of Evolution*. Montreal: McGill-Queen's University Press.

Lawson, Kay. 1968. *Political Parties and Democracy in the United States*. New York: Charles Scribner.

Leatt, Peggy, and A. Paul Williams. "The Health Systems of Canada." In M. Raffel, *Health Case and Reform in Industrialized Countries*, pp. 1–28. University Park: Pennsylvania State University Press, 1997.

Leclair, Maurice. 1975. "The Canadian Health Care System." In S. Andreopoulos, ed., *National Health Insurance: Can We Learn from Canada?* pp. 11–96. New York: John Wiley.

Lee, Sidney S. 1974. "Health Insurance in Canada—An Overview and Commentary." *New England Journal of Medicine* 290 (March 28): 713–16.

Lehmbruch, Gerhard. 1984. "Concertation and the Structure of Corporatist Networks." In J. Goldthorpe, ed., *Order and Conflict in Contemporary Capitalism*, pp. 60–80. New York: Oxford University Press.

Leman, Christopher. 1977. "Patterns of Policy Development: Social Security in the United States and Canada." *Public Policy* 25 (spring): 261–91.

Leman, Christopher. 1980. *The Collapse of Welfare Reform: Political Institutions, Policy, and the Poor in Canada and the United States.* Cambridge: MIT Press.

Leuchtenburg, William E. 1963. *Franklin D. Roosevelt and the New Deal.* New York: Harper and Row.

Lewis, David. 1981. *The Good Fight: Political Memoirs, 1909–1958.* Toronto: Macmillan.

Lichtenstein, Nelson. 1989. "From Corporatism to Collective Bargaining: Organized Labor and the Eclipse of Social Democracy in the Postwar Era." In S. Fraser and G. Gerstle, eds., *The Rise and Fall of the New Deal Order, 1930–1980*, pp. 122–52. Princeton: Princeton University Press.

Lijphart, Arend. 1971. "Comparative Politics and the Comparative Method." *American Political Science Review* 65 (December): 682–93.

Lipset, Seymour Martin. 1954. "Democracy in Alberta (Part 1)." *Canadian Forum* (November): 175–77.

———. 1970. "Revolution and Counterrevolution: The United States and Canada." In S. M. Lipset, ed., *Revolution and Counterrevolution: Change and Persistence in Social Structures*, pp. 37–76. New York: Anchor Books.

———. 1971. *Agrarian Socialism: The Cooperative Commonwealth Federation in Saskatchewan.* Rev. ed. Berkeley: University of California Press.

———. 1977. "Why No Socialism in the United States?" In S. Bialer and S. Sluzar, eds., *Sources of Contemporary Radicalism*, pp. 31–149. Boulder, Colo.: Westview Press.

———. 1983. "Roosevelt and the Protest of the 1930s." *Minnesota Law Review* 68 (December): 273–98.

———. 1986. "North American Labor Movements: A Comparative Perspective." In S. M. Lipset, ed., *Unions in Transition: Entering the Second Century*, pp. 421–52. San Francisco: ICS Press.

———. 1990. *Continental Divide: The Values and Institutions of the United States and Canada.* New York: Routledge.

Lubove, Roy. 1986. *The Struggle for Social Security, 1900–1935.* 2d ed. Pittsburgh: University of Pittsburgh Press.

Maioni, Antonia. 1995. "Nothing Succeeds Like the Right Kind of Failure: Postwar National Health Insurance Initiatives in Canada and the United States." *Journal of Health Politics, Policy and Law* 20 (spring): 5–30.

———. 1996. "Federalism and Health Care Reform in the Canadian Provinces." Paper presented at the Canadian Political Science Association Meetings, St. Catharines, Ontario, June 4.

———. 1997. "Parting at the Crossroads: The Development of Health Insurance in the United States and Canada." *Comparative Politics* 29 (July): 411–31.

Mallory, James R. 1965. "The Five Faces of Federalism." In P.-A. Crépeau and C. B. Macpherson, *The Future of Canadian Federalism*, pp. 3–15. Toronto: University of Toronto Press.

Manfredi, Christopher P. 1993. *Judicial Power and the Charter: Canada and the Paradox of Liberal Constitutionalism*. Toronto: McClelland and Stewart.

March, James L., and Johan P. Olsen. 1984. "The New Institutionalism: Organizational Factors in Political Life." *American Political Science Review* 78 (September): 734–49.

Marmor, Theodore R. 1973. *The Politics of Medicare*. Chicago: Aldine.

———. 1975. "Can the US Learn from Canada?" In S. Andreopoulos, ed., *National Health Insurance: Can We Learn from Canada?* pp. 231–50. New York: Wiley.

———. 1983. "Rethinking National Health Insurance." In T. Marmor, ed., *Political Analysis and American Medical Care*, pp. 187–206. New York: Cambridge University Press.

———. 1991. "Misleading Notions." *Health Management Quarterly* 13, no. 4: 18–24.

———. 1994. *Understanding Health Care Reform*. New Haven: Yale University Press.

Marmor, Theodore R., and James A. Morone. 1983. "The Health Programs of the Kennedy-Johnson Years: An Overview." In T. Marmor, ed., *Political Analysis and American Medical Care*, pp. 131–51. New York: Cambridge University Press.

Marsh, Leonard. 1975. *Report on Social Security for Canada 1943*. Toronto: University of Toronto Press.

Martin, Cathie J. 1991. *Shifting the Burden: The Struggle over Growth and Corporate Taxation*. Chicago: University of Chicago Press.

Martin, Paul. 1985. *A Very Public Life*. Vol. 2, *So Many Worlds*. Toronto: Deneau Publishers.

McAndrew, William J. 1978. "Mackenzie King, Roosevelt, and the New Deal: The Ambivalence of Reform." In J. English and J. O. Stubbs, eds., *Mackenzie King: Widening the Debate*, pp. 130–48. Toronto: Macmillan.

McConnell, W. H. 1969. "The Genesis of the Canadian 'New Deal'." *Journal of Canadian Studies* 4 (May): 31–41.

McLeod, Jack. 1971. "Health, Wealth, and Politics." In L. LaPierre, J. McLeod, C. Taylor, and W. Young, *Essays on the Left*, pp. 81–99. Toronto: McClelland and Stewart.

McNaught, Kenneth. 1959. *A Prophet in Politics: A Biography of J. S. Woodsworth*. Toronto: University of Toronto Press.

McRae, Kenneth. 1964. "The Structure of Canadian History." In L. Hartz, ed., *The Founding of New Societies*, pp. 219–74. New York: Harcourt, Brace and World.

McRoberts, Kenneth. 1993. *Quebec: Social Change and Political Crisis*, 3d ed. Toronto: McClelland and Stewart.

Morone, James A. 1990. *The Democratic Wish: Popular Participation and the Limits of American Government*. New York: Basic Books.

Morton, Desmond. 1977. *NDP: Social Democracy in Canada*. Rev. ed. Toronto: Samuel Stevens Hakkert and Company.

Morton, W. L. 1950. *The Progressive Party in Canada*. Toronto: University of Toronto Press.

Munts, Raymond. 1967. *Bargaining for Health Care: Labor Unions, Health Insurance, and Medical Care*. Madison: University of Wisconsin Press.

Myers, Robert J. 1970. *Medicare*. Homewood, Ill.: Richard D. Irwin.

Myles, John, and Jill Quadagno. 1994. "The Politics of Income Security for the Elderly in North America: Founding Cleavages and Unresolved Conflicts." In T. Marmor, T. Smeeding, and V. Greene, eds, *Economic Security and Intergenerational justice: A Look at North America*, pp. 61–85. Washington: Urban Institute Press.

Navarro, Vicente. 1989. "Why Some Countries Have National Health Insurance, Others Have National Health Services, and the U.S. Has Neither." *Social Science and Medicine* 28, no. 9: 887–98.

———. 1994. *The Politics of Health Policy: The US Reforms, 1980–1994*. Oxford: Blackwell.

Naylor, C. David. 1986a. "Canada's First Doctor's Strike: Medical Relief in Winnipeg, 1932–4." *Canadian Historical Review* 67 (June): 151–80.

———. 1986b. *Private Practice, Public Payment: Canadian Medicine and the Politics of Health Insurance, 1911–1966*. Montreal: McGill-Queen's University Press.

———. 1993. "The Canadian Health Care System: A Model for America to Emulate?" In A. E. King, T. Hyclack, R. Morton, and S. McMahon, eds., *North American Health Care Policy in the 1990s*, pp. 25–66. New York: John Wiley.

Neatby, H. Blair. 1963. *William Lyon Mackenzie King*, Vol. 2, *The Lonely Heights, 1924–1932*. Toronto: University of Toronto Press.

———. 1972. *The Politics of Chaos: Canada in the Thirties*. Toronto: Macmillan.

Nelson, Harry. 1994. "The States That Could Not Wait." In D. Fox and J. Iglehart, eds., *Five States That Could Not Wait: Lessons for Health Reform from Florida, Hawaii, Minnesota, Oregon, and Vermont*. Cambridge: Blackwell.

Neuschler, Edward. 1990. *Canadian Health Care: The Implications of Public Health Insurance*. Washington: Health Insurance Association of America.

Neustadt, Richard E. 1954. "Congress and the Fair Deal: A Legislative Balance Sheet." *Public Policy* 5, no. 2: 351–81.

Newman, Peter C. 1963. *Renegade in Power: The Diefenbaker Years*. Toronto: McClelland and Stewart.

Nice, David C. 1987. *Federalism: The Politics of Intergovernmental Relations*. New York: St. Martin's Press.

Noël, Alain. 1994. "Distinct in the House of Commons: The Bloc Québécois as Official Opposition." In D. Brown and J. Hiebert, eds., *Canada: The State of the Federation, 1994*, pp. 19–35. Kingston: Institute of Intergovernmental Relations, Queen's University.

Numbers, Ronald L. 1978. *Almost Persuaded: American Physicians and Compulsory Health Insurance, 1912–1920*. Baltimore: Johns Hopkins University Press.

Olson, Mancur. 1965. *The Logic of Collective Action: Public Goods and the Theory of Groups*. Cambridge: Harvard University Press.

Orloff, Ann S., and Theda Skocpol. 1984. "Why Not Equal Protection? Explaining the Politics of Public Social Spending in Britain, 1900–1911, and the United States, 1880s–1920." *American Sociological Review* 49 (December): 726–50.

Ormsby, Margaret A. 1962. "T. Dufferin Pattullo and the Little New Deal." *Canadian Historical Review* 43 (December): 277–97.

Page, Benjamin I. 1983. *Who Gets What from Government.* Berkeley: University of California Press.

Pal, Leslie A. 1988. "Prime Ministers and Their Parties: The Cauldron of Leadership." In L. A. Pal and D. Taras, eds., *Prime Ministers and Premiers: Political Leadership and Public Policy in Canada,* pp. 87–96. Scarborough, Ont.: Prentice-Hall of Canada.

Palmer, Bryan. 1983. *Working-Class Experience: The Rise and Reconstitution of Canadian Labour, 1800–1980.* Toronto: Butterworths.

Pearson, Lester B. 1975. *Mike: The Memoirs of the Right Honourable Lester B. Pearson.* Vol. 3, 1957–1968. Toronto: University of Toronto Press.

Penner, Norman. 1977. *The Canadian Left: A Critical Analysis.* Toronto: Prentice-Hall of Canada.

———. 1992. *From Protest to Power: Social Democracy in Canada, 1900–Present.* Toronto: James Lorimer.

Pepper, Claude D., with Hays Gorey. 1987. *Pepper: Eyewitness to a Century.* New York: Harcourt, Brace, Jovanovitch.

Perkins, Frances. 1946. *The Roosevelt I Knew.* New York: Viking Press.

Peterson, Mark A. 1993. "Political Influence in the 1990s: From Iron Triangles to Policy Networks." *Journal of Health Politics, Policy and Law* 18 (summer): 435–38.

Phillips, Susan D. 1995. "The Canada Health and Social Transfer: Fiscal Federalism in Search of a Vision." In D. Brown and J. Rose, eds., *Canada: The State of the Federation, 1995,* pp. 65–96. Kingston: Institute of Intergovernmental Relations, Queen's University.

Pickersgill, J. W. 1960. *The Mackenzie King Record.* Vol. 1, *1939–1944.* Toronto: University of Toronto Press.

Pickersgill, J. W., and Donald Forster. 1968. *The Mackenzie King Record.* Vol. 2, *1944–1945.* Toronto: University of Toronto Press.

———. 1970. *The Mackenzie King Record.* Vol. 3, *1945–1946.* Toronto: University of Toronto Press.

Pierson, Paul. 1993. "When Effect Becomes Cause: Policy Feedback and Political Change." *World Politics* 45 (July): 595–628

Poen, Monte M. 1979. *Harry S. Truman versus the Medical Lobby: The Genesis of Medicare.* Columbia: University of Missouri Press.

Pratt, Henry J. 1976. *The Gray Lobby.* Chicago: University of Chicago Press.

Pross, A. Paul. 1992. *Group Politics and Public Policy.* 2d ed. Toronto: Oxford University Press Canada.

Quadagno, Jill. 1988. *The Transformation of Old Age Security: Class and Politics in the American Welfare State.* Chicago: University of Chicago Press.

Rae, Douglas W. 1971. *The Political Consequences of Electoral Laws.* New Haven: Yale University Press.

Raffel, Marshall W., and Norma K. Raffel. 1997. "The Health System of the United States." In M. Raffel, ed., *Health Care and Reform in Industrialized Countries*, pp. 263–89. University Park: Pennsylvania State University Press.

Ragin, Charles C. 1987. *The Comparative Method*. Berkeley: University of California Press.

Rayack, Elton. 1967. *Professional Power and American Medicine: The Economics of the American Medical Association*. Cleveland: World Publishing.

Rayback, Joseph G. 1966. *A History of American Labor*. Rev. ed. New York: Macmillan.

Redelmeier, Donald A., and Victor R. Fuchs. 1993. "Hospital Expenditures in the United States and Canada." *New England Journal of Medicine* 328 (March 18): 772–78.

Reed, Louis. 1961. "Private Medical Care Expenditures and Voluntary Health Insurance." *Social Security Bulletin* 24 (December): 3–11.

Rice, James J., and Michael J. Prince. 1993. "Lowering the Safety Net and Weakening the Bonds of Nationhood: Social Policy in the Mulroney Years." In S. Phillips, ed., *How Ottawa Spends 1993–1994: A More Democratic Canada . . . ?* pp. 321–416. Ottawa: Carleton University Press.

Rimlinger, Gaston. 1971. *Welfare Policy and Industrialization in Europe, America, and Russia*. New York: John Wiley.

Rosenstone, Steven J., Roy L. Behr, and Edward H. Lazarus. 1996. *Third Parties in America: Citizen Response to Major Party Failure: 2d ed.* Princeton: Princeton University Press.

Rubin, Alissa J. 1994. "Two Ideological Poles Frame Debate over Reform." *Congressional Quarterly* (January 8): 23–28.

Rubin, Alissa J., and Beth Donovan. 1994. "With Outcome Uncertain, Members Face Critical Vote." *Congressional Quarterly* (August 6): 2201–12.

Rueschemeyer, Dietrich, Evelyne Huber Stephens, and John D. Stephens. 1992. *Capitalist Development and Democracy*. Chicago: University of Chicago Press.

Ruggie, Mary. 1996. *Realignments in the Welfare State: Health Policy in the United States, Britain, and Canada*. New York: Columbia University Press.

Sanders, Wilfrid. 1944. "Canada Looks Toward Postwar." *Public Opinion Quarterly* 8 (winter): 523–29.

Scarrow, Howard. 1962. *Canada Votes: A Handbook of Federal and Provincial Election Data*. New Orleans: Hauser Press.

Schattschneider, E. E. 1942. *Party Government*. New York: Rinehart and Company.
———. 1960. *The Semi-Sovereign People: A Realist's View of Democracy in America*. New York: Holt, Rinehart and Winston.

Schiltz, Michael. 1970. *Public Attitudes Toward Social Security, 1935–1965*. Washington: U.S. Department of Health, Education, and Welfare, Social Security Administration, Office of Research and Statistics (Research Report No. 33).

Schlabach, Theron F. 1969. *Edwin E. Witte: Cautious Reformer*. Madison: State Historical Society of Wisconsin.

Schlesinger, Arthur M., Jr. 1959. *The Age of Roosevelt*. Vol. 2, *The Coming of the New Deal*. Boston: Houghton Mifflin.
———. 1960. *The Age of Roosevelt*. Vol. 3, *The Politics of Upheaval*. Boston: Houghton Mifflin.

Shapiro, Robert Y., and John T. Young. 1989. "Public Opinion and the Welfare State: The United States in Comparative Perspective." *Political Science Quarterly* 104 (winter): 59–89.

Sharp, Paul F. 1948. *The Agrarian Revolt in Western Canada: A Survey Showing American Parallels.* Minneapolis: University of Minnesota Press.

Shillington, C. Howard. 1972. *The Road to Medicare in Canada.* Toronto: Del Graphics.

Simeon, Richard. 1995. "Canada and the United States: Lessons from the North American Experience." In K. Knop, S. Ostry, R. Simeon, and K. Swinton, eds., *Rethinking Federalism: Citizens, Markets, and Governments in a Changing World,* pp. 250–72. Vancouver: University of British Columbia Press.

Skocpol, Theda. 1984. "Emerging Agendas and Recurrent Strategies in Historical Sociology." In T. Skocpol, ed., *Vision and Method in Historical Sociology,* pp. 356–91. New York: Cambridge University Press.

———. 1985. "Bringing the State Back In: Strategies of Analysis in Current Research." In P. Evans, D. Rueschemeyer and T. Skocpol, eds., *Bringing the State Back In,* pp. 3–37. New York: Cambridge University Press.

———. 1996. *Boomerang: Clinton's Health Security Effort and the Turn Against Government in U.S. Politics.* New York: W. W. Norton.

Skocpol, Theda, and G. John Ikenberry. 1983. "The Political Formation of the American Welfare State in Historical and Comparative Perspective." *Comparative Social Research* 6:87–148.

Skowronek, Stephen. 1982. *Building a New American State: The Expansion of National Administrative Capacities, 1877–1920.* New York: Cambridge University Press.

Smiley, Donald V. 1987. *The Federal Condition in Canada.* Toronto: McGraw-Hill Ryerson.

Smith, Denis. 1973. *Gentle Patriot: A Political Biography of Walter Gordon.* Edmonton: Hurtig Publishers.

Smith, Miriam. 1995. "Medicare and Canadian Federalism." In F. Rocher and M. Smith, eds., *New Trends in Canadian Federalism,* pp. 319–37. Peterborough, Ont.: Broadview Press.

Soderstrom, Lee. 1978. *The Canadian Health System.* London: Croom Helm.

Sorensen, Theodore C. 1965. *Kennedy.* New York: Harper and Row.

Sparer, Michael S., and Lawrence D. Brown. 1996. "States and the Health Care Crisis: The Limits and Lessons of Laboratory Federalism." In R. Rich and W. White, eds., *Health Policy, Federalism, and the American States,* pp. 181–202. Washington: Urban Institute.

Starr, Paul. 1982. *The Social Transformation of American Medicine.* New York: Basic Books.

———. 1994. *The Logic of Health Care Reform: How and Why the President's Plan Will Work.* Rev. ed. New York: Penguin.

Stephens, John D. 1979. *The Transition from Capitalism to Socialism.* London: Macmillan.

Stevens, Rosemary. 1971. *American Medicine and the Public Interest.* New Haven: Yale University Press.

————. 1989. *In Sickness and in Wealth: American Hospitals in the Twentieth Century.* New York: Basic Books.

Stevenson, Garth. 1985. "The Division of Powers." In R. Simeon, ed., *Division of Powers and Public Policy*, pp. 71–123. Toronto: University of Toronto Press.

Struthers, James. 1983. *No Fault of Their Own: Unemployment and the Canadian Welfare State.* Toronto: University of Toronto Press.

Stursberg, Peter. 1978. *Lester Pearson and the Dream of Unity.* Toronto: Doubleday Canada.

Sundquist, James L. 1968. *Politics and Policy: The Eisenhower, Kennedy and Johnson Years.* Washington: Brookings Institution.

Swartz, Donald. 1977. "The Politics of Reform: Conflict and Accommodation in Canadian Health Policy." In L. Panitch, ed., *The Canadian State: Political Economy and Political Power*, pp. 311–43. Toronto: University of Toronto Press.

————. 1987. "The Limits of Health Insurance." In A. Moscovitch and J. Albert, eds., *The Benevolent State: The Growth of Welfare in Canada*, pp. 255–70. Toronto: Garamond.

Taylor, Malcolm G. 1987. *Health Insurance and Canadian Public Policy: The Seven Decisions That Created the Canadian Health Insurance System and Their Outcomes.* 2d ed. Montreal: McGill-Queen's University Press.

————. 1990. *Insuring National Health Care: The Canadian Experience.* Chapel Hill: University of North Carolina Press.

Thelen, Kathleen, and Sven Steinmo. 1992. "Historical Institutionalism in Comparative Politics." In S. Steinmo, K. Thelen, and F. Longstreth, eds., *Structuring Politics: Historical Institutionalism in Comparative Analysis*, pp. 1–32. New York: Cambridge University Press.

Thomas, Paul G. 1991. "Parties and Regional Representation." In H. Bakvis, ed., *Representation, Integration and Political Parties in Canada*, pp. 179–252. Toronto: Dundurn Press.

Thompson, John Herd, and Alan Seager. 1985. *Canada, 1922–1939: Decades of Discord.* Toronto: McClelland and Stewart.

Thorburn, Hugh G. 1996. "The Development of Political Parties in Canada." In H. Thorburn, ed., *Party Politics in Canada.* 7th ed, pp. 114–24. Scarborough, Ont.: Prentice-Hall of Canada.

Tolchin, Martin. 1989. "Sudden Support for National Health Care." *New York Times*, September 4, IV–4.

Tollefson, Edwin A. 1968. "The Medicare Dispute." In N. Ward and D. Spafford, eds., *Politics in Saskatchewan*, pp. 238–79. Don Mills, Ont.: Longmans Canada.

Toner, Robin. 1993. "Advocates of Canadian Health Plan Fight On." *New York Times*, May 4, A22.

Trofimenkoff, Susan Mann. 1982. *Stanley Knowles: The Man from Winnipeg North Centre.* Saskatoon, Sask.: Western Producer Prairie Books.

Truman, David B. 1951. *The Governmental Process.* New York: Knopf.

Tuohy, Carolyn J. 1988. "Medicine and the State in Canada: The Extra-Billing Issue in Perspective." *Canadian Journal of Political Science* 23 (June): 267–96.

————. 1989. "Federalism and Health Care Policy." In W. Chandler and C. Zollner, eds., *Challenges to Federalism: Policy-Making in Canada and the Federal Republic of Germany*, pp. 141–60. Kingston: Institute for Intergovernmental Relations, Queen's University.

————. 1992. *Policy and Politics in Canada: Institutionalized Ambivalence*. Philadelphia: Temple University Press.

Underhill, Frank. 1960. *In Search of Canadian Liberalism*. Toronto: Macmillan.

Valelly, Richard M. 1989. *Radicalism in the States: The Minnesota Farmer-Labor Party and the American Political Economy*. Chicago: University of Chicago Press.

Walker, Forrest A. 1969. "Compulsory Health Insurance: 'The Next Great Step in Social Legislation.'" *Journal of American History* 56 (September): 290–304.

Ward, Norman. 1967. "Saskatchewan in 1964." In J. Courtney, ed., *Voting in Canada*, pp. 125–29. Scarborough, Ont.: Prentice-Hall of Canada.

Wearing, Joseph. 1981. *The L-Shaped Party: The Liberal Party of Canada 1953–1980*. Toronto: McGraw-Hill Ryerson.

Weaver, R. Kent. 1986. "The Politics of Blame Avoidance." *Journal of Public Policy* 6 (November): 371–98.

Weaver, R. Kent, and Bert A. Rockman. 1992. "When and How Do Institutions Matter?" In R. K. Weaver and B. Rockman, eds., *Do Institutions Matter? Government Capabilities in the United States and Abroad*, pp. 445–61. Washington: Brookings Institution.

Weir, Margaret, and Theda Skocpol. 1985. "State Structures and the Possibilities for Keynesian Responses to the Great Depression in Sweden, Britain and the U.S." In P. Evans, D. Rueschemeyer, and T. Skocpol, eds., *Bringing the State Back In*, pp. 107–63. New York: Cambridge University Press.

Weir, Margaret, Ann Shola Orloff, and Theda Skocpol. 1988. "Introduction: Understanding American Social Policies." In M. Weir, A. Orloff, and T. Skocpol, eds., *The Politics of Social Policy in the United States*, pp. 3–35. Princeton: Princeton University Press.

Weir, Richard. 1973. "Federalism, Interest Groups and Parliamentary Government: The Canadian Medical Association." *Journal of Commonwealth Political Studies* 11 (July): 159–75.

Wheare, K. C. 1964. *Federal Government*. 4th ed. New York: Oxford University Press.

Whitaker, Reginald. 1977. *The Government Party: Organizing and Financing the Liberal Party of Canada 1930–58*. Toronto: University of Toronto Press.

Wilensky, Harold. 1975. *The Welfare State and Equality*. Berkeley: University of California Press.

Wilsford, David. 1991. *Doctors and the State: The Politics of Health Care in France and the United States*. Durham: Duke University Press.

Wilson, James Q. 1973. *Political Organizations*. New York: Basic Books.

Witte, Edwin E. 1957. "Organized Labor and Social Security." In M. Derber and E. Young, eds., *Labor and the New Deal*. Madison: University of Wisconsin Press.

————. 1962. *The Development of the Social Security Act*. Madison: University of Wisconsin Press.

Woolhandler, Steffie, and David U. Himmelstein. 1991. "The Deteriorating Administrative Efficiency of the U.S. Health Care System." *New England Journal of Medicine* 324 (May 2): 1253–58.

Young, Walter D. 1969. *The Anatomy of a Party: The National CCF.* Toronto: University of Toronto Press.

———. 1983. "Political Parties." In J. Morley, ed., *The Reins of Power: Governing British Columbia.* Vancouver: Douglas & MacIntyre.

Index

ABOUT THE AUTHOR

Antonia Maioni is Assistant Professor of Political Science
at McGill University.